DR. MARIO O. LAPLUME

WITH THE COLLABORATION OF GIAN LUCA LAPLUME

EMOTIONAL FRUSTRATION

THE HUSHED PLAGUE

A NOVELIZED ESSAY

« SUFFERING IS GOOD BECAUSE IT ENNOBLES YOU."
ISABELLE EBERHARDT

DEDICATED TO ALL THE GREAT WOMEN IN OUR LIFETIMES THAT HAVE CREATED, NURTURED, TAUGHT, WAITED FOR, FORGIVEN AND LOVED US.

DEDICATED TO OUR DEAR UNCLE JOSÉ LUIS, WHO TAUGHT US SEDUCTION TECHNIQUES FOR THE FEMININE GENDER WHEN WE WERE TEENAGERS.

Emotional Frustration
The hushed plague
All Rights Reserved.
Copyright © 2019 and 2021 Dr. Mario O. Laplume
v8.0

The opinions expressed in this manuscript are solely the opinions of the author and do not represent the opinions or thoughts of the publisher. The author has represented and warranted full ownership and/or legal right to publish all the materials in this book.

This book may not be reproduced, transmitted, or stored in whole or in part by any means, including graphic, electronic, or mechanical without the express written consent of the publisher except in the case of brief quotations embodied in critical articles and reviews.

emotionalfrustration Publishing

Paperback ISBN: 978-1-9772-2269-5
Hardback ISBN: 978-1-9772-2432-3

Copyright Registration Number: TXu 2-151-560

Front cover designed by: Noel Marie Laplume. nmlaplume.com.
© 2019 and 2021 All rights reserved - used with permission.

Back cover picture designed by: Wilson Araujo @wilsonaraujophoto.
© 2019 and 2021 All rights reserved - used with permission.

PRINTED IN THE UNITED STATES OF AMERICA

Disclaimer

Even though the contents of this Novelized Essay have been profoundly influenced by our longstanding clinical experience as a practicing physician, all the characters, characterizations, incidents, locations, and dialogue have been fictionalized and/or invented in order to protect our patients' privacy rights and illustrate the core issues.

Miami, October 5th 2021

Dear President Rosenberg:

LIST OF CONTENTS

If only one	pp. 1
After the pandemic	pp. 2 - 8
Acknowledgements	pp. 9 -13
Prologue	pp. 14 - 21
Chapter I – Casual talk over a flimsy fence	pp. 20 - 37
Chapter II – It's not only about sex	pp. 38 -75
Chapter III – The trolling toll of Technology	pp. 76 - 147
Chapter IV – The cyber chantage	pp. 148-187
Chapter V – The material girl	pp. 188 - 215
Chapter VI – The bad negotiator	pp. 216 - 243
Chapter VII – The Vegan Harta factor	pp. 244 - 282
Epilogue – What do women really want?	pp. 283 – 313
References	pp. 314 – 342

Thank you very much for granting us the privilege of studying and writing in the Creative Writing Program of the Department of English at FIU. It has made a real difference in our personal artistic lives.

Gian Luca and David C Laplume

IF ONLY ONE

If only one person reads this book…we would feel very satisfied.

If only one person gets the message…our mission would be done.

If only one person is distracted from the Horror…we would be happy.

We were about to deliver the final edited version of this manuscript for its publication when the Coronavirus pandemic brutally arrived in the United States. Initially shocked like the rest of the population, we went into strict social isolation. However, as a practicing physician, we had to continue our duties as best we could. In the relative safety of our desk, we pondered whether we should publish it or not. We knew that there had been a complete shutdown of most publishing initiatives.

People cloistered at home deserve the possibility of substantive reading. Terrified by the darkness swirling around, they might like this little piece of light. Emulating the heroic example of Anne Frank, we should garner our moral strength. Dismissing any commercial considerations, we will go ahead with its publication.

In one of the poor quarters of *Nàpule* —where some of our kin had lived —a neighbor lowered, with a little rope, a basket with a sign from the balcony: inside it, passers-by could drop groceries they wanted to offer for others to pick up.

"Chi può metta…Chi non può, prenda" [1]

After the Pandemic

« Il y a plus dans les hommes des choses à admirer que des choses à mépriser »[2]
La Peste, Albert Camus [3]

There are books that seem to be ageing in a rather dishonorable way—once deemed as essential reading, they nonetheless begin to show their little decadent details like a *former belle* that is cruelly assaulted by the passing of time—and we store them in the attic of our *Subconscious,* neglecting their still relevant messages.

La Peste, penned by the 1954 Nobel Laureate Albert Camus, is one of them.

Written in 1947, right after the end of World War II, it was supposedly a realistic exposition of how a *supernatural phenomenon* out of the *Dark Times* can ravage our communities and, in its aftermath. leave negligible redeeming changes. Critics argued that the plague was in fact a reference to the massive human and social destruction of Nazism in the European continent; in a January 11, 1954, letter to Roland Barthès, Camus did acknowledge it. Intellectuals were aghast that this *régime* could have appeared in one of the most educated societies of Europe.

In *Oran*—then the second largest city of *French Algeria*—a physician called **Dr. Rieux** sounded the alarm when he discovered unusually sick individuals in his ward. The epidemic arrived seemingly out of nowhere and rapidly destroyed the social, economic, and administrative fabric of the teeming city in just a few weeks.

In the beginning, the city inhabitants were *reluctant to accept* the Public Health threat as they could not face their own mortality and preferred to cling to their "normality." Slowly but steadily, *the warts of human nature* begun to surface into the open, exposing all kinds of miserly conducts in daily interactions.

One sick patient paradoxically rejoiced in the calamity of others as a way to mitigate his own solitude with a perverse *schadenfreude* [4] that undervalued Life. A priest said in a sermon that the scourge was God's penance for parishioners' sins. Many civil cadres cowardly abandoned their posts for the safety of isolation. Other individuals preferred to party before the inevitable demise would befall them. Dr. Rieux viewed the pest as "une interminable défaite" [5] and was ready to give up.

Then there was the redeeming character of **Rambert**, a common individual who, after trying to escape from the city in the beginning, decided to stay and help. He reminded us of **Katow**, one of the main characters of *La Condition Humaine,* [6] who sacrificed his life so his comrades could live on. Ever since we read André Malraux's book, the memory of the overriding *train whistle*—marking the eventual immolation in a cauldron of the prisoners taken by the Chinese Nationalists —has provoked an *uncontrolled shiver from head to toe* when it rose again in our mind. But it also exemplified the great capacity of humans to surmount our selfishness.

One of the most terrifying features of this kind of devastating disease is the gradual yet unrelenting invasion of **silence** in places hitherto occupied by humans.

All the physicians practicing in these terrible times have *a sickening feeling* in our stomachs when we traverse hospitals' sections that used to be bustling with patients and personnel—like children's wards—and we only hear *our steps' echo*. When we pass by a nurses' station, instead of the amiable greeting of colleagues and personnel, we are warily watched by a lonely nurse wrapped in protective gear. When we pass by patients' rooms, we see empty beds with no signs of occupation. Moreover, when we learn that one of our colleagues has fallen due to the disease, we have mixed feelings of sadness for the loss but also pride for their sacrifices. In Italy, more than 104 physicians—4 primary caregivers out of 10—passed away .[7]

Most of us have a relative, friend or neighbor that was infected while they were loyally on duty as **first responders** in the police, fire stations, pharmacies, supermarkets, etc. Thanks to them, we are duly supplied with services and goods. Without the *continued support* of county, state and federal authorities, our country cannot weather this terrible calamity and recover a semblance of "normalcy" after.

In the sad *2020 Easter*, **Pope Francis** gave a mass, seated on an illuminated podium in the middle of a totally deserted *Saint Peter's square*, to a TV audience. Instead of the elaborate *Via Crucis* [8]—traditionally held in the *Colosseum*[9] with the *thirteen stations of the Cross*—there was only a small procession of caregivers and corrections' personnel that offered a wooden cross to the Pope. He stood up and accepted it with a resigned but also *fierce resolve* to keep on fighting. *Coraggio*.[10]

After the Pandemic has hopefully passed, how will our world look like?

In 1348, at the height of the pandemic known as the **Black Plague** (Bubonic Plague) [11] that decimated the population of the European continent, a group of young women and men escaped from the ravaged city of Florence and took refuge in a countryside villa. In order to bear their forced isolation, they each narrated a different tale every night for two weeks—except one day for housekeeping and the religious holidays—which amounted to a final tally of one hundred tales. This is the script of *The Decameron* [12], a seminal book of Italian Literature, which foretold the coming of the Renaissance. Deeply influenced by *Numerology* and *Mysticism*, Boccaccio expressly chose **seven** (7) young women who represented the following:

a) Four cardinal virtues: *Prudence, Virtue, Temperance* and *Fortitude*.

b) Three theological virtues: *Faith, Hope* and *Charity*.

The **three** (3) young men represent theological virtues: *Faith, Hope* and *Charity*. [13]

Using the *allegorical writing method* of Dante Alighieri, this author engaged in a *satirical critique* of the prevailing socio-economic-political markers of that time, controlled by the *rancid patriarchal institutions* from feudal administrations and the Catholic Church. The exaltation of the *commercial values*—like intelligence, astuteness, and sophisticated goals—was an innovative common thread in them; up to that time, the European societies were dominated only by *piety* and *loyalty*.

The name *Decameron* is a composite of two classical Greek terms: *deka* (ten) and *hemera* (day) The subtitle of this work is a solid reference to *Gallehault*, a fictional king of the tale of *Lancelot*; he arranged the first clandestine meeting of *Guinevere*, King Arthur's wife, with his friend and bodyguard, thus abetting their tragic affair. In a provocatively subversive way, Bocaccio elevated the figure of this prince to showcase the *hard indenture of women* to their paternal figures. The escape of Guinevere represented the *possibility of movement, of love, of freedom.*

The recluse youngsters came out determined to build a better society with *more liberal values* and *tolerance for diversity,* including the participation of women in some community affairs, which started to chip away at the Patriarchate. The *Dark Night* of feudality would be wiped off by the coming of the *Renaissance.*

We are now living a humongous **sanitary and economic crisis** at the same time. Whomever thinks that we can go back to what we had taken for granted as "normal" is engaging in a most dangerous delusion. For example, the evident lack of proper preparedness regarding the *needed stocking of emergency supplies* of protective gear and ventilators exposed the disastrously short-sighted budgets cuts of governments. Who will defend the skimping on the critical social investments in order to have a low "supply on demand" policy for "just on time delivery"? That has condemned countless patients to a *lack of assisted respiratory therapy* plus *a deficient protection with disposable gear* for first responders and care personnel.

Most epidemiologists believe that *the initial host* of this dangerous virus was a bat, as had been the case with the *Ebola, SARS,* and *MERS* infections; the bats are asymptomatic carriers of many of these organisms, which do not sicken them but reproduce inside them. Supposedly the virus found the right opportunity to jump into another animal, and then into another one, and so on, until it finally landed on a human being in that infamously barbaric "wet market" of Wuhan in China. [14]

This **zoonotic disease**, which theoretically passed between animals and humans, was enabled by a *global trade of wildlife, agricultural intensification, deforestation,* and *urbanization* that bring us in *closer contact* with wild animals' habitats. Some scientists argued that the **re-engineered virus**—to make it more infectious— had accidentally leaked out from the *Wuhan Institute of Virology*.[15]

Another major upheaval is the change of the socio-economic coordinates of most societies regarding *the labor opportunities* that will be offered by employers. The purely physical labor will continue to keep downsizing in the *Information Age*, especially for positions that can be staffed by people working from their homes. The *remuneration of the heroes* that are now buttressing communities—physicians, nurses, care assistants, laboratory clerks, fire and police forces, operators of basic services, truck and delivery drivers, re-stockers of warehouse supplies, etc.—must be promptly, justly increased to reflect their *real value* for our mere survival.

Is a financier fiddling with numbers more valued than your local butcher?

As we are writing these lines, we are hearing the generalized hand clapping of the Parisians, exactly at their 8 PM time through the transmission of *Radio France Inter* [16] in honor of the medical and nursing personnel of their hospitals.

In a positive twist, the citizenry has stopped to subserviently follow the so-called "celebrities" of entertainment and sports that had polluted all public spaces. Who is the object of their dreams? The scientists that are working to bring *a safe and effective vaccine* against the Coronavirus. **The blessed saviors of Mankind**.

In the aftermath of this pandemic, the world all around us will feel "weird." Many of the familiar *physical and spiritual assumptions* that anchored our daily demeanor in our societies will either be transformed or gone forever from *Reality*. Tom Frieden, a former director of the *CDC* [17] said: "A new world is here. Hand sanitizers at building entrances, touch-free doors and elevators, health care that results in fewer infections of patients and staff, and similar measures are here to stay. Travel bans and quarantine of travelers will most likely continue until there is a vaccine, Vulnerable people may need to shelter in place even after others have re-entered our new world." [18] Whatever the magnitude of the challenges ahead, we have the firm certitude that **our dear women** will be at our side. Let us appreciate their precious devotion by enthusiastically giving them their due respect.

As President François Macron said in an address to the French nation:

"On doit se réinventer, moi le premier" [19]

ACKNOWLEDGEMENTS

*"If they don't want to give you something,
Get out in the street to make big trouble.
You'll always get something out of it."* [20]

In our list of needed acknowledgments this quote should take pride of place. It was casually uttered by our dear friend **Oscar Pérez**, a street-smart lawyer from *General Pirán* in Buenos Aires State, Argentina, that used to be a member of the *Peronist Party*. For its almost 70 years of existence that populist political party—composed of an heterogenous array of factions ranging from the extreme right to the left one—has been characterized by engaging in all kinds of massive protests.

When, after several years of assiduous daily toiling at our desk, we finally crafted a novel in 2016, we were flummoxed by the reluctance of literary agents and/or agencies—in spite of receiving some nice accolades for our writing skills—to represent us in order to secure its final publication. After the initial shock, we took a most bold step: we put the novel in a "holding area" as a *Kindle* book [21] and decided to create a *medical and literary web page* at https://drmolaplume.com

Spontaneously following primal instincts, we designed a few original series. One of them titled *Emotional Frustration* was perfidiously scheduled to go up at an early 7 AM EST slot on Saturdays, a time when we presumed some *overworked* and *under-appreciated homemakers* would get up to fix *a solo cup* of a hot brew and drink it quietly in the kitchen while their house coasts placidly in sleep mode. We guessed that these devoted women would be reflecting about their lives and *what was missing in them*. Often just a good listening ear (*Too much asking?*)

Hardly did we fathom at the time that it would turn into such a success, receiving the commentaries (in the page and in its associated e-mail address) of *emotionally frustrated ladies* from all over the planet, even as far away as Asia. These loyal readers even suggested the topics that we should cover. Somehow our accumulated experience of forty years as a medical practitioner and consultant furnished myriad anecdotes about critical issues that women have to contend with in our societies, especially *disdain* and *discrimination* for their real capabilities.

In order to get away *with a little trouble* (and more) in the dangerous Web, we could count on the help of **God Almighty**, who subtly protected us all along.

We must first honor our dearest father, **Mario Laplume Salguero**, and our dearest mother, **Gladys Josefa Garbarino**, who besides giving us our precious life and raising us with dedicated affection, had the visionary initiative to make us learn languages as a young child, with great financial sacrifices and commitment. When they send us to the *Instituto Cultural Anglo Uruguayo* to learn English, they gave us access to the *world's lingua franca* for our medical and literary careers. When the notoriously authoritarian authorities of the *Lycée Français* decreed in our first year of Primary School that we were not learning *calligraphy* fast enough and threatened us with a swift expulsion, our dear grandmother **Marta Salguero Laplume,** devotedly came to our apartment every afternoon to mentor us. As if it were happening now—and not sixty years ago—we watch our mother say: "Memé is coming up the stairs," before opening the apartment's door to greet her. With a heart condition, after shuffling two flights up, she had to sit down to rest.

In kindergarten we had the fortune of having a smart and gorgeous teacher called **Melita** who, intuitively knowing that we were born a rebel, took the time to coach us when we deviated from the strict path of a highly structured school. By the time we went to First Year, we had a certain *reputation of a troublemaker*; we wrote how our mother Gladys rescued us from the claws of "intolerant teachers" in this article: https://drmolaplume.com/2017/05/20/born-into-disobedience

After that incident we came across Melita half-way in the winding flight of stairs that went from the ground floor to the first one as she was coming down. The lovely brunette sat down on a tread, accommodated her long flowing black skirt, and pulled us towards her: "Come here," she sweetly said. "What's the problem?" Totally embarrassed, we welled up. She hugged us for a few minutes, caressing our head and whispering a few words that we cannot remember. Recalling that *unique sense of protection against any and all evil* , still makes us shake from head to toe.

From our Medical School studies in the *Universidad Nacional de La Plata*, we remember the bedside teachings of **Dr. Bernardo Manzino**, a superb clinician, who, with insight of clinical semiology and human nature, taught us many lessons. We also had the opportunity of befriending **Dr. Heraldo Tavella** who offered us mentoring in his specialty and loaned us the funds for the travel ticket to the USA.

In our studies of Health Policy and Management at *Columbia University*'s Mailman School of Public Health we had a superb Ad-Hoc Committee formed by *Dr. Lawrence Brown, Dr. Michael Sparer* and *Dr. Annetine C. Gelijns* who kindly advised us in the design of our doctoral dissertation about *Equality of Care Access*.

For the past few years we did consulting at *New Life Medical Institute,* a Miami care facility; we thank *Mr. Ernesto Rodriguez,* its owner, *Ms. Marilyn López*, its business manager, and *Mr. José Miguel Martínez*, its operations manager for it; we appreciate the kind help of *Ms. Madelin* and *Mr. Lemir,* our assistants, *Ms. Maya and Zoraya,* keepers of our tidiness, and *Mr. Antonio*, our chauffeur.

We could count on the guidance of *our lawyer-agent-friend* **Sandy Topkin**, from the top law firm of *Topkin and Parlow PI* https://www.topkinlaw.com, who is deftly assisted by *Ms. Carrol*, his secretary, and *Ms. Eva—*the *Golem Charmer*.

The publication of this manuscript was made possible by the priceless help of the staff of *Outskirts Press*, https://outskirtspress.com , that listened to all our concerns and advised us about the best course of action. Ms. *Allison, Jennifer,* and *Dana* were our fabulously empathic "handlers"; Ms. *Cheri* neatly edited our book.

Ever since we were medical students in La Plata, we have spent our long hours of studies and writings with the unobtrusive company of Meuci's invention. After we settle down with our *mate amargo* at our desk, we say our daily prayers. Then we tune in to either *Radio Mitre* of Buenos Aires, *Radio Montecarlo* or *Radio Carve* of Montevideo to get news updates, music, and interesting reportages. At noon we switch to the European continent, with *Radio Il Sole 24 Ore* of Milano, *Radio France Inter* of Paris; at 2 PM we listen to the *Radio Nacional de España*. Finally we watch *CNBC* for the market news and *CNN* for national developments.

From an emotional standpoint, the crucial support to carry out this task has been provided by *Noël Marie* and *Gian Luca*, our two children, and *Gustavo* and *Marcel*, our two brothers, who never failed to cheer us up when we wavered. Gian Luca wrote the section about "Violence in the Media and Aggressive Behavior", a subject that is relevant for most of us, parents, and our children in this digital age. *Noël Marie* masterfully drew with a few strokes the beautiful cover of this book; many artists have congratulated her for "saying a lot" while skimping on content.

Thank you very much for enabling this project to finally become a reality.

In these times of a brutal takeover by Silence, we must start talking again.

Trying to emulate the gesture of Adam in Michelangelo's painting, we are outspreading our index finger to try to touch God—the artistic ecstasy.

Prologue

"Women are meant to be loved, not understood." Oscar Wilde

We have a problem with a woman. A particular one. And it is getting worse.

Ever since we started our medical practice almost forty years ago, she has showed up every day—*rain or shine*—to share her multiple woes with us. She sits down across our desk, looks at us straight in the eye and says the very same words: "*I am emotionally frustrated.*" What is her name? Bovary. Emma. **Emma Bovary**.

When we read *Madame Bovary* [22] as a student in the *Alliance Française* [23] of Montevideo, we were mesmerized by the story of a beautiful and ardent wife of a country medical practitioner that could not find any solace in her grey existence. At the time we could not fathom how she could be so ungrateful to her partner.

However, the ensuing studies and practice as a medical doctor gave us the necessary insight to grasp—if still not fully agree with—the cause of her angst. Physicians watch births, deaths, and almost anything in between them. Including the big and small, yet none the less painful, incidents of women's humiliations.

We had left our copy of the novel in a box full of books in Montevideo but somehow, Emma sprung out of it to pursue us all the way to Miami to disturb us. Ever since her 1856 debut as a series in *La Revue de Paris* [24], this mischievously meek *petite bourgeoise* has been deftly manipulating ingénue men like us.[25]

Even in a hyper-connected age, she still cannot get her message through.

The plethora of mixed messages in the social media platforms has increased her confusion as her connections seem to be more tone-deaf than ever to her plight. As the **tragic trifecta** of *memory*, *love* and the *passage of time* relentlessly gnaws at her soul, she has been stubbornly nagging us to record her thoughts *verbatim* [26]. The Spanish language differentiates between the noble role of *escritor*—an artist inspired by a mission—and the mundane one of *escribiente*—an obscure agent that copies other people's writings or takes dictation.[27] Haggling with the most miserly of muses and fighting the meanest of demons, we turned into **Emma's escribiente**.

A strange phenomenon has occurred to us almost imperceptibly yet steadily: the causes of her *Emotional Frustration* have started to percolate into our mind. Moreover, the daily drill of listening attentively to women has developed in our brain one of the greatest gifts they have been endowed with: the *mirror neurons*.

Slowly, yet surely, we learned how to read any rictus of her face without exchanging words. We can anticipate how her mood is by just looking at the way she steps inside. Prodded by the cultural constraints of a supposedly "modern society" still controlled by men, women have been **more focused on association** rather than action like men had. In order to find out efficiently what their loved ones need, they have recurred to this edge ever since our Dark Times in the caves.

We can start to close the gap by following their advice: *"Just listen to me."*

Sigmund Freud [28] was perhaps the first man that tried to listen to women. In his medical cabinet, he sat down next to a lady that would **freely associate** to open her *mind* and *heart* to his clinical scrutiny. Thus, he had the courage to study what Dr. Jean-Martin Charcot [29], his mentor, dismissively dubbed as *la chose génitale* [30] when they saw hysterical patients in the Neurology ward of *La Pitié-Salpêtrière* [31].

The extraordinarily rich emotional armamentarium of a woman exposes her to many opportunities of frustration when her goals, or those of persons she loves, are not reached for sexual, familiar, financial, professional, or social reasons. After his workday, Freud had the temerity to go back home to listen to his wife and, if some unconfirmed reports are true, his sister-in-law too— his secret lover. *Brave.*

We have noticed the rising importance of **female bonding** in Emma's life. Women—historically, oppressed by all the patriarchal institutions and biologically burdened by the travails of the family—usually find the needed *emotional support* and social connectedness within their circle of friends, both male and female. Moreover, as women live more of their adult lives without a steady partner or a traditional family, they share more purposes and experiences with their friends.

Based on his solid experience as a physician, *Antón Chekov* [32] wrote about the paradoxical facets of our behavior. Humans are biologically hardwired for contradiction—the essence of the creative process—because we have **two brains** and **two minds**. The Left *propositional* Hemisphere is logical and analytical while the Right *appositional* hemisphere is perceptual and synthetic.[33] As a result, all the *sensory input* to the Right Hemisphere (originating in the body's left side) is stored without any hard analysis or judgement. Contradictions coexist in harmony there. Women have more neural connections via the Corpus Callosum, between the Right and Left hemispheres [34] —the basis of their *better integration* of emotional aspects.

We have patiently designed and written in a medical and literary web page at https://drmolaplume.com/, which has been a big success with a select public. We grouped our writings in series, one of which was named *Emotional Frustration*. It constituted the necessary scaffolding to slowly start constructing this sailing boat, besides gauging the reaction of our readers, and pleading for a propitious *hava* [35].

We would like to thank our children for their unfaltering support all these years besides helping us in concrete ways. **Noël Marie** designed the beautiful cover and **Gian Luca** helped us edit the text ; both have commented many articles. As Life is a *perpetual journey* along the treacherous channels to Wisdom that our kindred navigated before us, we would like to thank our parents and grandparents; **Yolanda**, *la Nonna*, and **Morizio**, *il Nonno*, endowed us with the Italian heritage.

Dear readers, trying to discern what the big causes of *Emotional Frustration* of modern women are might seem like an impossible task, especially for us, men. Parsimoniously retracing our steps to our days as a medical student in the clinical ward of the *Policlínico General San Martín* of the *Medical School of La Plata*, we remember how Dr. Bernardo Manzino, Professor of Medicine, sat down facing the patient, asked what was wrong and dutifully listened without ever interrupting. The theoretical and practical studies of **Semiology**—the compendium of clinical signs that are pathognomonic of sickness—gave us useful clues, not only about patients' physical ailments, but also about their psychological troubles. It was right there that we started to hone our intuition skills "to try to understand women."

Whether we like it or not, we are living in an **on-demand** environment. The time lapse between *awareness*, *desire* and *reward* has been reduced to an instant. If the streaming platforms release all the episodes of a series in a single day, we must realize that entertainment has taken a new dimension, especially for women. If you take a lady for a romantic dinner, she will scrutinize you closely for any faux-pas and quietly expect the right moves—verbal and physical. *Binge-watching-reacting*.

You must be able **to sell your brand** every time you interact romantically. Reality takes a backseat to the magic of entertainment. *It is what she sees in you.* To carry out this Houdinesque trick, you must combine the storytelling prowess of *brand marketers* with the action-driven stunts of *performance marketers*. Someone trying to market their brand has to leverage this new paradigm by learning the *best practices* advocated by psychologists, social researchers, philosophers, writers, etc.

The *Emotional Frustration* of women does not occur in a social vacuum but rather within **the constrictive corset** deftly set up by all the patriarchal institutions.

As there is absolutely nothing *natura*l or *biological* to justify the social, economic, and professional subordination of women in our societies, we will tackle this issue.

Being an admirer of Jerzi Grotowsky [36]—who sought to recreate the drama of spiritual/ religious practices by encouraging *spectators' participation* to exorcise our *Collective Unconscious*—we added a sub-section titled **A nugget of Wisdom** and some interspersed notes identified as the <u>Diary USS Awareness</u> ; we followed a "marine cadets' class" in their circumnavigation of the *Emotional Frustration*.[37] After discussing a major topic, we insolently broke the so-called "fourth wall" [38] to *proselytize directly to men* and try to shake their perennial, paralyzing torpor off. They look like the college notes on literary but hard to read classics like *Ulysses*. [39]

We can still remember the utter puzzlement and sense of loss we had when we raided the great library of our dear father Mario [40] and pulled that book out. "What is this? Why all this messy lay-out? Where do I start? Will I reach the end?"

Do not despair. Ignorant men can learn. Frustrated women can get relief.

We can overcome together the devastating consequences of this pandemic.

Only the concerted, sustained effort of all genders will rebuild our societies.

Every memorable adventure, and its printed saga, begins with a single step.

Please give us your hand and let us make that most humble, powerful move.

As Mario Benedetti [41]—a chronicler of the "little details of life"—said:

"Lo Imposible. Sólo tarda un poco más." [42]

Chapter I – Casual chat over a flimsy fence

What do women want? Can we understand them? Or is it a hopeless task?

If Sigmund Freud threw in the towel at the end of his professional career by confessing that, after long decades of analyzing hundreds of female patients in his office, he still did not know the right answers, how can we presume to have them?

With all due respect to the great Viennese neurologist, we will attempt to find, not a providentially encompassing single answer, but a series of smaller ones that might give us a glimpse of the complicated yet exciting feminine psychology.

Impregnable. The Janussian auto-antonym [43] that describes the woman's ethos: she can enable the precious creation of Life but also rebuffs any unwanted suitors.

She cannot be simple. She cannot be straight. She cannot be conformist.

If she were, Mankind would have disappeared a long, long time ago.

The *Oxford English Dictionary* defines **frustration** [44] as: "the feeling of being upset and annoyed of being unable to change or achieve something." We would respectfully add: "and to have something." That is the basis of *Emotional Frustration* in women. This begs the following question: "what do women want?"

The chapters in this book will be named after an article in our web page that we consider as a *blog bersaglio*, i.e. the target for our readers' attention. Once we are clear with the main concept, we can try to discuss all its florid ramifications.

With the didactic aim to unravel this Gordian Knot [45], we divided them in:

a) **Sexual dimension**, heralded by: *It's not only about sex.* [46]

b) **Family dimension**, heralded by: *The trolling toll of technology.* [47]

c) **Social dimension**, heralded by: *The cyber chantage.* [48]

d) **Financial dimension** heralded by: *The material girl.* [49]

e) **Labor dimension** heralded by: *The bad negotiator.* [50]

As we start discussing the major issues in these five critical dimensions, we must keep in mind that it is usually a *combination* and *cross-over of causes* from two or more of these dimensions—an **incrocio** *[51]*—that create chronic frustrations.

The *Dizionari Garzanti in Italiano* [52] defined that term as: "the intersection of two elements, particularly streets, that cross at a certain point." But it also refers to: "the hybrid final product from two different animal or vegetal species that mate." Likewise, the *crossing over of two causes* of *Emotional Frustration* can produce an altogether *new entity* that will start swirling around a woman's mind as a new composite one. For example, the lack of family support of single mothers—family dimension—will have repercussions in their careers —labor dimension— which will gravely limit their advancement and earnings—financial dimension.

<u>Diary USS Awareness</u> – *BUGLE CALL.* The training ship *Awareness* departs soon. Check list. Got your Dramamine pills [53] ? Life vest on? It will get really bumpy. Do not cry, ladies… Will either come back as *renewed men* or sink along the way.

In the chapter titled **The Vegan Harta factor**—one of the names assigned to *Lord Ganesh* [54], protector against evil—we will discuss the more relevant mixtures of critical issues that provoke *Emotional Frustration* in women, trying to find the proper solutions. A woman's inner realm is in constant *flux* and yesterday's cause of angst might not be what is vexing her now, or at least not to the same degree.

<u>*Diary USS Awareness*</u>—Some want to jump off ship and swim back to the pier?

We had hoped to end our task right there, but someone had other plans…

A few days ago, we were placidly sleeping when she came to visit us.

Our transition into REM sleep [55] *was halted by a familiar whispering.*

-"Hey, don't go there yet," Emma Bovary said. "Got to talk, buddy."

Rubbing our eyes, we saw her svelte silhouette sitting at the bed's edge.

-"What do you want now?" I replied. "Finished the manuscript already."

-"Yeah, it's good, but incomplete…Totally incomplete, my escribiente."

-"What are you talking about, eh?"

-"You did not discuss what women want…Must write the final chapter."

-"Oh, no! Freud couldn't do it…Almost went crazy trying to grasp it—"

-"Well, got an advantage over him—you're already totally screwed up."

What do you want me to say? Women can be so disarmingly convincing…

Prepare our admission to an asylum. We will write that chapter.

Our **Central Nervous System** is structured in three major levels. They are:

a) The Forebrain or Prosencephalon

b) The Midbrain or Mesencephalon

c) The Hindbrain or Rhombencephalon

Forebrain (Prosencephalon)

It is the largest CNS structure, housing *the final destination points* for all stimuli. It is embryologically divided into the *telencephalon* and the *diencephalon*. The biggest part of the telencephalon is the **cerebral cortex**—composed by the *frontal, parietal, occipital,* and *temporal* lobes—that processes all the inbound information. It also controls our motor functions and is the seat of reason/ analytical thinking. [56]

The *Frontal lobes* regulate the voluntary muscles' movement, our ideation and memory. The *Parietal lobes* efficiently receive and process all the incoming sensory information. The *Occipital lobes* analyze all the visual information that is furnished by the retina. The *Temporal lobes*, composed by the amygdala and the hippocampus, play a central role in perception of sounds, formation of memories and speech. In order to keep the *body homeostasis*—the physiological equilibrium of life—our autonomic, endocrine, and motor functions must be regulated by an *integrator* that tracks the nervous and endocrine stimuli—the *Diencephalon*. This is one of the *transportation hubs* where all the *incoming sensorial stimuli* and *hormonal signals* are integrated before they head to the respective cortical stations.

The **Thalamus** is a critical component of the Limbic System, integrating the sensory stimuli with the motor functions and regulating sleep-waking cycles. The *Hypothalamus* regulates the *autonomic* (unconscious) physiological functions like breathing, regulation of the peripheral blood pressure, body temperature, etc. Being one of the few organs with mixed nervous and hormonal tissues, it secretes *neuro-regulatory hormones* that affect our body metabolism, growth, and reproduction. [57]

Midbrain (Mesencephalon)

This waystation connects the Hindbrain—seat of Autonomic functions—with the Forebrain, seat of our major intellectual functions; it serves as a *giant distributor*. Its ventral portion is called **cerebral peduncle**, which contains the large bundles of the inter-connecting fibers (cables) in order to carry out that critical neural task. One of those bundles is the *reticular formation*, which connects the spinal cord with the CNS, relaying the sensorial and motor input for muscle tone and reflexes.

As the *oculomotor* and *trochlear nerves* are located there, it plays a major role in the processing of the visual and auditory stimuli. Its dorsal portion is called **tectum** and is composed of the *superior colliculi*—processing of visual signals—and the *inferior colliculi*—processing of the auditory signals. In its midst, there is the **substantia nigra** —cluster of cells secreting dopamine, a neuro-transmitter—which regulates our voluntary muscle movements and our general mood. [58]

Hindbrain (Rhombencephalon)

All the *incoming sensory stimuli* arrive at this "Grand Central Station" of the CNS where they are *triaged* to redirect them to the tracks abutting to a final destination; the linemen (*nuclei*) of many cranial nerves are servicing their assigned lines there. The *trigeminal, abducent, facial* and *vestibulocochlear* nerves are based in a subdivision called **metencephalon** and the *glossopharyngeal, vagus, accessory* and *hypoglossal* nerves are in another one called **myelencephalon**. As the *triage area* for stimuli from the **Autonomic Nervous System**, it regulates physiological functions like *micturition, sweating, defecation, temperature control,* etc.

The upper part of the hindbrain is composed of the pons and the cerebellum. The **pons** connects the cerebellum with the higher cortical areas, modulating our *sleep and arousal states*. The **cerebellum** regulates the *motor function* by relaying all the information of posture and strength to the motor cortex. As the seat of the vestibular nerves, it regulates *body equilibrium* and *coordination* of movements.

Our Cortex is inextricably linked with the **Limbic System**, the hideout of the "graffiti artists" spattering with a palette of *emotionally charged color hues* the passing convoys of *sensory stimuli going up* and the *motor commands going down*. Most sensory and motor signals must pass through the Thalamus—the CNS interconnector. Just below it, lies the Hypothalamus that regulates *mood, sexuality,* and *desires*; it reacts to external stimuli by sending signals to other limbic structures. [59]

Trainspotting. The ultimate tool for the concerned partner of any woman.

If we want to make a real difference in the lives of our dear women, we must first *observe* their moves carefully to learn the regular schedules and characteristics of their "sensory and motor convoys" so we can spare them (and us) frustrations. In their *Thalamic call to arms*, women recruit many more "graffiti artists" than we, men, ever could; thus their *arsenal of weapons-grade emotional paint* is superior.

We must check the daily, weekly, monthly variations in women's schedules, discarding what is *random* and registering what is *regular*. All their sensory stimuli and motor commands will be often modified by a plethora of associated signs from their *Autonomic System, Memory, Ideation*, etc. The *sensory convoys* going up to the CNS and the *motor ones* coming down from it are not in immaculate condition, but randomly "soiled" with the brush strokes of *feminine flowery emotionality*.

A nugget of Wisdom. So, you know a thing or two about her train routes?

When you see that all stimuli annoy her, her belly is bloated, she cannot eat carbohydrates, she is irritable, you know which train is slogging up to her cortex.

The pre-menstrual sensory cargo convoy. Get ready to give a massage.

When you see that she ignores you, she clutches her cell, she does not want dinner, she is riveted by TV, you know which train is careening out of her cortex.

The my-meddlesome-mom-called motor express. Get out of the way. Fast.

<u>Diary USS Awareness</u> – This ain't a cruise. Attention. Observe. Listen. Don't talk.

Can women "read" people's faces in a precise-all seeing-infallible way?

The historically archaic *division of labor* entrusted women with the care and nurturing of the weakest members of communities, i.e. the children and the elderly. In order to carry that critical task, the female brain developed a novel neurological network over the ages based on a group of specialized neurons: **the mirror cells**.[60]

Amongst all the millenary civilizations of the European continent, the Italian citizens—and particularly the Italian women—are more inclined *to watch and see*. Unlike the French and German cultures that emphasize the value of the written and spoken words, the Italians enjoy a *more visually oriented* culture.[61] Apart from the pioneering work of Dante Alighieri and some modern writers, there is a relative scantiness of books compared to a plethora of paintings from all the time periods. Since times immemorial, Italians like to sit at a café table to sip a drink and watch. They nonchalantly *see and scan* all the individuals walking past them and decipher their gestures; likewise, they like *to be seen* by friends, family and even strangers.

It is not surprising that the explanation for intuitiveness came from Italy.

Giacomo Rizollatti is a neuroscientist who has worked with his colleagues in the *University of Parma*'s lab where the mirror neurons were discovered in the frontal and parietal cortex of the macaque monkey—a scientific milestone.[62] When we interact with other people, we use our bodies to communicate our thoughts and feelings, our desires and frustrations, our ideals, and our wishes. *Our humanity*.

The gesturing with our hands, our facial expressions and the posturing of our body have been the basic necessary tools of our *social interactions* for ages. Without those signals, we end up *navigating* human relations *without a compass*. Mirror neurons are the only cells of the Central Nervous System that specialize in the *coding of the actions* of other people and our own in order to *provide meaning*. The *inner imitation* that the mirror neurons construct in our brains allow us to *replicate* the intentions and emotions that are underlying those manifest actions.

When our visual occipital cortex detects someone smiling in front of our eyes, our *mirror neurons for smiling* start sending electrical pulses that will replicate, in a milder form, the same experience that we are witnessing. The *inner image* in our brain recreates its *twin outside image* that first triggered the stimulus.

Like a child copying a model in the kindergarten, we get to understand it.

The neuroscientists are still debating whether these special neurons are a distinct class of cells or that *the mirror activity* is rather a specialized type of electrophysiological activity that will eventually facilitate certain coded responses of our motor system. Patricia Churchland, a neuro-philosopher, doubted that these neurons are solely responsible for understanding the intentions of other people and proposed that the final coding is done in a *higher, more complex level* of activity.[63] The function of these neurons is to provide meaning to actions, but they do not seem to play a role in non-social cognition; we should consider other mechanisms.

Our collective memory, molded by centuries of social interaction by our ancestors, will help us interpret the coded signals created by the human gregarious instincts.

Neurophysiological studies—using *Magnetic Resonance Imaging* (MRI), *Electroencephalography* (EEG) and *Magnetoencephalography* (MEG)—showed that certain areas of the Central Nervous System—the anterior insula, the anterior cingulate cortex, and the inferior frontal cortex—became active when we had an emotion or when we watched someone else's.[64] *It is the basis for human empathy.*

Yawei Chung et al. showed with sophisticated neurophysiological and MRI techniques, that women have a *stronger motor response* of the mirror system.[65] "Young adult females (n=25) had significantly larger gray matter volume in the pars opercularis and inferior parietal lobule than matched males (n=25) participants." Schulte-Ruther et al. showed in a study focusing on the emotional responses to certain events that the feminine participants had *stronger empathic abilities* than males. They studied gender differences in the emotional response to "emotion expressing faces" (*SELF-task*) or the "emotional state expressed by the faces" (*OTHER-task*) using functional *Magnetic Resonance Imaging* (MRI) They found that women rated SELF-related emotions *significantly stronger* than men as they recruited the right inferior frontal cortex and superior temporal sulcus much harder than the men did.[66] This study also showed that the ability to recognize the *emotions of others* was similar in both sexes, for which the better performance might be due to training. In cultural conditioning, women are reared to *express and recognize emotions* as an integral part of their traditional education; men, on the contrary, are usually taught to *withhold its open display* in the public sphere.

In the past two decades our understanding of how our brain basically works has changed as we found that the motor and sensory systems are *integrated*. Some data indicates that the Parietal cortex is linked to the Frontal cortex in a *specialized mirror system* that is part of the classical dorsal stream. This stream is further subdivided into a ventrodorsal part—associated with the *identification* of objects for recognition—and a dorsodorsal part—associated with *control* of actions. **Stable affordances** appear after our brain processes the visual input using our previous knowledge and experiences interacting with the same objects or persons. **Variable affordances** appear during a much faster processing of some features like positioning in space, changes in morphology, including the update for hand grasping. The dorsodorsal stream carries the signals for the coding of the variable affordances; the ventrodorsal stream carries the signals for the stable ones. [67]

Are women more capable of multi-tasking and integration of memories?

Studies [68] showed they have more **inter**-hemispheric connections between the **Left propositional**—logical and analytical—and the **Right appositional**—perceptual and synthetic—hemispheres, facilitating the integration of the analytical functioning of the Left hemisphere with the intuitive capacity of the Right one.

Men have more *intra-hemispheric* connections in the Left brain, which facilitates their *motor skills* while women's better *inter-hemispheric* connectivity enables them to combine the *analytical* and *intuitive conceptions* for personal memories.

Women are more skillful at *interpreting* the emotions expressed in faces, the *articulation* of integrated responses and the *safeguarding* of collective memories. In our families, we have watched our dear grandmothers and mothers prepare the religious season's meals to gather our families around a festive, celebratory table; even for non-believers, it constitutes a social excuse to re-connect with their kind. Those tender memories are safeguarded in our Sub-conscious for life. *Grazie*.[69]

Can a woman seamlessly pass from loving to hating, and vice versa?

Men are baffled by the feminine gender's power to *hop Tiger-like* [70] from feelings—and expressions—of affection to open disdain and even hate. It is as if there were **two long-time neighbors**—one residing in *the land of Love* and the other one in *the land of Hate*—just casually, amiably chatting over *a flimsy fence*. It does not take much physical effort or bad luck for one of them to accidentally trip and fall into the other person's property. A misjudged word. A misplaced stare. The most banal of circumstances can pit previously friendly neighbors against each other. Women are skillful at managing their Right Hemisphere—our intuitive half; the **apposition** of neuronal imprints for *Love and Hate* is perfectly plausible there.

No Right or Wrong. Never a judgmental stance. Only total harmony.

Is a woman's behavior influenced by her changing hormonal status?

We might be familiar with the hormonal **cycle of estrogen-progesterone** that determines the fertility in women on a rather regular basis. Their menstrual cycle begins at Day 1 with the *sloughing of tissue* off from the endometrial lining of the uterus and the drainage of a small amount of blood through the uterine cervix and then the vagina, lasting up to 2-3 days on average—**the menstruation**.

The Follicular Stimulating Hormone (FSH) from the hypophysis gland prods the *maturation of a follicle* in the right or left ovaries—**the follicular phase**. [71] At the same time the ovaries start secreting more estrogens, mostly estradiol, which *stimulate the growth of the endometrial lining* to form a welcoming mat for the potential lay-out of a fertilized follicle. Concomitantly the Luteinizing hormone (LH) rises to eventually induce the ova to detach from the follicle and travel to the Fallopian Tube in order to wait for the spermatozoids' invasion. The empty follicle starts to secrete progesterone, which together with the estrogens will prod the growth of the endometrium at day 14 of the cycle—**the luteal phase**.

From that time until day 28, *the ovum waits* for a spermatozoid to show up and fertilize it. If the latter does not happen, the hormonal secretions abruptly stop. Deprived of its hormonal support, the endometrium starts *shedding its outer layer* and another menstruation occurs. The fabulous feminine cycle that has created us.

Thanks Mom!

There is an **emotional variance** in the major phases of the cycle. In the two or three previous days to the beginning of the menstrual cycle, women are *excited* due to the hormonal changes and the retention of fluids in their bodies. From day 7 to 14, women have a *higher tolerance to pain*, but their *mistrust and edginess* rise. Between day 13 to 15 women become *sexually excited* to promote the coupling; after their ovulation, their *emotional lability* rises until the menstruation occurs.[72]

There are studies that claim that women did not lose the period of **estrus**—when an ovulating mammal advertises *her heightened receptivity for suitors*. Annie M. Paul said: "evolutionary biologists and psychologists have uncovered abundant evidence that women do, in fact, provide clues to the timing of ovulation, the moment when an egg is released and ready to be fertilized. Though these changes are far subtler than those in other species, they have a powerful effect on women's perceptions, preferences and behavior—and the reaction of others to her." [73]

Karl Grammar et al. studied the digital pictures of 351 women who went to Vienna's nightclubs and had a sample of their saliva collected to check for estradiol; women who were *dressed to kill* had much higher levels of estradiol—a telltale sign that they were *ovulating* at the time of specimen collection. [74] Nicholas Gueguen studied women's looks and gait, measuring their estradiol with an LH salivary test. Nearing ovulation, women *walked slower and sexier*, a sign that they unconsciously wanted to be more attractive to get better choices. [75]

Did you ever feel that your wife tightens up when you are ready to relax?

We are less aware of the *cortisol cycle* in women, which markedly differs from the masculine one. **Cortisol** is the hormone that regulates all the critical body functions in situations of *heightened activity* that provoke significant *stress*. [76]

Men are usually more stressed out in the *morning and afternoon hours* whereas women tend to be more stressed out in *late afternoon and evening hours*. They have different rhythms for this hormonal agent. **The cortisol's jump**. [77]

Men often derive most of their daily dosage of stress from the challenging work situations whereas women handle better the multitasking of modern labor. But the tables are turned when they go back home, and they face a stark reality. Children must be reined in to do their homework, family dinner must be fixed, their mothers are calling… Dreaded 4D. *Dismally. Droning. Domestic. Drudgery.*

Most couples *fight in the evening and night* when they are more tired and stressed out, besides facing the needs and demands of their young children.[78] In order to have *a healthy lifestyle*, people need a good night's sleep, something that will hardly materialize if they go to bed mad at their partners, feeling frustrated. An old aunt told us that she never went to bed angry with her fifty-years husband. Occasionally, they fought but they tried to reconcile before the end of the day.

When they could not, they would sit in bed in total silence the whole night.

<u>Diary of USS Awareness</u> – Use the sextant of ancient mariners to find a safe route.

A nugget of Wisdom. Just arrived home and dropped the keys on the table. We hear you. You had a tough time at work today and yearned for this moment: you are now safe in your own castle to unwind and relax. There is only one thing. Your wife is geared up to unload a *garbage truck-worth of complaints* on you.

Look at her tenderly in the eye and plant a furious kiss on her left cheek.

That hit of her skin receptors shoots up to her **Land-Hate game reserve**.[79] Tell her: "Please give me a few minutes, honey." Take full advantage of the brief confusion that you sowed in her rear-guard to skedaddle straight to safety ; change into comfy clothing and sit down in the sofa to watch the news or listen to music. Sip a soothing drink (absolutely no alcohol). Close your eyes to grab a quick nap.

Once you feel ready, take a deep breath, and get up to meet your *Destiny*. Playing dummy, kiss her and say: "what do you want me to help you with? Do all the laundry? Fix dinner? Help the kids with the homework? You decide, honey." Initially, she might view it as an empty gesture without substance, so be prepared to receive the brunt of the feminine sarcasm: "Really? Since when are so helpful?" Sulkily pouting with both lips, murmur: "There's always time to mend your ways."

Touché. She will quickly melt with a sudden rush of affection for her man.

And text her roster of friends about your Road-to-Damascus moment.[80]

As a sign of gratitude, she might even grant you cookie points in bed.

Easy...Very...So

"One side contains my exuberant cheerfulness, my flippancy, my joy in life and, above all, my ability to value the lighter side of things…This side of me is usually lying-in wait to ambush the other one, which is much purer, deeper and finer. No one knows Anne's better side."

Final entry dated August 1, 1944, "The Diary of Anne Frank" [81]

The martyred Anne wrote that three days before August 4, 1944, when a squad of the Dutch *collabo* [82] police burst into her family's hideout in Amsterdam and imprisoned them before sending them by train to the Auschwitz concentration camp. Together with her sister, Anne died of typhus in Bergen-Belsen in 1945. [83]

Bart van Es said: "Amid all this, as the years pass, Anne reads extensively and develops an increasing passion for her writing. She composes short stories, comic anecdotes, and begins a novel. Most important, after hearing a radio broadcast from the Dutch government about the need for records of the occupation. Anne started to revise her diary early in 1944, in the hope that it might be published…" [84] Anne Frank's life exemplifies **the moral strength** of women in the face of adversity. Even though a terrible terror was laying siege to her family, that heroic girl mustered enough serenity to write about her *psychological dichotomy*. Endowed by Mother Nature to carry on the precious task of reproduction, women spring a seemingly inexhaustible well of raw courage and determination.

There is a dimension of the feminine ethos that most health professionals—foremost amongst them we, the physicians—would rather avoid discussing it in any kind of public forum, let alone in a printed form like this essay, even though we have witnessed many clinical instances in which it manifested itself. By the nature of their own fertility, women are **more empathic** to the changing cycles of Mother Nature; many of them are what Dr. Orloff has dubbed as the *empaths*.[85]

Since Ancient Times, humans have been observing the stars above and the soil below to find if there were meaningful relationships that constituted patterns.[86] The Assyrians, the Egyptians, the Mayas, the Romans, the Chinese, etc., designed useful calendars based on the movements of the stars to determine the best timing for planting and picking up crops, to engage in warring campaigns, to marry, etc.[87]

There is a lot of skepticism about the value of *Astrology* and similar esoteric disciplines.[88] But if we have been so intrigued, there could be "something in there." We have observed that even the most rational of well-educated women often peek at their daily horoscope "to find out what it says." If it suits them, they might even whisper the discovery to another girlfriend; if it does not, they discreetly dismiss it. They might consider that even if the rational scientific methods have not developed enough yet to separate fact from fiction in these ancient premises, they are careful not to dismiss them outright—just in case there might be a hidden truth in there.

Standing firm, they scan for the orbiting Unknown above. En tout cas...[89]

Chapter II – It's not only about sex.

"I swear to Mr. the Marquis de Sade, my lover, of never belonging to anyone but him, of never marrying or giving myself to others, of being faithfully attached to him as long as the blood that I am using to seal this letter will flow in my veins. I offer him the sacrifice of my life, of my love and my feelings, with the same passion that I have offered him my virginity and I finish my oath by promising him that, if one year from this date, I am no longer a novice and as a result of that status, which I only embrace to be free to live with him and to devote everything to him, I swear… to follow him to Venice where he wants to take me, to eternally live with him as his wife" (signed with blood) December 15, 1769 [90]

Anne Prospère de Launay de Montreuil was born on December 27, 1751. At 11 years of age she became Sade's sister-in-law. At age 17, his lover.

Imprisoned for almost thirty years for his debauchery and cruelty, the Marquis de Sade [91] had a dark pull over women. [92] Chantal Thomas said that her favorite character was *Juliette* [93]: "because he puts a woman's voice as the first person. Sade fires up her text that passes from a programed series of orgies to a picaresque novel. Juliette travels. The libertines' invention is the invention of movement." [94]

Movement. The crux of the matter for conflicted women of all centuries.

Anne had been coached by her family and mentors to become a good wife.

Openly defying the supremacy of the patriarchal institutions, she ran away.

She decided to mate with the poster-boy of everything they had condemned.

Thrusting her hands in a pool of mud, she molded her own dream of a lover.

A common thread in almost all the causes of *Emotional Frustration* involving sex is the **presence or absence of movement** in the women's lives, with many facets. For the woman that submissively accepts a *quasi-passive* attitude in her erotic life, there is not a true engagement with her partner, leading to a loss of self-confidence.

On the opposite end of the spectrum, the woman that dares to defy the social conventions and *acts decisively* to find her space, becomes a target of bold critique. Either way, the subterranean torrent of misogynism that runs in the social media—despite all the patina of token respect for women—takes for granted the mobility of women, as if they were still dependent on other people's initiatives. She studies X. because her father said it… She marries Y. because her mother liked it… She has one kid because her mate chose it… She does not have one because he chose to.

Whenever a woman *changes the script* assigned to her, trouble will follow. Even though Anne's plight might seem dated, it is replicated in modern bedrooms.

Servility under the bed sheets fosters Sexual Dysfunction for both partners.
Only an emancipated woman allows a man to reach an Erotic Ecstasy.

Sex. A three-letter word that seems so simple and yet is so complicated. Especially for women. Not that they are not that interested or do not think about it. They do. Always. But they think and feel *in a different way* than we, men, do.[95] If we hope to try to understand *what women really want*, which Freud realized to be extremely difficult to grasp after decades studying their open and hidden sexuality, we must first determine *what they do not want* so we can thread carefully. *Very*.

The most common sex issues that foster feminine *Emotional Frustration* are:

a) Use of explicit pictures to stimulate the libido.

b) Take an inordinate amount of time in intercourse.

c) Hasty stimulation of the clitoris without a proper preamble

d) Refrain from moaning and other expressions of pleasure

e) Excessive attention to "romanticism" instead of passion

A. Use of explicit pictures to stimulate the libido.

In contrast to the insatiable masculine appetite for pictures/films with nudity, the feminine gender has a more nuanced and controversial view of pornography.[96] Women engage their imagination to *edit their own imagery* and bespoke sexual fantasies with their *subject of interest* instead of a crude body exposition.[97] Perhaps they are attracted to an intellectual type and would like to see you in a British prep school-tweed suit with a piece of chalk writing on the blackboard (*Still exist?*) Or perhaps they like the business type and prefer you in an impeccable Armani suit, dangling the keys of your luxury sedan. Or perhaps they like the muscular type and would melt at your sight in a football jersey or a Marine uniform. Or perhaps they are drawn to bohemian types and adore the neglected look of a bachelor pad…

Almost since they enter puberty, women start designing *the motion picture of their lives* with a central, dominant character and a few supporting ones as well. Every time she does an impromptu casting for roles, the film is rolling in her head. Find out what the features of her screenplay really are before making any moves.

Men usually have sexual desire almost uninterruptedly and when they find any kind of opportunity to mate, they become sexually excited. In contrast women do not live with the burden of *non-stop desire* and need to reach a certain point of erotic excitation before feeling sexual desire. [98] *Ready troopers, they are not.*

A nugget of Wisdom. Plenty of people take their clothes off. All the time. Tossing their garments off, they are paradoxically camouflaging their inner self.

What most women really mean when they ask you to "expose yourself" is not to send them a crude picture of your anatomy. It refers to an honest attempt to share all your thoughts, emotions, fears, desires, fantasies, etc.; eventually she will reciprocate with *her own nudity*. Easier said than done? How about her clothes?

Say "the right words" in her left ear. Tumbling down, they go. Abracadabra.

<u>Diary USS Awareness</u> – Stop trying to navigate "her emotionality" only with your eyes. Close them. Catch the *scent of her sea currents*. Like the Polynesians do.

B- Not managing the timing of the sexual intercourse

After the nice, exciting, foreplay is finally over, she might be ready for you. But the *vaginal lubrication* to avoid wall damage during the penetration will only last for a certain amount of time, after which she will feel pain during its rubbing. The *misguided macho* assumption that *you must pump* the vagina on and on, disregarding her pleas to go easier and even stop altogether, has harmful effects.[99] Not only she will resent that insensitivity, but she might avoid sex with you again.

It is better to save energy by taking time after the climax— hopefully, yours *and* hers—to cuddle in bed so you can both harmoniously stand down as a couple. Manly excitation quickly rises, peaks, and falls in just *a few minutes*. But the feminine one *rises slowly* and comes down with *a much gentler slope*, after coitus; her sexual organs, even in a shut off mode, still have a residual excitation.[100]

A nugget of Wisdom. Right on. You just had fabulous sex with your loved one and both of you reached an exhilarating erotic climax. Screaming included. You feel satisfied that you had treated her with affection and patience all the way. Beware. Your job is half-way complete. She is trying to unwind in her own terms. Resist with all your will that irresistible urge to turn around and fall asleep. Tough.

Gently grab her head and lay it on your torso while you caress her gently.

Whisper a few loving words that she can recognize as "intimately yours."

Once the flying carpet of your syllables takes off, you can start snoring.

C – Hasty stimulation of intimate parts without a proper preamble

Women have the only organ fully dedicated to enjoying sex: **the clitoris**. It is a *well-vascularized* organ with multiple nerve endings in order to transmit the sensations of the act to the *conscious processing* in the Central Nervous System.[101] Before touching it, her partner must suavely, rhythmically caress both the labia majora and minora of her vagina to incite it to come off under its *capuchon*.[102] Then he must attempt the *gentlest of contacts* to avoid the painful overstimulation. Each woman is different and her threshold for tolerance may significantly vary. It is better to start slowly, *finetuning* the intensity and timing of these parameters.[103]

The *good lubrication* of the vagina is a requisite for its safe penetration by the penis and to achieve a safe, satisfactory sexual arousal. When there is a dearth of liquid response, the act is flawed due to pain and the possibility of damage. [104]

One of the common causes of **sub-optimal lubrication** is a manly hurry to penetrate the cavity in a cruel *Attila-the-Hun-mad-dash-into-the-castle-to-subdue*. The time needed by any individual female to achieve the necessary lubrication might vary according to her age, her hormonal status, and her bodily connections. Moreover, as she ages, she *progressively* loses her natural load of estrogens, which will decrease her capacity to lubricate. A clinical study of 2400 women showed that use of lubricants, water-based or in gel form, improved the sexual satisfaction for 70% of those that used it with a partner and for 60% that used it alone. [105]

D – Refrain from moaning and other expressions of pleasure

The patriarchal repression indoctrinated men into avoiding overt expressions of sexual pleasure—supposedly not virile enough (sic)—which limited sex arousal. The *exchange of noises* and *exclamations* is of paramount importance to achieve a good excitatory state and an enjoyable orgasm for both partners.[106] The repressive paucity of the natural expressions of pleasure in men has **a mirror image** in some women who, to conceal their true dissatisfaction, tend to *fake an orgasm* to please their partners, using a mendacious maneuver that forestalls any frank discussion.

Gary Brewer of the *University of Central Lancashire* and Colin Hendric of the *University of Leeds* [107] developed a questionnaire for women ranging from 18 to 48 years old where they divided *female vocalizations in sex* into four groups:

1. Silence
2. Moan-groan
3. Scream/shriek/squeal
4. Instructional commands

They found that: "while female orgasms were most commonly experienced during foreplay, copulatory vocalizations were reported to be made most often before and simultaneously with male ejaculation. These data together clearly demonstrate a dissociation of the timing of women experiencing orgasm and making copulatory vocalizations and indicate that there is an element of these responses that are under conscious control, providing women with an opportunity to manipulate male behavior to their advantage." [108] Women used vocalizations, not to express pleasure, but to speed the process up due to boredom, fatigue, and time constraints; almost 92% said that this *little trick* boosted manly self-esteem.

More Machiavellian than what Niccolò Machiavelli [109] could imagine.

Some scientists said that the exteriorization of the female orgasm used to be critical to foster the ovulation of our ancestral women as it stimulated the release of prolactin and oxytocin. This *reproductive call to arms* became superfluous over the centuries due to cultural/societal conditioning, debunking its trigger role in mating. As a collateral effect, the clitoris slowly retreated backwards due to lack of proper stimulation; its central role in the female sexuality was shamed into camouflage. [110]

Pursued by its implacable foes, Maître Clito [111] had to join le Maquis [112].

E – Excessive attention to "romanticism" instead of passion

Men have in general properly learned how to treat women more respectfully in the past few years as the surge of Feminism has changed our social mores. The mellowing of the discourse about sex had the collateral effect of camouflaging the more passionate aspects of it as "too much information." But it is still charged with a florid emotional baggage that may include all kind of fantasies, which sometimes translate into actions. We used to assume that only men, saddled with the burden of non-stop sexual desire, were daydreaming about sex and conquest… *However.*

Women have wild fantasies that can match and even surpass those of men. A common feminine fantasy is some kind of relationship with other girls. Does that mean that women are in fact bisexual, instead of heterosexual?

Dr. Gerulf Rieger, lead researcher at the Department of Psychology of the *University of Essex,* found that, even though the majority of women might identify as straight, they are in fact **bisexual** or **gay**.[113] His research team used eye-tracking devices to capture the *pupil dilatation* (or lack thereof) in response to the sexual stimuli of showing videos of naked men and women to 345 participants. Straight women were *strongly sexually aroused* to videos of both attractive men and women, despite affirming that they were only interested in men. This contrasted with the response of lesbian women who showed a *stronger preference* for other women, making them more "male-typical" in their acts. The public appearance and discourse of women might not entirely coincide with their innermost preferences.

Adriana Arias, a Buenos Aires psychologist specializing in sex disorders, said that gay fantasies *should not be considered as bad* for a woman's well-being. "The imagination is the language of erotism. It connects us with our senses, these with our sensations and the latter with our emotions…Fantasies enrich us, stimulate our creativity, liberate us, decrease our tensions, allow us 'to play at being someone else' and are often an antidote to the sexual routine." [114]

L'imagination au pouvoir [115]

—"Doctor…Before serving a dish to a customer, got to try it myself."

Tanya X. is the feisty, lesbian sous-chef of a posh beach resto that jokingly told us that, despite having a partner, she used "self-stimulation" as an appetizer. There is a high prevalence of **masturbation** in the USA[116], both amongst the young and adults, but it is still considered as *a taboo issue* in most public forums.

Despite a strong social opposition, that practice is slowly "coming out."

The *National Health and Social Life Survey*, administered by the *University of Chicago*, showed that in the 18-60 years old segment, 38% of women and 61% of men said that they had at least one episode the previous year. The masturbation-partnered sex linkage had *a bimodal presentation* for both genders as it was both a compensation for an unsatisfying sex life and an addition to a satisfying one too.

Yvonne Fulbright, relationship expert and writer, said: "how to stimulate the 'hot spots', whether your own or your lover's, can be a piece of cake—that is once you know the recipe. The secret to becoming a rave-inspiring 'masterchef' in the bedroom is knowing when (and how) to throw in a dash of this or a pinch of that, let the things simmer a bit or even mix up the ingredients. It's also important to know why the right blend makes things so sweet." [117] *A personalized cookbook.*

Researchers at the *Kinsey Institute* [118] interviewed more than a thousand heterosexual Australians about what they usually hide below the bedsheets. The data showed that only 61.6% of women claimed to reach an orgasm during sexual intercourse compared to almost 85.5% of men that claimed they did. Almost 38% of the participating women said that they needed stimulation of the clitoris to reach an orgasm in 75% of the sexual encounters they had had; the investigators stated that previous clinical studies did not fully address the issue of clitoral stimulation.

—"Doctor…My hubby gave me a new dildo with a cute little ear—so nice."

When Saint Valentine's Day comes, physicians might teasingly ask their lady patients if their "significant other" remembered the date. Usually our patients would start "talking their heads off" about beautiful flower bouquets, or boxes of tasty chocolates or romantic dinner dates in tony venues… Or the three of them for a few. They did not tell us on how the action evolved the rest of the night, save for giving us a mischievous wink that said it all. *And we did not dare to ask either.*

Sadly, the mendacious **double morality**, and hence **double discourse** in society—on one hand cavalierly exposing us to vile forms of pornography and on the other one "playing prude" by dodging the discussion of our sexuality —has blurred the significance of **sensuality.** It originally refers to the human capacity to use all of our senses—vision, hearing, smell, taste and touching—to potentiate our regular sexual experiences in an innovative, fulfilling, and exhilarating way. [119]

Diary USS Awareness – Who is saying that this is *fake news*? That one with the MAGA [120] hat? Put him in the towed dinghy… Together with this one with the *No Malarkey* [121] T- shirt…We need to fast freshen up the deck so we can breathe.

In our still largely *phallo-centric societies* there is an over-reliance on the subject of **sexual penetration** as there is a lingering fear in males of not being able to satisfy the female desire and therefore *fail the test in bed*—in spite of the fact that only a fourth of women said they had an orgasm with penetration only.[122]

In women their sexuality is not limited to the vagina but *spread almost evenly* all over their bodies; *their skin* has a high concentration of receptors for sex steroids, which constitutes one of the best recipients to receive erotic stimuli.[123]

The concept of "good sex" entails much more that the penetration of a cavity to rhythmically rub its walls to excite receptors because we are both engaging in an intimate bonding with a baggage of *internal expectations* and *past experiences*.[124] In fact, it really starts when someone looks at another person in a different, original way and then approaches him/her/ihr [125] to start a significant emotional coupling. The mellifluous chatting, the overt flirting, the occasional touching, a furtive kiss, the sharing of exciting cultural/social events, etc., all form part of the sexual act.

What is a girl to do when she cannot find a ready way to sate her desire?

It seems that girls have been stealthily having fun for a long time indeed. In 2015 a siltstone phallus dating back 28,000 years was discovered in Germany. Phalluses made from stone, leather and camel dung were found in other sites. Initially labelled as mere decorative objects, the researchers eventually reclassified those instruments as the rustic forerunners of our present-day sexual artifacts.[126]

Despite the social censure for the regular practice of "the company of one", many women of all ages practice it on a regular basis; reliable social statistics are hard to find as the survey participants are often reluctant to tell the whole truth.[127] However, **the sex toys** are being slowly accepted in the mainstream as additives. The *special oils* for some relaxing massages, the *online stimulation* programs, the *vibrating ring* to prolong the erection, the *provocative lingerie* in black or red, the seductive *masks*, the various types of *vibrators*, etc. Even though many men still consider them as an unwarranted intrusion in the sex act that distract their partners from the action, more women are coming out in the open—first timidly suggesting, notching it up bit by bit and finally demanding it outright—in favor of them. [128]

There are bonafide personal considerations, including religious beliefs, that preclude the usage of the sex objects in many couples; however, if your partner is not *a priori* contrary to this playfulness, then it can be properly discussed as adults. In a couple there are hardly any issues—including sex—that cannot be considered. The most important aspect is to *respect the desires and concerns* of your partner, avoiding any kind of rushed move that will provoke a simmering grudge. Any innovation in the couple's regular sex schedule must be previously discussed to reach a consensus on *what to actually do* and *what not to even dream to do.* [129]

Before starting to play, the teams must define the boundaries of the field.

If there is any transgression, the game should be interrupted for a call.

No possibility of social encounters. Not even the platonic kind. What to do?

After months of *forced isolation* due to the *Covid-19 plague*, we are fed up. With *perturbed nights* and *never-ending weekends*, we feel entitled to a little fun. Under the auspices of the *Trojan* company—makers of the famous condoms—Dr. Robin Milhausen, an investigator of the *University of Guelph*, Canada, conducted a survey [130] to find the incidence and prevalence of **Masturbation.** They found that:

a) Men engaged in that practice at least once a week, *at a rate double* than women (65% to 35%) but women reported *a pleasurable experience* more frequently than men did (38% of women to 29% of men)

b) 43% of women that did it *on a regular basis* reported that their latest one was more pleasurable, compared to 27% of women that did not.

c) Men who considered that their last practice was pleasurable were more likely to be *more emotionally stable* in their couple relationships.

d) 47% of women and 39% of men who liked their latest drill were more likely to say that *they were satisfied* with their sexual lives.

e) 54% of women *used a vibrator*; of those 46% of them said that their latest drill was more pleasurable compared to 35% of those that did not.

The Japanese company *TENGA*—makers of the infamous sex toys—conducted surveys worldwide to prepare a **2019 Self Pleasure report**. [131] They found that:

a) Americans *ranked fourth* — 84% of respondents —behind Germany (89%), the United Kingdom (91%) and the world champion, Spain (93%)

b) The three more common reasons to do it were: *sexual satisfaction* (31%), *reach sexual climax* (25%) and *relief of stress* (21%)

c) Heterosexual and LGBT Americans *were more likely* to drill on a regular basis—91% and 94% respectively—compared to women (78%)

d) Men are more likely to start at *a young age*—13 years old on average.

e) Many women find it *more pleasurable* than the real thing; 37% of women considered that the solo act was better than sex, compared to 33% of men.

Dr. Julie Richters, investigator at the *University of New South Wales*, conducted a survey of almost 20,000 Australians to study their *solo practices*. They found that:

1. 72% of men and 42% of women had masturbated in the past year.
2. Half of the men (51%) and a 24% of women did it in the past four weeks.
3. In the past year, two-fifths of respondents—63% of men and 20% of women—browsed some pornography material in various presentations.
4. 21% of women and 15% of men had used a sex toy.
5. 19% of men and 15% of women had practiced digital-anal stimulation.
6. 7% of men and 4% of women had engaged in oral-anal stimulation.
7. 7-8% played sexual roles or engaged in cross-dressing.

A nugget of Wisdom. We get it. You are upset. You found out that your wife kept *a dildo* tucked away in the bathroom's cabinet. The one that you never opened because it was supposedly stocked with her stuff. Today you decided to be nosy. There it is. Behind a box of tampons, it was hiding. "Why does she need one?"

You can Olympically ignore it and make do as if you had never seen it. But she will likely notice a change in the way it was laid down again. She will know. When you can find an opportunity, fix a nice drink, and sit down to chat with her. After some initial trepidation, she will open up. She might tell you that, despite her raucous breathing and outbursts, she sometimes does not reach a good climax.

Without false prudishness you can both discuss how to improve your sexual life by upgrading the foreplay, taking more time with related activities like gently rubbing her breasts, kissing her neck, massaging her clitoris, whispering in her ear.

Be prepared to the possibility that, even though she has satisfactory bonding with you, she might want to include a sex toy in your couple's relationship. After the scandalous divorce of a Buenos Aires celebrity couple—a football player and a model—his new girlfriend impertinently snatched his Ex's toy. *Felipe*.[132]

<u>*Diary USS Awareness*</u> – A rogue wave of *women's secret lives* knocked you down? Got no warning? That's precisely why they call it rogue, dummies —Who's hollering? A married mariner has just connected all his wife's dots… It figures. Tie him to the mast and put a muzzle on. We got a good tailwind. Unfurl the sails.

Nora *(looking at her watch) "It is not so very late. Sit down here, Torvald. You and I have very much to say about one another"(She sits down at a table's end)*

Helmer. *"Nora—what is this? This cold, set face?"*

Nora. *"Sit down. It will take some time. I have a lot to talk over with you."*

"A doll's house" [133] *by Henrik Ibsen*

Nora, a traditional housewife in 19th century Copenhagen, summoned the spiritual strength—after her husband ostensibly failed to socially support her when an old misdeed became public—to confront him about her utter disappointment. She complained that her father had treated her as *his doll-child* and transferred the "possession of that toy" to him when they got married. A business transaction.

One of the frequent feminine complaints against men is that they view and treat women as mere **objects of desire** to satisfy their sexual appetite, giving short shrift to what they really think or feel. In the intimacy of the *medical office*, the *confession booth* or the quarter's *beauty salon*, women often vent this complaint. Women decry that society still views them primarily as *satisfiers* of manly desires and expectations that run the gamut from getting an orgasm to a salami sandwich. Only when they fulfill their arbitrarily assigned role in *society's division of labor*, they might be given some space—albeit limited and never without supervision—to express other concerns, including their cherished professional or artistic ambitions.

Women of all ages and classes have rebelled at being **sex objects** for men. On May 1, 1963, Gloria Steinem wrote her famous article *A Bunny's tale*.[134] Working undercover in the *Playboy Club* in New York City, she daringly exposed the *sexist* and *exploitative* working environment of this "gentleman's club." She was one of the first women to contest the prevailing societal "beauty standards", which started the still open social conversation about women's *raw objectification.*

Nowadays women are defying the high expectations of physical appearance that even our modern societies impose on them, whether explicitly or implicitly. A common source of *Emotional Frustration* for women of all ages is that, in order to advance in a society whose levers of power are still largely held by men, they must relent into accepting some kind of compromise: use make-up, trim nails, etc.[135] When they are young, they tire of the tremendous social pressure thrust on them. When they get older, they feel contrite about the spurious "horse trading" they did.

What is worth it ? Is that progress for us? What do I tell my daughter?

Jennifer Weiner said that: "even though the social media has been pivotal to allow the uncensored expressions of millions of women worldwide, it has had the collateral effect of pressuring them into 'looking good' at all times. Being out in public means 'being looked at', and possibly photographed, in a way that men are still not, and maybe will never be."[136] However, there is still a glaring **disconnect** between the protests of *objectification* and the *admiration* of the "celebrities."

—"Doctor…After years of marriage, I still get so anxious when I undress."

Graciela X. is an attractive middle-aged housewife with a wonderful family that confessed her lingering sexual fear in the intimacy of her bedroom. In our age of sexual liberation with non-stop exposition of all kinds of audacious poses in the social media, this frankness seems so quaint. However, **the sexual fears** (and the related pathologies in the form of *phobias*) are a cause of *Emotional Frustration* in women of all ages and social segments. The anxiety over being considered as a mere object of sex for men's pleasure might worsen the sexual fears in the bed.

Making love is much more than a penis that makes contact with a vagina.

When we make love, we are bringing along our socio-cultural baggage with all the connotations of *faulty perceptions* and *biased opinions* we have acquired. Modern Sexology states that, except for a few clinical conditions, there are no sex pathologies but common complications that need fixing—sexual desire, foreplay, orgasm, and pain at the time of penetration, proper relaxation techniques, etc. [137]

The two most common *sex dysfunctional syndromes* in modern times are:

1 - Lack of lubrication: this problem is especially annoying as the woman experiences severe pain at the time of outright penetration in a dry receptacle. The use of gels and a laser treatment with the segmented CO_2 can alleviate it. As the woman ages, her estrogen endowment may decrease, producing vaginal dryness. Women should consult their gynecologists in order to get good treatment.[138]

2 – Localized pain during intercourse: this is a common occurrence post-partum as the surgical stitches can alter the vulva's anatomy and provoke a re-alignment of the sexual cavity. It can also be rightly fixed with laser therapy. [139]

Even though the sensitive terminals in our sexual organs collect the signals, they are ultimately *processed* in the brain to deliver its *final conscious message*. One of the most common sexual dysfunctions occurs when a woman, after delivering a child, is being bullied by her partner to resume their sexual bond.

In a woman's post-partum subconscious mind, the perception of her vagina as a conduit for new life cannot quickly *switch* to one as a source of pleasure; it still hurts after the taxing physical and emotional demands of the delivery. Their partners must assist them in that psychological transition with a lot of affection.

Two women with contraposing perspectives are sharing a single cavity.

Our sexuality is progressively construed since childhood with the influx of the household, the school, the media, the circle of friends, the associates, etc. These social influences interact with our powerful trove of animal instincts to achieve a *socially acceptable expression* of our sexuality. Usually we enter into a relationship with fear and anxiety, which is a perfectly normal response; but each couple must design their *mutual* psychological and physical familiarity. Once it ceases to be purely casual, there is a "switch" in attitudes—emotional and social—that condition the partners' psychological awareness henceforth.

In steady couples **the sexual fears** surface or become much more manifest. Dr. Walter Ghedin [140], a psychiatrist and sex therapist in Buenos Aires—a city with one of the largest assemblages of psychological therapists [141]—said: "there are still women reticent to show what they feel, to ask for what they like or to move in sync with the erotic moment…Men are also conditioned by their desire to perform appropriately, to have a sustained erection and to make women moan during penetration." [142] The surreptitiously, steadily seared social conditioning does alter our sexual behavior. When the anxiety and fear become extreme, the clinical presentation evolves into the **sexual phobias**, which limit the pleasure of sexual bonding. Dr. Debra Kaplan, a licensed sex therapist from Tucson, Arizona, USA, described the twelve most common **triggers:** [143]

1. To touch or caress the body (especially breasts, nipples, or thighs)
2. To look at the genitalia (your own or those of your partner)
3. To touch your partner's genitalia.
4. To kiss the breasts, the mouth, or the genitalia.
5. To be penetrated (by the penis or another object)
6. To smell the sexual secretions (semen, vaginal fluids, breath)
7. To feel excited (with your own odors or the ones of your partner)
8. To have an orgasm (loss of control)
9. To (give or receive) oral sex.

10. To become pregnant.

11. To catch a contagious disease.

12. To the nakedness of your body or the one from your sexual partner.

There are multiple reasons for the emergence of sexual phobias: restricted education, religious beliefs, sexual abuse, physical violence, personality disorders, inferiority complex, social anxiety, fear of social critique, physical handicaps (real or perceived), and the unreasonable expectations of top performance. Paradoxically one of the less studied pathologies is **the obsession with sex**, something normally attributed to men; however, in these egalitarian times, women are close behind. [144]

Do some women feel the same irrepressible sexual urge as most men do?

In our "modern" society, where there is a hypocritical **disconnect** between the *abject availability* of raw pornography and the *prudish avoidance* of a serious discussion of our sexuality, the *masking of female desire* is methodically enforced. In 2002, Eric S. Blumberg turned the mike on and registered in-depth interviews of 44 highly sexual women aged 20 to 82 years old. [145] They admitted that their sexual desire was so strong that they organized their life around it; due to society's double discourse, they would have paid a hefty cost if they had dared to own it up.

Sleazy men dare to put a muzzle on the mouths of a few honest women.

A transposition out of "Animal Farm"[146]

—"Doctor…Got to make love every night—my husband has to keep up."

Solange X. is a gorgeous thirty-something lady that has a loving husband and a small child, besides working as a business manager. She consulted us for a painful bursitis in the right shoulder that she attributed to a very fancy sexual pose. The issue of *desire discrepancy* is common in partners and can radically change as we age; a *Luvze study* affirmed that it might affect 80% of couples sometimes.[147]

The issue of **sex addiction** is being hotly discussed in professional circles at present, which led to a conflict on whether to include that entity in the *DSM III*; the lack of clear-cut clinical evidence tipped the balance against including it (for the time being)[148] An addiction implies the existence of *two factors*, which are:

1. The search for a compensation or pleasure.
2. The existence of a conflict surrounding this behavior.

An *addiction* is different than an *obsessive-compulsive* behavior because in the latter pleasure does not figure as its final goal. Some psychologists argue that in these addictions, there could be physical/psychological harm like it happens with the *food obsession* or *gambling* that are considered as separate clinical entities.

Dr. Walter Ghedin said: "in the addiction to sex the desire is mixed with the impulse, pleasure with anxiety, the temptation with moral values, danger or the risk sensation with the sense of self-preservation. The sex addiction is an irrepressible, repetitive behavior that carries the stigma of guilt and sensation of void that appear once the sexual tension has come down." [149]

Notwithstanding that the majority of Millennials were raised in a *culture of hypersexuality*, many of them are paradoxically reluctant to try intimate relations. Santiago Gómez, a psychologist from the *Centro de Psicología Cognitiva* of Buenos Aires, said: "it may be that on one hand they have lost the habit of personal interactions with someone else, or simply because everything seems to be channeled through the social media nowadays, the young people are devoid of emotions and affection." [150] The over-stimulation of the senses might blunt the sensory receptors and produce a "shut-off phenomenon" for further stimuli.

Does the nymphomaniac predisposition really exist in modern women?

Robert Weiss, a licensed sex therapist, said that: "after more than 20 years spent treating and writing about sex and intimacy issues, I can assure you that women like Joe (he refers to the main character in *Nymphomaniac: Volume I* [151]) definitely do exist, and the film is deadly accurate in its portrayal…provides a spot-on depiction of the types of adult female sexual behaviors that can manifest as a delayed response to the neglect, emotional abuse, and other forms of trauma that sometimes occur during childhood." [152] This frenzied pursuit of multiple sexual targets may be a crude compensatory mechanism to mask a sentimental vacuum.

Une fuite en avant [153]

Robert Sternberg proposed a **triangular theory of love** where the three angles represent a critical component of it: *passion, intimacy, and compromise*.[154]

Passion represents the libidinal, erotic, and sexual factors in a relationship—the *emotional* baggage. It evokes our sexuality, physical attraction, eroticism, pure skin contact; it is the most fascinating component in the beginning of relationships.

Intimacy represents the slow yet solid acquisition of a *close bonding* with a partner; it allows us to show our true self, with virtues and defects, to our partners. Still keeping our individual traits, we safely proceed to know more about theirs.

Compromise is the result of a *solid combination* of passion and intimacy. It is the naturally expected result when two individuals care deeply about each other; they voluntarily make the rational choice to protect their budding relationship. To improve their bond, individual desires are vetted for the common good, fostering *a social contract* between two consenting adults; progressively they will appear as a single, indivisible entity to others.[155] *One plus one is much, much more than two.*

Some women, especially those vaunting *the glories of their youthful power*, may willfully prioritize the acquisition of objects, advance their careers and/or social standing in detriment of their emotional needs, which are relegated for later. A dangerous wager. Progressively they grow tired of the possession of those goods and feel totally bored. Devoid of humanly comfort, they feel a sentimental angst.

Hedonic adaptation.[156]

—"Doctor…Need to see him every week—he's my oxygen mask."

Sheila X. is an attractive middle-aged nurse, supposedly happily married to a good, friendly, affectionate man and with two teenage children still living at home. But something is sorely missing in her life. She confessed to us that the only way to slog through all her routine is to clandestinely date an also-married physician regularly in a cheap motel in the *Calle Ocho* area of Miami. Hardly her cup of tea.

Is she unfaithful because she does not love her husband? No, she does.

Is she unfaithful because she does not like sex with him? No, she does.

Why on earth would she do it then? Because she loves the sheer trill of it.

Even though men still top the *Two-timing* chart, women are closing that gap.[157] The surge in **feminine infidelity** might be related to their *financial liberation* that has freed their libidinal impulses without the fear of being economically penalized. The social censure for a woman found *in fraganti*[158] with a lover has waned down, for which she might be more willing to discreetly try out with a *Coup de Coeur*[159]. Dr. Jane Greer, a marriage/sex therapist in New York City, affirmed that unfaithful women want to feel like *they are special again* and adored by their lovers.[160]

Antoni Bolinches, an expert in Human Sexuality from Barcelona, said in his book that if someone *does not get it right the third time*, he would surely fail in the following relationships.[161] In an interview for the *Clarín* newspaper, he was asked to clarify that statement: "if we want to have success in love, as in all other realms of life, we have to learn from our failures and be aware that the good times are for enjoyment and the bad ones, for learning…instead of laying the blame on the other person, which is the commonest attitude in couple conflicts, what we have to do is rectify, which entails engaging in a self-critique." [162] For all those who have failed in a couple relationship more than once (*like yours truly*) his words are a reminder of a basic lesson gleaned from human endeavors: **the virtues of failure**.

We reviewed [163] the homonymous book written by the French philosopher Charles Pépin [164], where he compared the stultified French learning system to more dynamic ones where failure is viewed as *a pre-requisite for success*. "The name crises derives from the Greek verb 'krinein', which means 'to separate'. In a crisis two elements separate and suddenly create an opening; it is a chance to discover something different. The Greek philosophers called 'kairos' that special moment where a new reality appears… That moment and its re-evaluation might be the *raison d'être* [165] of depression as we are forced to stop and change gears." [166]

Antoni Polinches said that for any couple to succeed, we must go through "a process of personal growth, finding harmony between the sufficient pleasure with the needed obligations. The great school of learning that allows us to grow is the couple. No other relationship is this complex, but at the same time so conflict-prone as there is a mix of roles: friends, parents, lovers…"[167] When they asked the Catalan psychologist and author what the biggest problem of traditional couples was, he responded that it was a good venue for partnership but not so much to enjoy sex. Moreover, the gender equality provided *opportunities to come across* other persons who were not our partners but attracted us precisely because of it. He said that: "we all have defects and virtues, and with our cohabitation the rules make that whatever I see good in you becomes less good as I grew accustomed to it, and whatever I saw as being bad is becoming worse as I grew tired of it." [168]

Men brag about their affairs, but women—much better at histrionics as they *internalize the script lines* to give the illusion of veracity—are truly perfidious. For men, the **feminine infidelity** can be puzzlingly cryptic. What are its telltale signs? <u>*Diary USS Awareness*</u> — Stop goofing around on deck… Great danger lies ahead.

1. Suddenly having her cellular phone out of the reach of her partner.
2. Excessively worry about her personal appearance.
3. Make plans with "friends" that are unknown to her partner.
4. Being unusually emotional and happy.
5. Arrive home late from work and being hard to reach.
6. The irrepressible impulse to hide her feelings.
7. Being sarcastic and indifferent in her formal relationship.
8. Lack of interest in her partner and common activities.
9. Flirting with other men (or women) that might be old friends.
10. Loss of libido and disdain for her partner. [169]

The last feature might be the easiest one to conceal, as supposedly women might be less keen on sex than men are, for which the latter often miss the mark. Antoni Bolinches said that some shrewd women before being unfaithful might fabricate a false couple crisis—based on real tenets or not—in order to buffer their guilt complex after their misdeed.[170] *Men are not the only ones having fun.*

Esther Perel, psychotherapist, and author, said that since the 1990s, the number of women who have cheated in their couples increased by 40%.[171]

A nugget of Wisdom. Your wife stopped nagging you. Did the storm pass?

Beware. It is the eye of the hurricane before its outer ring comes crashing.

Didn't you notice that she cares more about her waistline and started a new diet?

Didn't you notice that she has some furtive chats in a phone unavailable to you?

Didn't you notice that she has new, exciting friends that are unbeknownst to you?

Didn't you notice that she works until late and comes back home with a smile?

Didn't you notice that she seems absent-minded and hums ballads all the time?

Didn't you notice that she looks at you with a mischievous glint in her eyes?

Didn't you notice that even the family dog looks at you in a funny way lately?

Men try to callously conceal their transgressions by hook or crook.

Like a reverse-Sherlock Holmes, women blow clues to the four winds.

<u>*Diary USS Awareness*</u>– Discussing your dogs' looks at lunch? It's a start.

—"Doctor…Finally I made up my mind…I'm divorcing my husband!"

Susan X. is a young secretary—with a nice partner and a small boy—that fell in love with her boss. Just a little detail…*Happens to be her brother-in-law.* Ready to come clean with the affair, she was turning into **a loose cannon on deck**.

In the 18th and 19th centuries, the warships of seafaring nations like France, England, and Spain carried cannons as their primary offensive weapons that were mounted on rollers to avoid structural damage in the brutal recoil after firing.[172]

Victor Hugo in his novel *Ninety Three* [173] described the mayhem provoked by a cannon after it got loose from its ties: "The cannonade, hurled forward by the pitching, pushed into this knot of men and crushed four at the first blow…The enormous cannon was left alone. She was given up to herself. She was her own mistress, and mistress of the vessel. *She could do what she willed with both.*"[174]

The writer's use of the feminine gender is informative and insinuating at the same time as the word cannon sports the masculine one in the French language.

Listening to her, we knew it was a *break-glass-in-case-of-fire-moment* and we had to mind our words…What to say? (*Thinkie…Thinkie*) Long, long time ago, before we became *a monk of Medicine*, we might have been in a similar scary spot.
–"Mmm…Tread carefully," we said. "Your kid can't understand this situation—"
-"Think so?" she said, demurring. "Perhaps I should wait until he's at least three."

Delaying the débâcle, our magic incantation tied the loose cannon back.

—"Doctor…I'm always fab for him, unlike his wife—stinking of garlic."

Marcela X. is a young, beautiful, feisty, and smart woman that has had a strong attraction for a particular man—against the advice of her friends and family. Ignoring good prospects, she made an unorthodox choice: **dating a married man**. Despite all her critics, she is so totally smitten to the point of starting to love him.

Kristen Houghton said that: "being part of any couple can be challenging and unpredictable. But when the man with whom you're involved is part of another couple… then the challenge and unpredictability can make your life a messy, unhappy waiting game that you will rarely win." [175] Married men hardly ever leave their families to set up another household with what they consider just *a love tryst*.

Even though they would never admit it openly, it happens to many women. They did notice he had a wedding ring, but they were still interested. Very. When the right opportunity arose, they gleefully jumped right into his arms.

Why would a woman with many choices pick, of all men, a married one?

1. Because he has what she wants: a spouse, a house, a job, a family.

2. Because she is convinced that he only made the wrong choice.

3. Because he has been vetted as a sex partner and good father.

4. Because there is no better lover than the one solving frustrations.

5. Because she can play the martyr's role—critical leverage with him.

6. Because he looks like a kid in a candy store. So happy, so grateful.[176]

-"The beauty of it ," Marcela X. said, "is that after listening to his droning, I dispatch him out… As I don't have to find solutions, I sleep like a baby."

—"Doctor…I finally acted on my dear old fantasy…I slept with two men."

Claudia X. is an attractive middle-aged divorced mother of two teenagers that has a stellar career as a corporate lawyer. After dating another colleague for a while, she finally mustered the inner strength to pop this most delicate question:

-*"How about if we invite your pal Ted for a threesome? Do you mind?"*

Even though the issue of **group sex**, either hetero or homosexual, has always swirled in manly minds, it is only now appearing in women's radar screens, usually with the masculine encouragement. The couple's fantasies may now include a *third player*: male, female, or transgender. [177] The fantasy of *one man with two women* still ranks first but increasingly women are demanding *a quid pro quo*; however, they must deal with their partners' reticence for it and their own homosexual fears.

Dr. Walter Ghedin said: "the woman that dares to try erotic games with two or more men likes her sex intense and varied. No conventional poses. No romantic wording. Far from a 'passive' role, she asks, does, and acts. Her behavior fulfills her fantasies. And more." [178] But a daring woman that has *multiplex-mode-sex* is careful because she does not want an unwanted pregnancy or a disease contagion.

Unlike the manly "lapses", the feminine ones are scrutinized more tightly.

Does it seem unfair to you?

—"Doctor…My husband likes to watch me making love with another man."

Lucy X. is a nice looking, middle aged professional who had consulted us a few years ago for the treatment of a lower urinary tract infection; she claimed that her membership in a swingers' club might have caused that "wear effect." Her husband, a successful professional, often hinted that they should try "something new" as he was obviously getting bored of their sex routine; his listless lassitude in bed prodded her to act. It was her, not him, that arranged their admission details to that club. The excitement of **voyeurism** has rekindled their passion. *Times change.*

One of the commonest sexual fantasies of adults is that "our significant other" is having sex *with another person* but that often stays in our dreamworld. To make the fantasy real, there must be audacity and an unequivocal understanding of the pre-arranged parameters for such an adventure. Those that participate in the swinging lifestyle usually have had extensive chats with each other where the rules of interaction are clearly defined in advance. No room for any improvisation. [179]

What used to be a permissive prerogative of the wealthy has become much more mundane and accessible due to the democratizing power of the social media. According to the prevailing **swinger's credo,** the *taken for granted fidelity* of the monogamous couple prods the bored partners *to try a tryst* with the inevitable pain when the truth surfaces. Swingers claim they can keep their emotional allegiance for their partners if they *frame the experiment* with previously defined parameters.

Their arousal often depends on **the double role** of actor and spectator in the act—the *voyeurism* factor, which seems critical to achieve their sexual satisfaction.

Their partner of convenience becomes an *object of pleasure*; in French swinging is called *échangisme*, which typifies an "objectification of sorts." The use of proper protection like condoms is mandatory as well as the understanding that a partner can say "no" anytime. The engagement with "non-vetted partners" is discouraged.

The discreet practice of **poly-loving** has been spreading in modern nations, first in North America, then in Europe and now in traditional societies. Alessandra Rampolla, an Argentine sex expert and author, said: "Yes, people are looking for swinger experiences, threesomes and all the rest. It is the type of activity and play that allows a lot of variety. It is a novelty, a strong fantasy, because it is a taboo, and it goes against the social mandate of monogamy… we know that monogamy is not a human condition and that not everybody wants to be monogamous." [180]

(*How's that for straight talk, eh? Girls can grow really big balls*)

In Sénégal there is a distinct social phenomenon whereby young women maintain *parallel relationships* with all the men that had fathered their children. The term **Mbarane** is derived from the Wolof language—widely spoken in that country of Western Africa. Loosely translated as tentacles, it refers to the practice of some young women that *collect many paternities without attachments* in order to brazenly hoard alimony payments so they can enjoy a posh lifestyle.[181]

A *mbaraneuse* explained why she invited all her lovers for one of her son's birthdays. "If they hadn't contributed a little each, I wouldn't have been able to organize it. I don't have relationships with them. I manage my attachments." [182]

The Senegalese intelligentsia has decried the social influence of the native soap operas (like *Dinama Nekh* or "Happiness") that feature *mbaraneueses* in their star roles and teach young girls all the tricks to become a successful player. They show how they should never appear in any picture that might get wide diffusion in social media, how they must carry multiple phones and avoid sending SMS, etc.

Dijby Diakhate, a Senegalese sociologist, said that the series' emphasis only on the glamorous aspects of that dubious social practice has the collateral effect of giving a dangerous seal of approval to a habitude that might harm the children.[183] While the poor young girls see it as a way out of their misery and social exclusion, Diakathe says that they are misinterpreting the message of the program… Really?

<u>Diary USS Awareness</u>– When the ship resupplies in Dakar, do not disembark.

The practitioners of **poly-loving** claim that they can honestly fall in love with *more than one person* at the same time and maintain a healthy emotional attachment; the *sine qua non* [184] condition is that there should not *be any secrets*. The forced loosening of the strict restrictions of women's movements imposed by the patriarchal institutions and the expansion of the digital media have enabled the *relative anonymity* to try these clandestine relationships for men and women alike.

Andrea Orlandini, a Buenos Aires psychologist, said: "in their interpretation there is no treason because there is freedom to include third-parties…the polis have certain codes of conduct where the honesty, communication and negotiation are of paramount importance." [185] She claimed that these persons have more empathy.

A nugget of Wisdom. You had so many missed opportunities. Remember?

When she expected some timely words of comfort when she was ill…

When she asked you to stop kissing her because she wanted to sleep…

When she asked you to come to bed as you were watching a movie…

When she asked you to take a little more time before penetrating her…

The critical organ in your couple is not her vagina or your penis. It is both brains. They are the central computers where the incoming information is being processed.

Your wife's mind is eager to travel to exciting, new places. *Like Anne's did*.

—"Doctor…I'm not that much into sex—too difficult to understand?"

Luciana X. is a beautiful and charming lady in her late thirties that works as an administrative assistant in a county office, which she likes very much. She is still single because she has had trouble maintaining a stable couple relationship. She does like a manly company, and she enjoys sex to the hilt, but she does not want to do it on a *regular basis*, let alone *against her mood*. She enjoys the little details of a love bond. She likes to read novels. She definitely dreams. However…

Her mother and girlfriends do not quite understand her apathy towards sex, even suggesting therapy. Nothing is "wrong" with her. Save that *she is asexual.*

Dr. Anthony Bogaert, professor of Health Sciences and Psychology at *Brock University,* studied different aspects of sexual orientation for twenty years; he was the first author to put forward the term **asexuality** as a variant of sex conduct. He wrote a book titled *Understanding Asexuality* [186] where he detailed the condition; it is not a pathological state but a *life choice* like many others that must be respected.

Besides being a minority whose rights should be acknowledged to develop a greater tolerance in society, the asexual people represent a counterbalance to the *hyper-oppressively-exhaustingly-sexed-media-message* that would not allow you to watch TV without being ambushed by a busty blonde peddling a cheap car wash. Their sedated approach should make us reflect about our societal indenture to sex. <u>*Diary USS Awareness*</u> – Take your mind off "it" with a hobby. Painting, perhaps?

Why do Millennials have even less sexual satisfaction than their elders?

Living longer with their parents, the proliferation of smart phones and social media messaging, the accessibility of pornography and the higher stress levels might be some of the reasons for the big **decline of the Millennials' sexuality**.[187]

Maximiliano Martínez Donaire, a psychoanalyst and former secretary of the *Asociación Psicoanalítica Argentina* [188] said: "it's clear that the modern times afford more direct and accessible pathways for sexual enjoyment than before…The way relationships are organized today shorten the distance for a sexual encounter…Those possibilities exist and nonetheless people continue to stumble with the difficulties of their sexuality, an issue not entirely resolved yet…" [189]

A 2018 *Berkeley Institute* report said: "nearly 34% of U.S. adults aged 18 to 64 will develop an anxiety disorder at least once in their lives. Data also reveals that anxiety disorders are the most common mental disorders among today's adolescents in the U.S., with approximately 32% of 13 to 17-year-olds having met criteria for an anxiety disorder at least once in their lives." [190] **The Anxious Gen**.

Oftentimes Millennials complain that they are lacking the most basic sexual education, which is being supplanted with the *fallacious messages* of pornography. Instead of treating the latter as entertainment, they might use it as a learning tool; they feel frustrated when they cannot emulate that *doctored depiction* of sex.[191] The cacophony of hysterical shouting for fictitiously never-ending orgasms is the bellwether for the basic instruction of Millennials who want to "learn about sex." Moreover, they watch the *jarring juxtaposition* of a brutalized depiction of bodies in the media with a hypocritical plea from their elders to engage in safe sexuality. There is a new urgency as they receive an "alternate instruction" behind our backs.

An insidious hacker is posting a confusing syllabus in their small screens.

If we give up our parents' mentoring role , usurpers will shove us aside.

Chapter III – The trolling toll of technology

She was a woman of extraordinary beauty and a unique sexual prowess.

Novella Primigenia was the most famous prostitute in the city of Pompeii.

The *RAI* [192] TV channel presented a program titled *Stanotte a Pompeii* [193] where Alberto Angela recreated the wee hours before the eruption of the *Vesuvius* volcano in 79 B.C. that entombed the Roman cities of *Pompei* and *Herculanum*. In this series the presenter visits archeological sites and museums at night when there are no boisterous crowds of visitors that interfere with the enjoyment of viewing.

After extensive archeological work from the Italian experts, new sections of them have recently opened to the public. One of them is the *lupanar* [194], a "house of pleasure" belonging to a tough former legionnaire nicknamed *Africanus* [195], which stood in a prominent city corner. Upon entering, we observed the numerous small rooms that functioned as meeting places for the clandestine sex encounters; on the waiting area's walls there were well preserved frescoes with hot tales. One of them extolled the legendary accomplishments of this *Grande dame du Plaisir*.[196]

Even if we do not know what actually happened to Novella Primigenia when the asphyxiating cloud of ash and fire hit the city that fateful morning, her memory rightfully reached us, untainted by the passage of time and pristine for our viewing.

Growing wings, her contemporaries' opinions flew away to Posterity.

—"Smile…Say cheese!" said the woman holding the cell phone aloft.

The family members huddled together at the beach for that lasting memory; then each one of them went back to watching their little screens in total solitude. No funny banter of any kind. No looks of love. Or hate. Gawking. *Just gawking*.

Sherry Turkle, clinical psychologist, and sociologist at the *Massachusetts Institute of Technology* (MIT), asserted that our transformation into some kind of **device people** has happened with unprecedented celerity since the invasion of the iPhones in June 2007, followed by Android a year later.[197] (*Only 14 years ago?*)

We clutch our smartphones because we feel safer, more productive, and less bored. Turkle said that the digital media put people *in a comfort zone* where they believe they can share "just the right amount of themselves." Not an ounce more. The firm *eMarketer* [198] stated that Americans spend an average of five and a half hours with digital media, more than half of it on mobile devices like the phones. The frequency of that connection is much higher in the 15-25 years-age group.

As a result, Turkle affirmed that, as they are not learning how to be alone, the young people are losing their *ability to empathize* even with their close ones. She said: "it's the capacity for solitude that allows you to reach out to others and see them as separate and independent." [199] They have a **disconnection anxiety**. Turkle said that for young people the art of friendship is increasingly becoming the art of *dividing their attention* in an efficient way to get the *best online impact*.

What is the only thing they never do? Engage in person with one another.

They believe that the back-and-forth of unrehearsed real-time conversation makes them *vulnerable*, exposing them to *the risk of social censoring*. Nir Eyal, a game designer, writer, and professor of Applied Consumer Psychology at *Stanford University*, wrote that a successful app creates *a behavioral loop*—it both triggers *a need* and provides its *ready satisfaction*. Social networks encourage *FOMO*, i.e. fear of missing out. The social status—and self-esteem— is related to the numbers of *likes*, *comments,* and *friends*.[200] This indenture to social opinions beyond their control is a common cause of Anxiety for the Millennials and the Gen. X's.

A nugget of Wisdom. You come back home with a delicious meal and a bottle of *Veuve Cliquot* from your favorite deli; your wife's daughter is celebrating her birthday at her Ex's home. Alone. A romantic date you both were dreaming of.

When you arrive home, instead of being greeted at the door, you find her in pajamas, slouching in bed, gawking at a screen, haltingly sobbing, and not talking. You casually peek at it to find out what might be bothering her. Her daughter is enjoying a totally fun event organized by her young stepmother… What's wrong?

Look again. Her successor is casually flaunting her incredibly thin waistline. Don't make a move. Don't say a word. Lay down next to her. And hug her.

It's a girl thing.

One of the most troubling new facets of *Emotional Frustration* for women is the inability of some of their closest persons to identify and/or exhibit the *proper emotional response* to common events. It is a clinical entity called **alexithymia**.[201] This personality disorder is characterized by the following main features:

a) Inability to *identify emotions* and *differentiate* them from bodily sensations.

b) Trouble to *express, communicate* or *describe* feelings in them and others.

c) Difficulties to *imagine* and *construct* abstract concepts.

Persons with this disorder have difficulty in identifying the emotions expressed by other people, which can lead to *lack of empathy* and *improper behavior*.[202] Devoid of the emotional responses to common situations, they *overuse logical thinking*; their seemingly operational adjustment to reality is *masking* an emotional void.[203]

Alexithymia is *more common in men* than women, with a 1:5 preponderance. Considering that manly displays of emotional responses have been repressed due to the archaic norms of the *paternalistic education*, this higher incidence is coherent. The *overload of external stimuli* and the *urging to react fast* worsen this condition because affected persons cannot process them to find the right emotional reaction. Dr. Ghedin said: "the urgency to solve all the conflicts, even the most basic ones, the inability to tolerate the incertitude of life and to evaluate the priorities lead to a mad dash to reach the target, without evaluating which is the best alternative." [204]

—"Doctor...Even when I'm alone, I feel they're always watching me."

Sarah X. is a single young lady, working as a secretary in a car dealership.

When we were having breakfast, we watched her as *her addlepated attention* was flitting butterflylike from one screen to the other and she was typing countless texts in furious salvos, while waiting for her tuna salad wrap to arrive. When it did, she hardly raised her eyes, save for a perfunctory look at it. **She was in a trance.**

Mesmerized by the intense glow of her little screen, she was tacitly abetting *the observation* of her moves at a distance by strangers. All the time. It smacked of the dramatic effects of Charcot's therapeutic hypnosis in *La Pitié-Salpêtrière*.[205]

Bernard Harcourt said that the civic damage inflicted on citizens' privacy by the worldwide spy agencies and data processors is quite substantial. It is being involuntarily abetted by the *non-stop online posting* of updates about ourselves and everything we do, think, feel, fear. "We are not being surveilled today," he wrote, "so much as we are exposing ourselves knowingly, for many of us with all our love, for others anxiously."[206] He described a new kind of *human conscience* that is constantly seeking people's approval via its *virtual self* in the social media.

Wendy Hui Kyong Chun exposed the *reactionary tendency* of digital input: using a screen rather than printed matter gives preeminence to critical keywords.[207] Our attention tends to jump *from one magic word to the other*, only confirming our previous associations with them in both our Conscious and Unconscious minds.

As we do not read arguments questioning what we already know, we get a fallacious confirmation. By accessing the web, we obtain an incredibly rich trove of useful information at the mere click of the mouse. But we also relinquish to the "camouflaged crowd out there" our own judgement as we are being subliminally influenced by the so-called **social consensus**, which can be—and often is—wrong.

It is a *reinforcement* of our old knowledge but also of our rancid prejudices. Sadly, most of the public *is being corralled* into "mentally isolated holding pens", unaware that there are other opinions out there that at least merit to be considered.

In Ancient Times, a homemaker usually had to get out of her house to meet other women at the market in order to exchange news, gossip, etc. Our mothers and grandmothers had the benefit of using *Antonio Meucci*'s invention.[208] Even though working women had better connectivity, it was still done via *Analog media*.

Our social indenture to the *Digital media* has shortened the time intervals that some alternate—and even opposite—opinions spring up in our minds. The penchant of women **to pivot** amongst different points due to a *richer emotionality* and better *inter-hemispheric traffic* was potentiated; they can seamlessly shift from one position to another one in a few seconds. *Le basculage émotionnel.* [209]

<u>Diary USS Awareness</u> – Be ready. The lady that will be greeting you back at the dock might not be the very same one that had bid you farewell at the moorings.

At dawn, raise your index finger and check the *prevailing winds' course*.

A nugget of Wisdom. You come back home, ready to watch the big game. Earlier on, you had finally settled a big issue with your wife during breakfast. After a few jousting rounds over a cup of coffee, you finally reached some consensus. At the time it seemed like a good compromise solution. You were both satisfied.

On your ride back to your little castle, you feel like a tournament's winner. You imagine the expected hero's welcome with *plenty of cheer, beer, and boar.* But when you open the door your heart sinks. No delicious aroma. No soft music. Defiantly enthroned at the round table, she is ready to re-start the game. *Not again.* The *court zester* intercepts you. Sneering, he says: "You're in so much trouble—"

What happened? After she kissed you and waved goodbye to you at the door in the morning, she started texting the basics of your agreement to "her network." Some agreed that you earned her favors cavalierly enough, but others contested it.

-"Dear," you say, kneeling down to rekindle a vassalage. "What can I do?"

Sniff, sniff. "You should not take so much advantage of me (sic)," she says.

A clarion call echoes through the hall…She languidly points at the *Lists.*[210]

Breathe deeply, don your armor, and jump back in the *champ d'hônneur.*[211] You are given an old donkey and a sawed-off lance to face the Black Knight. What's a man to do? Imitate the chevaliers of yore. Only one way out of it.

Man up. Smile. Charge.

—"Doctor…My family drains me. So demanding—and how about me?"

Betty X. – a wife, mother of two and caretaker for her elderly parents—blurted a complaint about her inner circle that is commonly heard in our practices. Many patients, burdened by home and labor obligations, feel overpowered by some unreasonable family demands—from their own side and their partner's one as well.

Any system consists of several *individual parts* that are *essential* and *related to one another* when a certain outcome is desired. Members of **a family system** fit together to form a functional unit; examining that close association uncovers some patterns. When we join into it, we are assigned *a defined job* with expectations.[212] Virginia Satir, an American psychiatrist and author, said that "the presenting issue" was not the "real problem" but rather the "particular way" the members coped with it—therapists should shift their focus to relationship education.[213] We should first connect with "one another" and then extend those connections to "other people." Her motto was *peace within, peace between and peace among*. There are 5 roles:

- The **Hero**: successful, a decision maker, an initiator, a natural leader; challenged by perfectionism, inability to play, and fear of mistakes.
- The **Clown**: good sense of humor, flexible, and ability to relieve stress; challenged by need for attention, bad behavior, and poor decisions.
- The **Scapegoat**: creative, shows feelings, sense of humor, less denial; challenged by inappropriate anger, intrusiveness, and rebelliousness.

- The **Lost Child**: independent, flexible, ability to follow, easy-going; challenged by inability to initiate, sense of isolation, and confusion.
- The **Caretaker**: empathetic, good listener, sensitive, giver; challenged by an inability to receive, self-denial, and martyr resentment. [214]

These patterns have predictive value and can be modified to avoid repetition; most of us have played one (and maybe more) of these roles in family units. As keepers of the hearth, women often carry their family obligations over to their new homes.

A nugget of Wisdom. This time you got it right. You left work early so you could do the shopping to fix a fresh Bolognese sauce for her favorite pasta dish; you did not forget to pick a bottle of Malbec and fresh bread for the romantic meal. Humming *Love of my life* as if you were Freddy re-incarnate, you are laying your *plat de résistance* [215] on a nice tray when a thumping stiletto's staccato startles you.

Exuding spousal devotion, you stop to greet your wife as she well deserves. She barges in while she keeps arguing with her Mom in her phone, ignoring you. Without a word, she pushes you over to cruelly dip a morsel of bread in the sauce. Snubbing you, she walks out, leaving you in sentimental shambles. *So insensitive.* Angry? Take a page from women's playbook of building up leverage for later use.

Store it quietly in the only-grudges-against-her cupboard of your mind.

When the opportunity arises, retrieve it back and rub her nose right in it.

—"Doctor…Was transferred out from the prison at home to the one at work."

Melanie X. has a white-collar job and a big family: a husband , two children and three creatures with special needs… A cat. And a dog. And a mother-in-law. She hired an efficient maid that comes regularly to do her laundry, dust the furniture, clean the bathrooms, cut the yard's grass, and do some healthy cooking. Her husband does help with the children's activities, becoming *a soccer dad,* and her own mother shows up on weekends so she can take a night off with her partner. Once she arrives home from work, her workday *is only half-way done* as she must check that all the team members pitched in and to make amends, when necessary.

The sociologist Arlie Russell Hochschild [216] said that the economic crisis of the early 21st century has tightened **the time bind**: the actual workweek of salaried professionals increased from a standard of only 40 hours *to 50 plus*, not counting the regular catch-up of work, e-mails, phone calls, etc., done at home after hours. It is a corporate onslaught that is sabotaging the boundaries guarding the *family life*. Women in blue-collar jobs have fared the worst as, lacking the hitherto *protective umbrella* of unions, they must bear the *unpredictable work schedules*— preventing them from planning ahead family's activities— the lack of comprehensive medical and dental benefits plus the sinking purchasing power relative to inflation.[217]

This maelstrom envelops the most vulnerable tighter. The working poor.

Aside from their tasks at home and the role of *helicopter moms* outside of it, white and blue-collar women are struggling with the **abusive demands at work** . As incomes and sense of self-worth erode, the *Emotional Frustration* progressively degrades their quality of life and poisons their family dynamics at various levels. <u>*Diary USS Awareness*</u> — See how little room for maneuvering most women have?

Judith Shulevitz said that women need a new kind of feminism that she labelled as **caregiverism**. She described it as: "a demand for dignity and economic justice for parents dissatisfied with a few weeks of unpaid parental leave and strive to mitigate the sacrifices made by adult children responsible for aging parents." Besides improved childcare benefits and public services, she asked for some *Social Security credits* for caregivers that want to cut work hours or just opt out.[218]

Pamela Druckerman relished that the experience of raising her kid in Paris was a much more relaxed experience than back home in the USA, even though French children can be just as boisterous as the American ones. She claimed that French mothers assume that even the good parents should not be at the constant service of their children and there is no need to feel guilty about it.[219] The French State has provided a social net since the times of the *Front Populaire* in 1936.[220] However, the ravages of globalization and the financial crisis had curtailed those benefits in an ageing society that had lacked market dynamism, which caused a grave *de-industrialization* and *delocalization* that only now has started to revert.[221]

In 2019, the citizens of *la France profonde*—the mythical reservoir of the *Gaulois spirit* in the hinterland—started to mobilize in small groups wearing their **gillet jaunes**—the yellow chest vest emblematic of all the *emergency responders*. They started to spontaneously assemble in road intersections and shopping venues. What initially started as a quiet grass-roots protest against the increase in oil prices planned by the French administration in January 2019, has extended and expanded. The protesters first rallied against *la fiscalité* [222] and *le pouvoir d'achat* [223], which unduly affected the elderly retired, the single mothers and the young unemployed.

Every evening the French TV showed the protesters demanding state reform. Stoically standing in the cold , they had two traits. Educated. And women.

The French bureaucrats made the mistake of trying to ignore them as rogue outliers, ignoring that it was mostly *a feminine protest* fighting for their families. Finally, they relented to meeting with their representatives and halted the rise in the oil prices; President Macron designed a new package of economic measures.[224]

Politicians should tread carefully when spontaneous barricades resist them. Especially if they are manned by women… Or "wonned", should we say?

Once the food they lay on the table is menaced, women become fearless.

<u>Diary USS Awareness</u> – You must sail through a canal with two obstacles: one piece of ice with a smiling woman on top and another one with a gruff man. Which one to coast by? The guy's one, of course. She is on the tip of an iceberg.

—"That one," I said to Lita. "Get that big fat one to make nice sausages."

The relatives from our dear mother's family side—either Italian immigrants largely from the region of Campania or their descendants—used to meet for a whole day in a farm owned by Raúl, an uncle, and Lita, an aunt, located in Colón—a northern suburb of Montevideo—in the dead of winter for a millenary ritual. Being Italian Americans—with an insatiable *fame di terra* [225]—we prepared pork cuts and sausages in a gathering that started at dawn and ended with a nice dinner.

When the time to choose *a candidate* came, Lita grabbed my hand and we walked together, piercing the early morning thick mist, to the pigpen; amongst the sounder, a white elephantine pig with a marked limp of its left hind leg stood out.

—"Which one should we choose, eh?" Lita always asked me with a tender smile. Resolutely pointing at the monster-creature, I always said the same: "That one!" It could have been our child's imagination… But we had the impression that in that instant the beast zeroed its sight on Lita with *a plaintive look* that pierced her heart.

—"Oh no, poor thing," she said, shaking her head. "Let's choose another one—"

She then picked the healthiest, fattest resident to pass it under the sharpest knife.

Year after year, that *thespian pig* performed the same life-saving histrionics.

It had an unusually long life and was interred by a sobbing Lita in the field.

The Limping Pig. My first mentor in the perplexing feminine psychology.

"*Hacerse el chancho rengo.*" [226]

Carmen Maganto and Mayte Garaigorbodil published the results of a study with 140 participants—parents aged from 45 to 60 years old, and the children aged 17 to 25 years old—to observe their behavior. **Empathy** is our human capacity to recognize *the thinking and feelings of others* so we can "immerse our conscience" in their reality to appropriately react. [227] The study showed that women are better at forgiving than men in general as they show *a greater capacity and readiness* for empathy vis-à-vis other ones. Even though parents and children agreed that there is a *need to forgive* in close personal relationships, the capacity for forgiveness takes time to develop in earnest. Overcoming negative feelings is an act of volition that requires certain effort, but it may be beneficial for our psychological well-being. The *capacity for forgiveness* is a tool for a healthier lifestyle, akin to the nutritious eating and good sleep; people that can forgive have far fewer signs of stress. [228]

A nugget of Wisdom. You come back home after a demanding workday. You want to put your pajamas, grab a beer and slump in the sofa to watch a movie. Your wife is giving you *that look*, which means she has other plans for you tonight.

—"Hon, got a bad headache," you say. "How about watching a stand-up?" She gives a long hard look at the Coors in your hand. No sweat. Grab her left hand. look her in the eye and wistfully whisper: "Barley is so good for Migraines (sic)" She demurs for a few seconds…Then she smiles, snuggling up with you ¡*Olé!* [229]

Who taught you how to hit her Achilles' heel? A pig did. Never forget.

—"Doctor, I adore my son…But taking care of him daily drains me—"

Verónica X. is a young mother of three children that decided to postpone her graduate studies to take care of her eldest son—he has *Multiple Sclerosis*.[230] This neurological disease is one of the commonest causes of non-traumatic disability of young adults in the Northern Hemisphere and can manifest itself with a broad range of *chronic clinical symptoms*—vision loss, muscular weakness of the limbs, sensory alterations, bowel, or bladder dysfunction and worsening limited mobility.

As there are frequent *cycles of remissions* and *poussées* [231], the caregivers might feel miffed by unpredictable outcomes. The MS patients need the permanent assistance of some *informal caregivers* to remain in their homes as their functional dependence rises with their symptoms and disabilities. The *Emotional Frustration* of these caregivers arises from their *progressive sense of isolation* and the *forced lowering of their social expectations*, which lead to a much lower quality of life.[232]

Compassion fatigue—also known as the *secondary trauma stress*—is a psychological abnormality affecting those caregivers that have an intense and close relationship with someone they care for; the symptoms include *isolation, physical ailments, bottled-up emotions, substance abuse,* and *recurring nightmares.*[233] Moreover, the professionals that regularly care for them—neurologists, critical care specialists, hospice nurses, aides—can show symptoms of this affection too.[234]

Sweeping these signs under the rug only worsens the cadre.

The *empathy-altruism hypothesis* [235] states that the human empathy-related processes are influenced by two different, and often antagonistic, groups of factors:

1. **Motivating factors**: the physical and emotional deficits of the sick.
2. **Inhibiting factors**: the mental and mood limitations of the caregiver.

Sedipeh Poyan et al. published the results of a descriptive, cross-sectional pilot study with the caregivers of non-institutionalized individuals living with MS in Canada—a country with a high incidence and prevalence of the disease. [236] They used the *POMS 2 35 item questionnaire* to capture their *mood status*. Of the 55 family caregivers that responded, 23 were women, most of them were their spouses, lived with them and had done it for more than 2 years; 15 caregivers had elevated total mood scores, being the highest for *Fatigue-Inertia*, followed by *Anger-Hostility*, *Depression-Dejection* and *Anxiety*. The burden of taking care of a chronically sick person takes **a heavy emotional toll** on close family members, the majority of whom are women in their prime years and with their own families.

—"Doctor…I hide in the bathroom—so my children can't hear me cry."

Susan X. is a nice, intelligent, and hard-working mother of a small child who must shoulder the entire burden of her household all alone, even though she was diagnosed with Multiple Sclerosis. Her husband works as a salesman and has had a chronic back problem since he was injured in a previous stint as a truck driver.

Her family cannot help her economically but her mother pitches in occasionally. Oftentimes she puts her child to bed, finishes her household duties and, before her husband arrives for a late supper, locks herself in the bathroom to well up at ease. It is a simple ritual that gives her emotional relief. **Crying alone in the bathroom**.

The tried-and-true escape valve for women in angst. Like Gladys did.[237]

Modern women, who are employed full-time in demanding jobs, usually must return home to complete the house chores with little or no help from their live-in partners; to make matters worse they might not have the support offered by close family members or friends. In our hyper-connected age, where most of the rooms at home are taken over by the obnoxiously-pinging **squatting devices**, they must retrench to the bathroom—their "panic room" to do an exorcism of sorts.

Welling up, they slump on the floor and hug the cold toilet with passion.

Isn't it sad that they had to anoint a disposal unit as a default confidante?

A nugget of Wisdom. You planned a nice vacation for the whole family. In the middle of the night, a muffled sound creeps in from the bathroom. Opening the door, you see your wife crying, with her hands on her face.

-"What's wrong?" you say, hugging her. "Nothing, don't worry," she says. Finally, she tells you that her father told her that her Mom's symptoms worsened. What do you do? You cancel the trip as she must find an alternative care for her.

Your wife is her family's hero (and yours too)

—"Doctor…My husband is so possessive—he wants to totally control me."

Mary X. is a nice, young woman that, for rather mysterious reasons, has not taken full advantage of her upbringing and education to get a better job opportunity than the lowly clerical position she has had. It looks as if she deliberately chose to "downgrade herself" to match the blue-collar identity of her less gifted partner. She appeared occasionally in our office with a *different and vague complaint* each time about headaches, gastrointestinal problems, urinary disturbances, etc. One day, watching her *evasive looks* and the *ridiculously long sleeves* she was wearing in a hot South Florida afternoon, we decided to pop the question: *"Is he abusing you?"*

The issue of **domestic violence** is tragically present in our modern societies, crossing all the ethnic, cultural, and socio-economic boundaries; it is still one of the most serious Public Health issues in the USA with more than 27% of women and 18% of men aged 18 years old and higher as the victims of it. [238] It can be defined as the *victimization of an individual* with whom the *abuser* has or has had an intimate and/or romantic relationship; it is also referred as *spousal abuse*, *battering* or *intimate partner violence* (IPV) [239] Victims of this abuse suffer various types of injuries and will seek care in hospitals, clinics, and medical offices. [240]

A 2003 *CDC* report stated that its economic cost—estimating the cost of the injuries, the charges of care facilities and the lost labor hours—was approximately U$ 8.3 billion per year in the USA; no updated information is available now. [241]

A report by the *U.S. Department of Justice* found that between 1993 and 2011 the rate of *nonfatal domestic violence* against women *declined by 73%* and the rate of *violent crime* in that same time period *decreased by 60%*.[242] This same study attributed these statistical drops to the *lower marriage* and *domesticity* rates, the *improved access* to federal and state-funded shelter facilities, the *rise* in women's economic profiles and the *ageing* of the population. As a collateral effect of the 2008 financial crisis, more women are "wearing the pants at home", which has robbed abusive men of their economic leverage to blackmail their partners.

In 2000 the enactment of the *Florida Statute 741.316* finally summoned the *Florida Department of Law Enforcement* (FDLE) to publish a yearly report based on data from the *Domestic Violence Data Resource Center* (DVDRC) a statewide tracking system of those instances of domestic abuse that ended in a fatality.[243]

In the 2016 *DVDRC* annual report based on the summary of 62 violent Florida cases by the *Fatality Review* teams, they found the following indicators:

a) A majority of the abusers were male, 95%, and 50% of those individuals had *previous criminal records*; for domestic violence, the rate was 47%.

b) There was a 24% incidence of *do not contact orders* for these abusers; also 22% of them had a *permanent injunction* filed by other victims.

c) In 47% of the cases there was a history of *substance abuse* of various types and 30% of them had a history of *Mental Health* disorders.[244]

The *psychological traits* of perpetrators have been less thoroughly studied than those of the abused individuals, but some studies suggest they are also *heavy abusers of alcohol*, even though they might not have been intoxicated at the time of the violent incident. [245] Other studies showed that men who engaged in episodes of domestic violence are *possessive, jealous, insecure,* and even *paranoid*. [246]

We, physicians, have a special responsibility to properly **screen for signs** of abuse as the sickly *dynamics of abuser/abused* might not be that easily identified; they might have shallow *symbiotic bonding* that fools us into *clinical complacency*. Apart from the most flagrant acts of abuse—lesions in the face, thorax, abdomen—there are *more subtle physical signs* like minor lacerations to the face, neck, face, breast, or abdomen, which are different from the injuries suffered in accidents, which usually involve the extremities. [247] The victim may present with the signs of an *agitated depression syndrome*—fatigue, restlessness, insomnia, loss of appetite—or *multifaceted physical complaints*—headache, backaches, etc. [248]

A nugget of Wisdom. Yeah. Yeah. Yeah… We hear you. Enough excuses. Office hours kill you. Paperwork sucks. F****** appointments do not show up… More paperwork. Payors are Scrooges. And your Ex is taking you to the cleaners… Stop. Even though your staff swears that you never did, you once had a mother too.

Do not give an attitude to the patient seated in front of you.

Can't you see that her eyes are crying out for help? Focus.

—"Doctor, my daughter's mind is in another planet—don't know why."

Maria X. does not understand why her teenage daughter—who did not have to go through the hassle of immigrating to a country with a culture and language so different than hers—seems to hover in a completely different reality. She rightfully senses that those **hidden distractions** might endanger her mental/physical health.

Nancy Jo Sales, after interviewing more than 200 American teenagers, said that the *sexist and erotic culture* of the modern social media is damaging them.[249] Even though they feel much *more socially empowered* than their elders, they are in fact treated as *mere sexual objects* in a perverse way that our ancestors never knew.

Maniacally glued to their little screens and waiting for an equivocal approval of the latest postings, they might be assaulted with *misogynist jokes*, *pornographic images* and *horrible comments* that will inevitably damage their own self-esteem. This *low intensity-sexual harassment* precedes a more aggressive coercion, which entails the *rating of their physical traits* in the web and a *demand for nude photos*.

While physical bullying is largely directed at young boys, **digital bullying** usually targets the *young girls*.[250] The implacable gaze that the social media train on the girls' evolving sexuality fosters their continuous anxiety about their physical appearance—assessed by the "likes" they get for the posted photos—that smacks of *a self-objectification* harking back to the Homo Sapiens' times in the caves.

<u>Diary USS Awareness</u> – Out there, unfathomable monsters are bidding their time.

It is not that easy for young people to *make the right choice* nowadays as they are being bombarded by the enticing advertisement of a consumerist society. In his 1970's book titled *Future shock*, Alvin Tofler warned about the potential health risks for the individuals exposed to an excess of choices: **Overchoice.**[251]

In almost all major decision-making situations, the presence of equally good choices can lead to *severe mental stress* and *paralysis* for us. As we rationally try to determine *the pros and cons* of each choice, we are mentally and emotionally burdened. Even though initially people feel happy that the number of choices is rising—something common in the dating apps—eventually they tire off and feel depressed. Too much variety can increase the complexity of the selection process.

This is a common occurrence for those Millennials trying to find a romantic partner in the dating apps. As they *masquerade themselves* with an implacable self-photoshopping [252], the large number of good possibilities can, and will, overwhelm them. One of our patients, who was looking for a simple date for a Friday night, got more than 1500 hits in her inbox. She is certainly an attractive lady… But still.

This exuberance coincided with the demise of a social role: **the agony aunt**. For centuries girls relied on the sage advice of an experienced woman that checked their romantic requirements and vetted the new candidates; first they disassembled them *piece by piece* to find the *right character traits* in the intimacy of the boudoir.

Without her, the assemblage of "the right one" became more agonizing.

Peggy Orenstein said that these girls' generation had been induced by a porn-saturated culture "to reduce their worth to their bodies and to see those bodies as a collection of parts that exist for others' pleasure; to continuously monitor their looks to perform rather than to feel sensuality." [253] Even though many of them had an active sexuality (and said they liked it) *few of them ever had an orgasm* ; in a humiliating twist, almost half of them gave *oral sex* but never had any reciprocity.

(And then we wonder why Sally always looks so pissed off)

-"Doctor…My Ex is blackmailing me to get laid—those d*** pictures."

Thelma X. is a nice, clever medical assistant that, after a few failed romantic relationships, has finally met whom she firmly considers as "the man of her life." Unfortunately, she had the bad idea of allowing her Ex to take some suggestive poses of her during intercourse, which at the time seemed like intimate pranks. But he re-surfaced again, threatening her with **digital blackmail** if she refused him sex.

The smartphones cheapened the access to expressions that were hitherto a preserve for the wealthy: the communal *sharing* of racy, explicit physical portraits. We must remember that *L'origine du monde* –a tableau of the external aspect of an exuberantly bushy vulva made by the French painter Gustave Courbet in 1866—was commissioned by Khalil Bey, an Egyptian diplomat of the Ottoman Empire.[254] Some of the hung masterpieces in European museums have shown some hidden images of *nude women*—a comic diversion—when examined with x-rays.[255]

Many men of all ages have shown a readiness to take and send pictures of their intimate parts to female recipients—some of them underage girls—a practice dubbed as **sexting**, which constitutes a criminal offense in many jurisdictions. [256]

This social media practice has crossed the gender barriers. As another sign of the feminine empowerment in modern society, *the vulva* also became fair game. Lauren Stover said: "the V-selfie, though very much here, is perhaps less insistent (than the male counterpart). Shared on dating apps or in texts, it has been sent to create longing and a sense of intimacy; a missive of lust and promise to lovers who are separated."[257] An unorthodox version of the epistolary correspondence of yore.

The women practicing it consider it as a bold statement that they are *in full command* of their sexuality and how they will decide to share it. Those images also are used in the practice of *cyber-infidelity*, which may or may not be consummated. Some exalted feminists are calling for the final baring of all the physical mysteries surrounding a woman's body, including her most intimate parts, to challenge the repression of the patriarchal institutions for the expressions of their sexuality.[258]

Does the blatant exposure of a woman's intimate parts excite all the men?

As medical students, we studied the Human Anatomy with the magnificent 19th century *Testut-Latarjet textbook* [259] and the *Netter illustrations* [260], which did not elicit any kind of arousal on us. Without the context of eroticism, those medical illustrations were only what they were supposed to be: a practical learning tool.

Mary Cassatt [261] was an American painter that had joined the *Impressionist movement* [262] right at its beginning in the late nineteenth century and, being a close friend of Edgar Degas, she was the inspiration for his painting titled *In the loge*.[263] In the 1870s, women were not allowed to sit in the orchestra section of the *Paris Opera* and could only be accompanied by a man in the rear stalls in the *matinée* function, not the *soirée*. Julian Barnes said that: "at evening performances, women were allowed to attend in pairs or in groups, when they might sit together in the upper loges, or boxes…No respectable woman was allowed backstage, where only the entitled male—a self-declared 'connoisseur' of women, whether as lecher, or in rare cases, as painter—might tread." [264] Mary Cassatt—both in her life and in her depiction—was only allowed to sit alone at a box, leaning on the balcony rail; in the painting's background there is a man blatantly training her binoculars on her.

A nugget of Wisdom. Your wife has been chasing your attention for days. Not the innocuously domestic version that inquires if you want bacon for breakfast. The protective version of her wants to talk about your teenage daughter's behavior. You do not see anything unusual. You are kind of relieved that she seems subdued. Wrong. Women have a better intuition of any looming threat against their families. With a conformist sigh , you turn sideways in bed and say: "OK…Spill the beans."

—"Worried about Megan…So distracted. And her grades are plunging."

It may be the only indication that your daughter is being cyber-bullied.

What are the dangerous aspects of Millennials' and X's communications?

Even though most of us—the Baby Boomers parents—are quite ignorant of the new paradigms of communication, we put *an excessive amount of trust* in them. As they slam their bedrooms' doors shut on our faces, barricading themselves with the *sole company of their phones*, we are being duped into a *risky sense of safety*. There are three *major features* of their communications that should concern us:

1 – The dark anonymity of the Web

2 – The rigidity of the Web messaging

3 – The social isolation of the Web

1- **The dark anonymity of the Web**.

The pioneering Web designers had an *esprit de corps* [265] that encouraged the popular expressions without censuring. John Haughton said: " In the 1980s, 'cyberspace' was… a geek preserve, with a social ethos that was communal, libertarian, collaborative, occasionally raucous, anti-establishment and rich in debate and discussion. It had no commerce, no hierarchies, no crime and no spam, and in general it was populated by people who either knew one another, or at least knew others' institutional affiliations…Cyberspace and the real world existed as parallel universes." [266] *A nerdy Nirvana.*[267]

This author also said: "two developments eroded the distinction between the two universes and caused them to merge. The first was the commercialization of the network achieved by the NSF's decision to hand out the backbone over to ISPs. This meant that lay people could now access the network-generally via slow dial-up connections. The second development was the arrival of the network's second 'killer application' – the World Wide Web." [268]

From that seemingly quaint origin as just an amiably libertarian mode of expression for likely-minded, respectful people, we arrive at our present reality, which has *inextricably meshed together* the physical and virtual components. At present the *World Wide Web* sadly affords multiple ways for shady, malicious operators to *spread messages of hate* and *intolerance* with *quasi-total impunity*.

The **masquerading of the identities** is a strategic choice to avoid all civil and legal responsibilities for what they say, no matter how outrageous, false, or nasty. Martha Nussbaum, professor of Law and Philosophy at the *University of Chicago*, said that the purpose is: "to create for themselves a shame-free zone in which they can inflict shame on others…the power of the bloggers depends on their ability to insulate their Internet selves from responsibility in the real world, while ensuring real-world consequences for those they injure." [269]

Ultra-malicious adults posing as "same-age buddies" set up *games, chats,* etc. to *harass your kids, demand pics* or arrange *clandestine dates*. **Grooming.**

2 – The rigidity of the Web messaging.

Since times immemorial, women, and especially the younger ones, have been meeting in twos, threes, or larger groups to chat, gossip and share feelings. However, the invasion of the *small screens' mind snatchers* in Planet Earth in the past few years has curtailed that longstanding habitude and generated a new form of clinical pathology: **the addiction of young people** in front of their little screens.

When a girl buys a new blouse, she is likely to take *a selfie* and post it in the social media for her friends' network. Then she waits for *some blessing of sorts*. That seal of approval might come in the form of a "like" or despairing indifference.

Reviewing Jia Tolentino's *Trick Mirror*, Maggie Doherty said: "Social media makes us feel as if we're perpetually onstage; we can never break character or take off our costumes. Channeling the sociologist Erving Goffman, Tolentino explains how 'online, your audience can hypothetically keep expanding forever, and the performance never has to end." [270] *Luigi Pirandello* [271] *could not fancy it*.

Those that rely solely on the *Manichean opinion of others*, are missing a critical component of bonding: **the critique**. If we do not get any feedback about *what is right* or *wrong*, we cannot learn . Mark Thomas said: "If someone has a criticism it means they want to give you feedback on what you're doing for them – that means an opportunity to learn more about the person you're working for and how to convert them into a satisfied customer or audience member." [272]

3 – The social isolation of the Web

One of the most useful and at the same time dangerous features of the World Wide Web is that it enables us to make contact with many people almost anywhere without ever leaving "our comfort zones." However, some individuals may get *addicted* to that advantage and decamp from our physical reality to *settle down* in its virtual counterpart; they create a "sheltered profile" for their **social isolation**.

Josep Matali-Costa, from the Department of Child, Adolescent Psychiatry and Psychology of *Hospital Sant Joan de Deu* in Barcelona, studied adolescents with **Internet Addiction,** dividing them into a *sheltered* group that used it to escape, cope, or feel safe and a *non-sheltered* one without those motivations. They found: "sheltered subjects were significantly younger, had more comorbid disorders, more previous interpersonal problems and an increased loss of contact with friends, used the Internet more often to cope with interpersonal problems, had received prior treatment more frequently, and more often required a combined approach to treatment. Moreover, their motivation was less likely to be a feeling of offline boredom…they had greater multiplayer role-playing game (MMORPG) use, night-time use, increased school failure and loss of contact with peers." [273]

When you give an I-phone to "your little princess", you are *uprooting her* from the *safety of her bedroom*, to plant her right smack in the *middle of a jungle*. Holding a puny device, she is standing all alone, trying to fend off many monsters.

Steven Spielberg managed to exorcise but also worsen our fears about sharks by playing a dirty trick in *Jaws*: they do not appear in the beginning.[274] Instead of showing the monster-fish right away, he drags us along several scenes where its presence *is felt, but never seen*, including the opening *girl's scary dip in the water*.

Similarly, the burrowing of malicious web operators is not evident at first glance, but we must assume that they might be likely lurking there. On the prowl. Savvy users will install defensive mechanisms to fend off unwanted spam, hate messaging, hidden predators. But that might not be enough. And our kids know it.

In 2014 the *Pew Research Center* conducted a survey of parents of 13-to17-year-olds to find out the wide range of actions they take to monitor their online lives and how they encourage them to use the Web in a responsible way. It showed that 39% of parents used parental controls for blocking, filtering, or monitoring, and that 94% said that they talked with their teens about what to share online. [275]

A nugget of Wisdom. Your wife keeps nagging you about your daughter… But in your eyes, Megan is just another teen, distracted by girls' gossip. Women… Close your eyes. Go back to the very first time you saw Spielberg's *Poltergeist*.[276]

Do you recall that cute little girl mesmerizingly touching the grainy screen?

Do you recall her kin's angst when she was gobbled up by "the other side"?

Do you recall the halting line whispered by the exorcist hired to rescue her?

—"S*he's not alone…Someone is with her… And he is lying to her."*

—"Doctor…I need to consult my husband on everything—can't help it."

Paola X. is a successful physician that had happily settled in South Florida after completing her training in New York City a few years ago. We met in an Italian American social event, and we have been friendly ever since. She married another successful physician, and they have a nice family with three children. However, her upbringing under *über-archaic traditions—w*here their *father figure* loomed too large in all family issues—had marked her. *Padre Padrone.*[277]

She has invested *her energies* and *time availability* to recreate a welcoming hearth for her partner, even though she is a busy professional too. Being the perfect homemaker, she finds time to plan her family's schedule. However, all that wifely devotion came at an extremely heavy *personal price* as she does not have any kind of independent activities, let alone friends. She has an **emotional dependence**.[278]

A loving relationship entails sharing time and activities with your partner.

But do you have to share everything, even the most negligible of events?

In a closely-knit couple, there is a danger that *any attempt of decoupling* for the most menial task in a banal period by one partner might be construed as a sign of *disloyalty* by the dependent one. Individuals that have suffered unusual verbal and/or physical abuse as children are much more likely to experience what clinical psychologists call *anxiety of separation.*[279] The need to be in constant company of your partner, without any respite, can lead to great anxiety and stress in the couple.

Moreover, to preserve that tight bonding, the dependent individual might come to accept some forms of abusive behavior as an unavoidable trade-off. One of the sad social tenets of abused women is that they sometimes feel that *they need their partners*, delaying a rescue. A report by the *Florida Department of Children and Families* said that **domestic violence** is: "a pattern of behaviors that adults and adolescents use against their intimate partners or former partners to establish *power and control*. It may include physical abuse, sexual abuse, emotional abuse, and economic abuse. It may also include threats, isolation, pet abuse, using children…to maintain fear, intimidation and power over one's partner." [280]

—"Doctor…Whatever I do or tell him is always wrong—I'm exhausted."

Isabel X. is a gorgeous, young graduate student that had a big, big problem. She fell madly in love with a dashing classmate, and they started to live together. Initially she felt that her dream had come true but soon found out that the *pretty packaging* was in fact concealing an obnoxious personality trait: **Narcissism**. It is easy to like a narcissist because they *seem to be* so much fun. They are sociable, eager to meet new people, have wonderful conversations, show courtesy.[281] But a unique clue always blows their cover away: *they talk too much about themselves*. Their friendliness hides an insatiable urge to catch an even larger captive audience.

Isabel found out that it was always "about him", never "about her."

Worse, when she opened her mouth to say something, he interrupted her. Her angst was gnawing her self-esteem; her friends encouraged her to dump him. She continued to give, give, give…In return she only got **toxic feelings of guilt**.

"Is it my fault?" "Do I talk bad?" "Do I ask too much?" "Do I merit him?"

Jeffrey E, Young said that the only way to break off negative life patterns is to *re-evaluate your relationships* and start to appreciate those persons, who, despite being not that glamorous, listen to us.²⁸² A companion, who might be a little bit too thrifty with his words, but takes the time to cuddle with you in the sofa, is precious. The *always fun-always attractive-always loving hero* of the romantic movies might not really want to stoically listen to *your all-too-pedestrian tale* of toilet troubles.

Isabel asked us what to do. "Move out and cut all contact," we told her. When she left our office, we did not imagine she would follow our advice. She did.

That same day she said to him: "we need to talk." Just like Nora had done. He became aggressive and refused to even listen to her. But she stood her ground. In the morning she gathered her belongings and moved out with a girlfriend; she re-connected with her old friends' network and went back home for a weekend. Despite his frantic efforts to reach her, those that loved her *circled the wagons*.

Recently she met a good listener. A keeper. She is learning how to cook.

<u>Diary USS Awareness</u> – Ignore the sirens' calls to shift from your set course. When your knees start to wobble, put some wax in your eardrums. Like Ulysses did . ²⁸³

—"Doctor…It's not how much he pisses me off—but rather how often."

Sheila X. is a jovial, good mannered nursing aide that had chronic migraines for years; almost all the therapies failed and now she participates in a clinical trial. The trigger for her headaches lies close to her. She has an *uncooperative husband*. Occasionally she bursts out with anger, which does not elicit any real changes in him but ends up worsening her headaches. Silently soldiering on, she gave up.

A French chef recently explained in a TV program the advantages of a slow burning fire to tenderize hard-to-cook meats like game and fowl; when we watched him, we could not help comparing that technique to the way Sheila's husband is slowly sapping her strength, a little abuse at a time. Gently. **L'abus au petit feu.**[284]

The *low-intensity abuse* is a sum of little acts that damage our self-esteem. A flutter of the hand that never lands… Or perhaps a not-so-subtle-threat in a chat… Or, worse still, a stony silence after only asking for an explanation for a misdeed. Women might be subjected to many instances of verbal and physical abuse that taken individually do not reach *the threshold of intensity* to elicit a firm response. But the baneful buildup of angst from small incidents can test their patience as its *cumulative effect* may be as (if not more) toxic than the one of bigger incidents.

In Japan, due to the *Narita syndrome*—named after the Tokyo airport—some young Japanese women coming back from a foreign trip —where they were exposed to other cultures with kinder men— dump their boyfriends on the spot.[285]

Famadihana. The ceremony of *turning of the bones* of the Malagasy people. The highland people from Madagascar take their dead relatives out of their burial place every seven years for a ceremony aimed at renewing their social bond. Only after their corpses go through this ritual , the *Dead* will be allowed to enter the *Afterlife* with their ancestors. It is not a moment of sorrow, but of happiness.[286]

The recent spate of feminine censure—against their verbal and physical abuse—that has swept the social media was long in coming.[287] Finally, there is an open discussion of the *highly abusive behavior* of many men in positions of power; the camouflaged nature of that crime makes it easier to conceal it for many years. One of the commonest equivocal rebukes of these denunciations—used to discredit the victims—is the *supposedly long time* it took for them to come forward and talk.

"How come she's doing it now?" "Why didn't she denounce it earlier?"

When a woman suffers such a heinous crime, her age of innocence is over. She must insulate off what—pestilent as it is—forms part of her life and move on; she swiftly shoves that event into *a hermetic sarcophagus* in her *Subconscious*. Not to destroy it. Only to contain it. Whenever she feels she is ready, she will allow the *Conscious* half of her mind to recover it; feeling secure in the company of loved ones, she will take that *cadaveric memory* out in the open for its final disposition.

An abused woman wants to design her healing ritual in her own terms.

A famadihana fai-da-te [288]

—"Doctor…Got to have a shot before I go to bed…Can't sleep if I don't!"

Carol X. is a divorced middle-aged mother of three that looks much older than her chronological age due to her **chronic abuse of alcohol** and smoking. Paradoxically she kicked her husband out of their house due to heavy drinking but *his bottle*—a callous counsellor of sorts—stayed behind in a cupboard's top shelf. Like for many women, it started as a *self-medication* for her resilient *depression* and *insomnia*, furtively used at home, without nosy witnesses; slowly she became hooked on that habit, even after having *Detox* and joining *Alcoholic Anonymous*.[289] <u>*Diary USS Awareness*</u> — See how she ended up as a castaway in a faux island?

A study [290] by the *National Institute of Alcohol and Drug Abuse* shows that 60% of US women have at least one drink a year; 13% of the latter group have more than seven drinks per week. This level is above the "Dietary Guidelines for Americans" [291], issued by the *Health and Health Services Department*.

Women's bodies have *less water* than men's ones, which makes it harder for them to disperse the toxic by-products in brain, liver, digestive tract, and kidneys. Even with small intakes, they are at a *higher risk* for car accidents and abuse.[292] Even though it is illegal in all states, underage women engage in it, especially in American colleges.[293] Alcohol temporarily blunts all the sensory input to the brain, which brings an *illusory sense of relief*; it enables the onset of the *first superficial* phase of the sleep process, but it decreases the duration of the *REM* phase. [294]

—"Doctor…Don't want him to see my scars—I undress and plunge in bed."

Sandra X. is the lady that set up a painter's atelier in the Wynwood section and has a boyfriend who is 20 years younger. However, she still feels ashamed of the small striae in her belly , a post-partum sequela: for all her derring-do, she has not mentally shed the *ridiculously perfect model* of women's bodies in the media.

Women have a much more **holistic vision of their bodies** than we, men, do. They can scan themselves quickly in the mirror and swiftly detect *something* that is not quite right. It could be the color of their hair, the size of one of their breasts, the symmetry of their thighs, etc.; they usually try to conceal that supposedly *ugly aesthetic feature* and constantly worry about it.[295] The hurried pace of modern life and their erratic choice of sexual partners will enable them to avoid the sexual foreplay altogether and jump straight in the act—cutting their satisfaction short.

Some institutions [296] have been teaching women for years how to accept their bodies—defects included—and develop a more tolerating attitude for them. The media pressure to conform to a fallaciously idealized, trimmed down version of their bodies must be rightly considered as a relatively recent enslaving tool to keep "problematic" women in check—*a self-made virtual, yet suffocating corset.* Women who spend too much time watching their bodies, dismiss what lies outside.

A cowered person can be manipulated. Remember Fahrenheit 451 [297]?

Bradbury's tale of a Neofascist Police State is more relevant than ever.

Dr. Walter Ghedin said: "the entire body can be an object of internalized critique and camouflaging. When the malaise progresses, it is impossible to remain open-minded to engage in a sexual encounter. The experience of undressing together (a practice that is generally being dropped due to the modern daily haste), of touching ourselves, of allowing us the time to discover our bodies, becomes a feared event that must be avoided, recruiting the bed sheets and the bedroom darkness as our allies in the conceit." [298] He claimed that our attention becomes fixated in "that thing" and distracts us from enjoying sex. Our anxiety about "our defect" makes us second guess our partners' thinking as *we take for granted* that they are sharing our obsession and do not speak out in order to avoid hurting us.

The incidence of **anxiety and depression** in modern women is increasing. Why is depression more prevalent in women than men? Paul R. Albert said: " the triggers for depression appear to differ, with women more often presenting with internalizing symptoms and men presenting with externalizing symptoms. For example, in a study with dizygotic twins, women displayed more sensitivity to inter-personal relationships, whereas men displayed more sensitivity to external career and goal-oriented factors." [299] High anxiety might lead some women—especially those with chronic diseases—to consider the possibility of suicide. In the next section we will discuss that socially underestimated yet unfolding drama.

Mutatis mutandis [300]

—"Doctor…He never said anything to us—didn't even leave a little note."

Pamela X. is a nice middle-aged housewife from Coral Gables—one of the posh quarters of Dade County with leafy boulevards and large houses smelling of magnolia—that cannot accept that one ordinary Saturday morning, her son Mark put the barrel of his father's hunting rifle in his mouth. And he pulled the trigger.

He was a handsome, affable, clever teenager that was supposedly enjoying his privileged lifestyle— a top school, outings with friends and his Netflix series. He never touched any alcohol or illegal drugs as he had been treated for a mild form of Epilepsy in his childhood; but he had been seizure-free for years, which allowed him to get a driver's license. He did not talk much but his parents knew that he was taciturn by nature and kept a low profile by choice. What provoked it?

In the USA, 42,773 Americans die by their own hand each year, being the 10th leading cause of death. The annual age-adjusted suicide rate is 12.93 per 100,000 individuals and men die 3.5 times more often than women; there are 117 suicides per day. [301] Even though it is more frequent in mature males, *young people attempt it 25 times* more per each act compared to *4 times* in the older individuals. More *women* attempt it than men do, peaking between *45-54 years old*. Suicide was the second leading cause of non-natural death in young people, surpassed only by accidents and crimes. Suicidal thoughts, depression, bipolar and panic disorders are clinical risk factors that must be thoroughly evaluated by professionals.[302]

Since the times of Saint Augustine, **Suicide** has been considered a mortal sin for the Christian ethos—a censure that would also taint the social standing of the victim's family.[303] Emile Durkheim, a 19th century French sociologist, considered suicide as *an objective evidence* of a deep malaise of the milieu where it occurred. He divided it in three major categories: *selfish, altruistic* and *without a name*.[304]

Marzio Barzagli, a professor of Sociology at the *Università di Bologna*, said: "the processes of social breakdown were not the only cause, let alone the main factor underlying the rise in the suicide statistics up until the beginning of the 20th century…Suicide depends on many psychosocial, cultural, political and even biological causes…It must be analyzed from different points of view." [305]

However, one of the leading causes of suicides and attempted suicides in the younger population of modern nations has been long under-reported in the official statistics: its *association with chronic diseases* that might provoke depression.[306] Dr. Harley C. Gorton directed a study [307] in the United Kingdom that canvassed two large primary care-data sets—the *Clinical Practice Research Datalink* (CPRD) in England and the *Secure Anonymized Information Linkage Databank* (SAIL) in Wales—in order to find out the *real rate of unnatural deaths* in epileptic patients. Oftentimes the certificate of death of patients do not list Epilepsy as a contributing factor, which *underestimates its real impact* in the morbidity/mortality rates. Those databases are linked to *hospitalization, outpatient care centers* and *death* records.

They suggested that physicians must consider **the co-morbid conditions** like *anxiety*, *depression,* and *substance abuse*—they must check the patients' use of opioids and psychotropic medication. The researchers matched 44,678 participants with Epilepsy in the *CPRD database* to 891,429 participants without it in a period spanning from 1998 to 2014; they matched 14,051 participants with the disease in the *SAIL database* to 279,365 people from 2001 to 2014. Epileptic patients were 2.77 times more likely to die of an unnatural cause, 2.97 times more likely to die of unintentional injury or poisoning, and 2.15 times as likely to die of suicide. People taking medication had 4.99 times higher risk of collateral effects and 3.55 times higher risk of drug misuse—opioids (56.5%) and psychotropic agents (32.3%)

The researchers stated that: "patients should be adequately advised about unintentional injury prevention and monitored for suicidal ideation, thoughts and behavior…The suitability and toxicity of any concomitant medication should be considered when prescribing for comorbid conditions."[308] Health Care providers should understand that *an excessive focus* on seizure control will sideline *screening* for serious behavioral and psychiatric issues, which might delay a timely referral.

A *CDC survey* done in the pandemic's lockdown showed: "18-to-24-year-olds reported the highest levels of anxiety and depression, and a quarter of them said they had seriously considered suicide." [309] In the worst possible timing, they are trying *to figure out their* lives, as the ground violently shifts under their feet.

Health Care providers have a **unique fiduciary duty** to do a thorough job when we see a patient that we suspect might have any kind of suicidal ideation. The first order of action is: give the patient all the necessary time to *open up* to us. Notwithstanding our full schedules, we must allocate more time for that interview. The initial questions should be open ended—"you seem to be upset today... are you?"—and we should listen to their answers, showing empathy for their plight.[310]

Once we establish *a good rapport* with the patient, we can ask more pointed questions like: "do you feel desperate?" or "do you feel life is not worth living?" When we confirm that the patient has suicidal ideation, we must inquire about its *frequency* and *severity* to determine **the level of risk**: *low*, *medium,* or *high*. It is of paramount importance to find out if the patient has ready access to medication or firearms to carry out the act of suicide. We should ask *what, how and when.*[311]

A suicidal patient has the potential to harm some other persons who might be "influencing his/her/ihr thoughts" or are totally innocent like family members. Moreover, when a patient, who was totally agitated for days, appears to calm down caregivers must consider the possibility that *the decision to act* was already made. If a concerned family member tags along, the initial impression could be of denial. If there are any indications of drug or alcohol abuse, the patient *should be referred* fast to an urgent care center.[312] There is no excuse whatsoever for any delay.

Docs, remember that, at our graduation, we swore the Hippocratic oath.

-"Your family knows that you tried to kill yourself?" I asked, point blank.

-"How do you know ?" she shot back, angrily. "I was completely alone at home that Sunday afternoon....Never told anyone—not even my sister."

I had invited a lovely girl for dinner at one of my favorite French restos. Nibbling at amuse-gueules [313], she broke a dam of complaints about how she had been frustrated of trying to convey her true feelings to her family. Her detached demeanor seemed so dissonant. As if she were an orchestra member that had given up on the score... For the ebb and flow of Living.

That is precisely when I knew that she had tried the "final escape route."

One of the most disseminated fallacies is that someone that attempts suicide has to be in a manifest state of *anxiety, depression,* or *despair*. A misleading assumption. Many patients are clinically depressed but only a minority have *suicidal ideation*; similarly, some with suicidal thoughts *never show* signs of a major depression. [314]

Moreover, when they decide to act, they reach *a state of tranquility* — akin to a suave Buddhist peace of mind. **Depression is not synonymous with Suicide.**

Alas, what was supposed to be *a hot date* turned out to be *a therapy session*; fortunately, she eventually favorably discussed those thorny issues with her family. But scared of *our gift*, she then avoided us [315] (*And you wonder why I am writing*)

Gabriel García Márquez said: "escribimos para que nos quieran." [316]

Friedrich Nietzsche wrote about the caged tiger that, after being mercilessly beaten up by its master with a whip, suddenly snatches the instrument of torture from his hands and starts to beat itself with élan.[317] *The abused mimics the abuser.*

We could not help recalling that parable when we read the *New York Times* article about the suicide of British TV host Caroline Flack at only age forty.[318] Why would a sexy, smart, successful lady like her chose that disgraceful way out?

Derrick Bryson Taylor wrote that: "In a 2019 Instagram post, Ms. Flack wrote that she was 'in a really weird place' and that she found it hard to talk about it. She said when she reached out to someone to talk about her feelings, they called her 'draining'…'I feel like this is why some people keep their emotions to themselves." When *emotionally frustrated* women "internalize" the repressive mechanisms to silence them—"normalizing" the system's irrationality to a certain degree—they become *walking pressure cookers* that could one day burst out.

The über-false mantra of "sheer happiness" peddled by social media—and repeated parrot-like by the bobos—gives some credence to a *dangerous delusion*. It is *simply not human* to be permanently in the "happy, care-free and fun mood." When there is *a valid reason* for our emotional angst, we should be able to share it with our close ones, without the risk of being unfairly labeled as "too draining."

Do not squander your emotionality with counterproductive self-censoring.

Speak out, lay it out in the open, even at the risk of fretting "the happy."

The stressed-out E.R. personnel of the New York-Presbyterian Allen Hospital

Got used to the company of the little sparrow flying over their place of penance

She was always the first one present when the doors of the ambulance opened

She was always the first one present when they took a patient to an exam table

She was always the first one present when they hooked the whirring machines

She was always the first one present when the drilled routine of care kicked in

One day her tender heart could not resist so much suffering and stopped beating

Plunging into the depths of their sorrowful spirits, she gave them a final cheer.

On April 27, 2020, **Dr. Lorna Breen**, chair of Emergency Medicine at the Columbia-affiliated hospital, committed suicide in her parent's home in Virginia. She had been diagnosed with a Coronavirus infection, but she fully recovered; she had a leave of absence from work, and she decided to spend it with her family. In a communication with *The New York Times* her father said: "She tried to do her job, and it killed her…Make sure she's praised as a hero, because she was. She's a casualty just as much as anyone else who also died." [319] He said that she told him that many patients were already dead when they opened the ambulances' doors. She never had a history of Mental Health issues, but she *seemed detached* to him.

Once a suicidal patient decides to act, a Buddhist peace of mind sets in.

Lorna was screaming for our help. But we were not properly listening.

Physicians have been mentored to face most of the stressful situations of our careers with *a stiff upper lip* and the *steely determination* to carry on. Nonetheless. If the moral values of fortitude and resiliency were drilled into physicians' minds during their schooling and training, they will be *the last ones* to ask for help. As a result medical personnel are hard hit by *an unusual incidence* of suicidal acts and attempts, which will worsen during the course of this protracted pandemic.

Unfortunately, there are *institutional barriers* that are blocking the remedies.

In a 2008 *Health Affairs* article [320], Donald M. Berwick, Thomas W. Nolan and John Whittington coined the term "triple aim" to define the simultaneous pursuit of three objectives—improving the *experience of care*, improving the *health of populations,* and *reducing per capita costs* of health care—to fix the care system. In a follow-up article in 2014, considering the increasing dissatisfaction of physicians and nurses with medical practice, Drs. Bodenheimer and Sinsky argued that: "the Triple aim be expanded to a Quadruple Aim, adding that the goal of improving the work life of health care providers, including clinicians and staff." [321]

Professional burn-out is characterized by a most evident but ignored *tragic triad*:

a) High emotional exhaustion

b) High depersonalization

c) Low sense of personal accomplishment

A - High emotional exhaustion

The *increasing demands* of payors, administrators and patients on the time and resources of the health care personnel produces a generalized dissatisfaction with the perceived quality of their delivered care services. The level of *resilient frustration* is so pervasively high in our system that physicians, nurses, technicians, receptionists, and other ancillary personnel are literally "counting the days" until the end of their *silent martyrdom* eventually comes—their retirement date.

B - High depersonalization

The negative feelings and bad vibes will inevitably foster the emergence of *cynicism and sarcasm* in the ranks of providers, with the resultant degradation of their rapport with the patients and families. It is a self-sustaining vicious circle. Patients complain that they are being ignored and/or mistreated, which triggers *more negativity and disdain* for the staff. As a result, the latter continue to react negatively without the possibility of pausing for a moment and reflect calmly.

C - Low sense of personal accomplishment

For the majority of us who have chosen the medical career, profit and social standing are secondary considerations. What we most value is the *possibility of helping* our fellow human beings and at the same time enjoy the *unique standing* conferred by possessing a voice of authority. With the landing of the abominable "bean counters" in both the public and the private payor system, our maneuvering room has been drastically curtailed. Our decreasing satisfaction not only pushes us into early retirement but also into all kinds of *drug* and *alcohol abuse* in our ranks, plus the possibility of one day to casually start mulling about "the unthinkable."

Shanabelt et al. studied the *incidence of burnout* with work-life balance in the US physician and general workforces in 2011 and 2014 to compare the results and significant trends, using the *Maslach Burnout Inventory*; they invited more than 35,000 physicians to participate and 19% completed the survey. [322] They said that: "54.4 % (n=3680) of the physicians reported at least 1 symptom of burnout in 2014 compared with 45.50 % (n=3310) in 2011.Substantial differences in rates of burnout and satisfaction with work-life balance were observed by specialty." They found minimal differences in the general workforce between those years.

Early on in our flight training, a silent hitchhiker steps into our cockpit.

Douglas A. Mata et al. conducted *a meta-analysis* of 31 cross-sectional and 23 longitudinal studies of the *incidence and prevalence of depression* in resident physicians. "The overall pooled prevalence was 28.8 % of participants, ranging from 20.9% to 43.2% depending on the instrument used, and increased with calendar year." [323] Lisa S. Rotenstein et al. extracted data from 167 cross-sectional studies and 16 longitudinal studies from 43 countries. "The overall pooled crude prevalence of depression or depressive symptoms was 27.2%...Depressive symptom prevalence remained relatively constant over the period studied…In the 9 longitudinal studies that assessed depressive symptoms before and during medical school (n=2432), the median absolute increase in symptoms was 13.5 %." [324] They also found that only 15.7% sought medical treatment for their symptoms.

Amy M. Fahrenkopf et al. studied the *incidence of medical errors* among resident physicians of three urban children's hospitals by evaluating the depression with the *Harvard National Depression Screening* day scale, the burnout using the *Maslach Burnout Inventory*, and the rate of *medication errors per resident* per month. They found: "24 (20%) of the participant residents met the criteria for depression and 92 (74%) met the criteria for burnout. Active surveillance yielded 45 errors made by participants. Depressed residents made 6.2 times as many medication errors per resident month as residents who were not depressed…Burn-out residents and not-burnt out residents made similar rates of error per resident month." [325] There are several factors that *block physicians*, and other medical personnel, to seek the needed counselling. The *crazy work schedule* of physicians and residents, the *confidentiality issues* that might affect the licensing status of practitioners, the personal issue of *loneliness* and *divorce*, all might contribute to it. However, there are solutions that can be implemented by the medical institutions.

We have dawdled about writing a book on Physician/Nurse burn-out.

Lorna's sacrifice has shaken our torpor and put us immediately to task.

—"Doctor…Can't stand my husband's mother… She's simply impossible!"

The mother-in-law is often the *bête noire* [326] in even the happiest of couples, as both members might resent her usual impertinent intrusiveness in their intimate affairs. Sri Ravi Shankar, the Indian musician, said that the greater number of break-ups of couples in our times was causally related to our *lack of patience*.[327]

We are mentally wired for fast solutions to our problems; we cannot wait for issues to unravel on their own, fearing unpredictability. The **rush for a resolution** of any conflict dooms the chance of a more labored but better lasting solution. In the newly formed couples, the *husband's family* is an unknown factor in a wife's realm that must be tactfully dealt with. What does that woman want? So simple.

To keep her sons' love and not to be excluded from his life after marriage.

She might watch you and second-guess you and whisper behind your back.

But there is another one that has done it with impunity. Who? *Your mother*.

If you reached *an entente cordiale* [328] with her, why not try the same with this one? Where there is a sense of belonging and intimacy, there is some kind of friction. When the critique is not justified or is malicious, a patient attitude might be wiser. One quick way to increase our capacity for tolerance is to fine-tune our breathing techniques like they teach in the soothing practice of modern Yoga. Why not try it?

Take the chance to practice sitting on a bed of nails for her garish garbling.

—"Doctor…Can't stand my husband and his mother —they're both crazy."

Erica X., a smart middle-aged lady that we were treating for headaches, told us that she could not tolerate her *mother-in-law's mollycoddling* of her partner, besides suspecting that "those two" were *in cahoots* to pan her behind her back. Besides the fact that many men are *Momma's boys*—infuriating their partners—there is a psychiatric condition that affects individuals in intimate contact. What appears as a wifely delusion is in fact *the little cousin* of a rare but real disorder.

The **folie à deux** —a shared psychosis—is a syndrome that manifests itself in *delusions* and *hallucinations* transmitted from one individual to the other. The *DSM-V* identified it as "shared psychotic disorder" [329] and the *ICD-10* called it "induced delusional disorder." [330] It was described by Charles Lasègue and Jean-Pierre Falret, two 19th century French psychiatrists, who divided it:

- **Folie imposée**: a dominant individual (the inducer/the principal) creates a delusional belief and imposes it on another one (the acceptor/the associate).
- **Folie simultanée**: two psychotic individuals co-influence the content of their delusions and their co-morbidity can trigger symptoms in each other.

Some of these individuals had criminal careers like *Bonnie and Clyde* [331] (the *inducer* and the *acceptor)*. When two persons with a *folie imposée* are separated, often the delusions in the acceptor resolve without recurring to any medication.

<u>The following section was written by **Gian Luca Laplume**, our dear son.</u>[332]

Can we predict the possibility of violence by studying certain personality traits?

In *Section III of the DSM-5* [333], a dimensional model of *maladaptive personality traits* has been proposed; the **personality trait** can be considered as *a recognized tendency* to feel, perceive, behave, and think in a relatively consistent way across different situations and periods of time. The *new model* is formed by *25 lower order* personality features that are grouped into *five higher order* groupings:

a) Negative Affectivity

b) Detachment

c) Antagonism

d) Disinhibition

e) Psychoticism

These broad categories are *maladaptive variants* related to the domains of the well-studied *Five Factor* personality model—the **Big Five**—which is divided into:

a) Emotional Stability

b) Extraversion

c) Agreeableness

d) Conscientiousness

e) Lucidity

This inventory of basic personalities was developed to evaluate the impact of the maladaptive personality traits that had been proposed in the *Fifth Edition* of the *Diagnostic and Statistical Manual* (DSM-5) [334] Vanessa Gongora and Alejandro Castro Solano said: "there is an increasing body of research that supports the psychometric properties of the PID-5, with an internal consistency alpha more than .70 for all its dimensions. Evidence of the five-factorial structure has been found in student, community, and clinical sample." [335]

These authors studied 1,032 participating individuals from the metropolitan area of the city of Buenos Aires with the *PID-5-BF*, the *Big Five Inventory*, the *Mental Health Continuum-Sort* form, and the *Survey on risk factors*. "A five-factorial structure that explained 59.48% of the variance was found, with reliability values higher than alpha= .86 for each factor. Convergence among pathological personality traits and the five-factor personality model were found, except for Psychoticism and Openness to experience." [336] The researchers found *a low incidence* of mental health problems with the severity of those traits.

Emily Dowgwillo, Kim Meanrd, Robert Krueger, and Aaron Pincus studied the associations between some common *pathological personality traits* identified in the *DSM-5* [337] and the *intimate partner violence* among a sample of male and female American college students. They said: "For both genders, detachment was positively associated with relationship violence. Antagonism was uniquely associated with relationship violence for women, whereas disinhibition was uniquely associated with relationship violence for men." [338]

Sigmund Freud, the father of *Psychoanalysis*, studied the *neurotic features* of his patients and how they might had become *the trigger* for some of their inner frustrations and/or anti-social behavior. He said that Psychoanalysis aims to find out: "what (a neurotic patient's) symptoms mean, what instinctual impulses are concealed behind them and are satisfied by them, and what course was followed by the mysterious path that has led from the instinctual wishes to the symptoms." [339]

In his book *Civilization and its Discontents* [340], Freud exposed his theory of a **two-sided pleasure principle**, which regulates the lives of humans as *our Id* [341] is in continuous collision with the outside world. Human beings suffering from the angst of some unsatisfied desires recur to certain *defense mechanisms* that would blunt their impact in their daily lives. *An inner, self-regulated control mechanism.* To manage the incompatibility, we deploy the following defensive mechanisms:

a) Deflections

b) Substitutive satisfactions

c) Intoxication

Freud proposed that the frustration in our lives derives from three major realms: *our bodies*, our *natural elements,* and *our social relationships*. Initially he proposed that, considering than we have little leeway in controlling factors from the first two realms, we should concentrate on the third one. However, the clinical practice in his Vienna cabinet taught him that *our ways to relate with each other* can be as unyielding to long-term reform as the other two, especially because there is a **clash between the libidinal and aggressive instincts**. Freud believed that the existence of civilization is enabled by the *active suppression of our instincts* in order to foster *a harmonic co-existence* with other individuals that also have their own interests; the individual interests *are sacrificed* for the larger societal good.

Is our Id solely responsible for the overt display of anti-social behavior?

Freud established that the *Super-Ego* [342] can be as tyrannical and damaging for human psyche as the *Id*, capable of burdening our psyche with excessive, irrational demands. In the case of Raskolnikov, the murderer in *Crime and Punishment* [343], his hypertrophied Super-Ego makes him believe that he has the right to kill the pawnbroker in order to "sanitize society"—an act that should be "appreciated" by all citizens. Only after he actually committed the heinous crime, will he start to have resiliently remorseful second thoughts about it. Eventually he will confess his crime and subject himself to the punishment of the society he so deeply abhorred.

<u>*Diary USS Awareness*</u> – Beware of the close company you keep aboard the ship. Some of them might have a shady personal background that can gravely affect you. Rest like the seasoned sailors of yore: with only one eye closed.

Violence in the media and its effect on **human behavior** is a topic that has long been hotly debated. [344] For almost fifty years, social scientists, psychologists, pediatricians, and psychiatrists have been discussing whether the ever-increasing violence in the mass media has had some real, meaningful impact on the increasing levels of citizens' aggression and the ensuing episodes of violent acts. [345]

Even though professional associations have claimed that there was a direct link between violence in the mass media and tragic social events [346], many experts have questioned the true *scientific validity* of those position papers, accusing the authors of distorting the evidence. [347] In a perverse turn of events, the mass media seems to be more interested in debating whether their shamelessly violent imagery (including the gratuitous assault on our senses) has any bearing on impressionable young minds rather than taking practical, incremental steps to *cut the sludge off*. [348]

After the *Columbine shooting* and other similar mass shootings in the USA, our collective *imagination* has been fixated on this issue in an effort to categorize and explain these tragedies. It is known that both Columbine shooters were active video game players, who particularly enjoyed watching the violent games. Even though violence in the media has a clear-cut effect on our behavior, it is however only a *significant factor* amongst many others that can lead to increased aggressive cognition and behavior. [349] We should take a bird's view of the whole ensemble.

The modern evaluation of individual and communal violence is based on the **General Aggression Model** (GAM) which is an integrative theoretical scaffolding to study the role of the social, cognitive, personality, developmental, and biologic factors that determine the final outcome. [350] *Human Aggression* encompasses all the acts whose aim is to cause immediate harm to other persons. [351] Anderson and Bushman said: "people acquire the aggressive responses the same way they acquire other complex forms of social behavior—either by direct experience or key observations." [352] The General Aggression Model has three major pillars:

A- Inputs

B- Routes

C- Outcomes [353]

A -<u>Inputs</u>

They are composed of *personal* and *situational* factors. The personal factors are:

a) **Traits**: for example people with inflated self-esteem (narcissism) are prone to feel anger and react angrily when their self-image is threatened.

b) **Sex**: men and women differ in their mode of aggressiveness—men prefer *direct aggression* while women prefer the *indirect aggression*—and there is 10:1 ratio of male to female violence.

c) **Beliefs**: efficacy-related beliefs will predispose people for violent behavior.

d) **Attitudes**: unbecoming positive and tolerant attitudes towards violence will encourage the emergence of more aggressive acts.

e) **Values**: socio-cultural differences in the USA may explain a "more benign vision" of violence in the South and the West.

f) **Long-term goals**: using it as a brutal enforcer of crime, gangsters want to be feared and respected with violence. [354]

The situational factors are:

a) **Aggressive cues:** objects that prime the recall of aggression-related concepts in our memories, i.e. guns.

b) **Provocation:** it constitutes perhaps the single most important cause of overt aggression; it includes the verbal forms like insults, the printed forms like slanderous articles, the physical forms like workplace abuse/bullying and, more prominently in our age, the digital bullying.

c) **Frustration:** defined as the blockage to obtain an object or a special status in society.

d) **Pain and discomfort:** certain physical variables like temperature or noise provoke it.

e) **Drug:** caffeine and alcohol can foster aggression in individuals.

f) **Incentives:** they can be either objects or services. [355]

B – **Routes**

They are composed of:

a) **Hostile thoughts**: some specific sensorial stimuli will increase the relative accessibility of some aggressive concepts in our Memory; their chronic activation facilitates their ready accessibility.

b) **Scripts**: some basic processes favor the development of aggressive stories in our minds.

c) **Mood and Emotion**: some sensorial stimuli affect our aggressiveness. i.e. horror movies.

d) **Expressive motor responses**: some bad experiences will activate motor-related responses.

e) **Arousal**: it acts with three different mechanisms. First, arousal from an irrelevant source can potentiate the then prevailing aggressive response. Secondly, arousal provoked by physical exercise might be misconstrued as anger in situations involving provocation. Thirdly, a high or low level of arousal may provoke aggressive behavior.

f) **Interconnections**: emotional responses can spread through various levels of our brains, after passing through integrative structures like the Thalamus. [356]

C – Outcomes

The third pillar includes *complex neural information processes* that range from the relatively automatic to the heavily structured. They can be divided in:

a) **Immediate appraisal**: automatic, spontaneous, and relatively effortless without an accompanying mental awareness; depending on the given circumstances, a certain stimulus (i.e. being hit in a crowded place) can produce either an *automatic response* (i.e. aggressive response) or a *situational inference* (i.e. understand that it was merely an accident)

b) **Re-appraisal**: the person engages in a totally different understanding of the stimulus, based on the memory of previous experiences, prejudices, ideology, etc. (i.e. a Black person fending off a White Supremacist)

c) **Personality processes**: the stimuli can reinforce previous held beliefs (i.e. Racism) or influence future behavior (i.e. disdain for Minorities) [357]

Despite the link between aggression and media violence, the latter is only one of the many factors usually present in extremely violent individuals. Craig Anderson, a noted psychologist who has studied the effects of violent media, said in a *Psychiatric Times* interview [358] that the link between media violence and aggression is strong and observable from every significant type of study design, including randomized experiments, longitudinal and cross-sectional studies.

Does the supposedly observed link have any statistical significance?

In 2017, Anderson et al. reviewed relevant research published in the past 60 years to determine if there was any significant relationship between violence in the screen entertainment and *short-term/ long-term harmful effects* on young people; the study focused on longitudinal studies about the effects of violent video games. They concluded that the majority found that violent media exposure produced *an increase* in aggressive thoughts, feelings, physiological arousal, hostile appraisals, desensitization to violence, decreased pro-social (civic) attitudes and empathy. The research showed that both young men and women who played violent video games excessively showed a change in their behavior, which became more aggressive. [359]

Anderson said: "there now are numerous longitudinal studies by several different research groups around the world, and they all find significant violent video game exposure effects." According to this author, studies from developed countries such as Japan, Singapore, Germany, Portugal, etc., showed that "the association between media violence and aggression is similar across cultures." [360]

Alarmingly, Anderson also said that the *frequent exposure to fast paced violent images*, frequently found in videogames, can change the way our brain processes violent imagery. It can lead to a dampening of our emotional responses to violent stimuli. Indeed, violence in art can produce a *defamiliarizing effect*. **Bertolt Brecht**, the German playwright [361], used this technique when he created the *alienization effect* in modern theater. He wanted his audience to be removed from the lives, motivations, and actions of his characters so his plays could touch directly upon the audience's subconscious and spirituality—not often revealed or acknowledged. However, one could argue that violence in art is defamiliarized *by express design* in order for us, the audience, to enjoy it in good faith. In contrast, real violence is horrendous and is not meant to be enjoyed by any well-adjusted individual. Its *artistic defamiliarization effect* is precisely the artificial means by which we watch violence in art but do not feel personally touched or disturbed.

Although there is a link between media violence and aggression, Anderson said: "media violence is only one of many risk factors for later aggressive and violent behavior. Furthermore, extremely violent behavior never occurs when there is only one risk factor present. Thus, a healthy, well-adjusted person with few risk factors is not going to become a school-shooter just because they start playing a lot of violent video games or watching a lot of violent movies."[362] The central point argued by Anderson is that, although exposure to media violence (like the contents of video games and films) is one of the known risk factors for future violent action, it is *usually not* the single motivating factor. There is a summation of many factors. Moreover, also an individual with low risk factors for violent action and cognition *is not likely* to turn unusually violent solely from the exposure to violent media.

Douglas Gentile, one of Anderson's colleagues at the University of Iowa, found in a different study that media exposure is only *one of six factors* useful for predicting future aggression. Besides media violence, they included the following:

a) bias towards hostility

b) prior aggressive behavior/fights

c) physical victimization

d) sexual disfunction/trauma

e) low parental involvement. [363]

In a literature review, this author stated that research on media violence has to move away from solely determining the effects and tackle *the underlying factors* that stimulate these reactions like "cross-cultural differences to neurophysiological effects, and the interplay between media, individual and contextual factors." [364] Gentile said: "The best single predictor of future aggression in the sample of elementary school children was past aggression, followed by violent media exposure, followed by having been a victim of aggression."

If exposure to the media does not foster violence, then what really does?

Modern psychology has long been dominated by the Freudian theories [365], but in the 1950's, 60's and 70's a Canadian Psychologist named Albert Bandura [366] took a different approach and changed its evolution. He analyzed means of treating aggressive children by identifying sources of violence in their lives.

In 1961 Bandura conducted a study known as the **Bobo Doll experiment** where the researchers physically and verbally abused a clown-faced inflatable toy in the presence of preschool-age children to watch their reactions.[367] In his experiment, carried out when he was a professor in Stanford University, Bandura and his assistants enrolled the participation of preschoolers at Stanford University's nursery school who were divided in three groups:

a) **First group**: observed aggressive adult behavior.

b) **Second group**: observed nonaggressive behavior models.

c) **Third group**: not exposed to any models [368]

Furthermore the three groups were divided *by masculine or feminine genders* into two sub-groups each with a resulting six sub-groups; half of these sub-groups would observe *a same-sex behavior* and the other half would observe an *opposite-sex one*. The study was divided in three stages:

a) **First stage**: the children were first seated in a corner table with interesting activities (stickers, pictures, etc.) Then the behavior models were transferred to a table which had a Tinkertoy set and a Bobo Doll. "In the aggressive model groups, the model abused the Bobo doll both physically…and verbally. In the non-aggressive behavior model groups, the model ignored the Bobo doll and instead quickly assembled the Tinkertoys." [369]

b) **Second stage**: the children were led to a room that had some interesting toys and were encouraged to play with them. After a brief period of two minutes, they were told to stop playing and were led to another room in order to prod their *aggression arousal*. To find out whether previously observed violence fostered aggression in the observers, they were shown aggressive toys (like the Bobo doll) and non-aggressive ones.

c) **Third stage**: each child's behavior was studied for 20 minutes to determine whether there was an aggressive attitude or not in each sub-group. [370]

When the children, who watched an actor act aggressively to a doll, were in turn left alone with it, they *adopted the same aggressive behavior* and acted accordingly. However, children that were not exposed to that behavior towards the doll were in turn *not aggressive* towards it.

Even though the data was similar for both genders, there were some differences if the behavior was *sex-typed*—considered more appropriate for a specific gender. Males were *more prone* to imitate physical aggression than females were; there were no differences in the expression of verbal aggression, which is less sex-typed. Regarding physical aggression both male and female groups were *more imitative of the male behavior model* but with the verbal aggression both male and female groups were *more imitative of the same-sex models*. [371]

Bandera et al. proved that children **learn by imitation** and by adopting the behavior of what they were exposed to in their learning process, especially the adult models. He affirmed that violence is learned, but that *non-violence* could also be. Our societies must develop sound strategies to avoid violence as well, including the tragic repetition of mass shootings of innocents.

The Bobo Doll experiment has been used to justify or rather highlight the role of media violence on human behavior, arguing that violent images could influence them, encouraging them to act violently. Children show an increase in violent cognition when they are exposed to it. However, the disseminated violence in media does usually have that necessary *degree of artistic separation*.

After all, the majority of spectators understand that it is only a fantasy, which is meant to be watched, not glorified, and let alone imitated in real life. However, real life-violence does not have that degree of separation, except for psychotic people that commit crimes, representing a diagnostic challenge for psychiatrists that are asked to evaluate them in Emergency Departments. [372]

The Bobo Doll experiment proved that children are more likely to be violent if exposed to violence, which is **a learned behavior** passed on by their educators—parents, teachers, family members influencing their future adaptation.

Every time there is a mass shooting , the same perverse question arises again.[373]

Does the ubiquitous violence in the mass media enable that criminal behavior?

In the beginning of their book chapter *Media and Violence*, Valkenburg and Pietrovski said: "No topic in the field of communication has been more heavily investigated than media violence and its effects on aggression. Every time a child or teenager committed an act of violence in recent years, the debate about the effects of media violence on aggression flared up again. Can children and teens indeed become aggressive, or even criminal, from seeing violence on television, in movies, or in games? And if so, are some children and teens particularly vulnerable to media violence effects?" [374] These authors put forward many examples of mass shootings , starting with the example of Adam Lanza, who, after killing twenty schoolchildren and six adults in Sandy Hook Elementary School in Newton, Connecticut, in December 2012, then killed himself. [375]

The above-mentioned authors stated that, in order to establish *a definitive causality* between media usage and criminal behavior, two criteria must be considered:

a) **First criteria**: person's exposure to media violence must predate his or her criminal behavior.

b) **Second criteria**: all other possible explanations for that behavior can be excluded.

They claimed that a good research might unveil some *alternative explanations* for that criminal behavior, besides the media exposure. In the case of the crime of two-years old James Bulger by two 10-years-old in Liverpool in 1993, they had watched *Child Play's 3*, a violent film; however, they both were problem children who had been severely neglected by their parents. [376] Given that there are co-morbid causes like Anxiety/Depression disorders, developmental issues, etc., these incidents *do not unequivocally prove* that that the media violence will lead to heinous crimes. These authors made the *critical difference* between aggressive thoughts and aggressive behavior. "While criminally violent behavior is illegal behavior, and therefore punishable by law, aggressive behavior is not illegal-unless it becomes extreme." [377]

They also stated that few studies have focused on **indirect aggression**—camouflaged acts that seek harm and are perfidiously delivered. They are especially relevant for Millennials and Xers' who might suffer the assault of rumors, innuendo, or sexting in their little phone screens. While *physical abuse* is generally directed at males, females of all ages suffer the worst consequences of *digital abuse*, enabled by the dark connectivity of the Internet.

Digital dating abuse (DDA) is a variant of an extremely aggressive modern behavior where camouflaged individuals try to *coerce or cajole* known individuals using the web's anonymity. Lauren Reed et al. surveyed 365 college students and found that, even though there were *no gender* differences, women complained of *more negative effects* of sexual messaging than men. [378]

In the literature regarding this issue, there are two types of experiments:

a) **Laboratory experiments**: they take place in artificial conditions and their results cannot be easily extrapolated to other settings found in everyday life—they *lack external validity*.

b) **Field experiments**: they are usually conducted in places teeming with participants. Even though they reflect real-life conditions, they also have *difficulty establishing a direct link*.

One of the best-known field experiments was conducted by Dr. Jacques-Philippe Leyens with institutionalized teenagers who were exposed to violence in TV viewing; half of the group was exposed to violent film viewing for a week and the other half watched neutral ones. They found that viewing of violent films *did increase the aggressive behavior* of young spectators. [379]

In order to bring clarity, there are two scientific approaches for collected data:

a) **Correlational studies**: they are also called cross-sectional correlational studies. Assuming that there is in fact a direct link between the media violence and aggressive behavior, researchers *collect data* from schools or communities.

b) **Meta-analyses**: they use *statistical techniques* to analyze the vast amount of data collected by the correlational studies.

In the correlational studies the researchers asked the participants and/or their family members if they watch violent movies or play video games, the frequency, the circumstances, etc. Then they observe the individuals to find out if there any aggressive signs. Even though they might establish the link between violence in the media and aggressive behavior (external validity) their *internal validity* is minimal. The egg dilemma: *what came first? The egg or the chicken?*

This can be ameliorated with **causal correlational** or **longitudinal studies** where the measurements are taken in *two or more points in time* to determine if the trend persists. Researchers have a better chance to determine if the aggressive behavior was *a precursor* or *a consequence* of exposure to media violence.

Valkenburg and Pietrovski said: "while the internal validity of these designs is certainly stronger than that of cross-sectional correlational studies, it remains possible that unmeasured third variables (for example, a child's temperament, peer and family circumstances) may explain potential associations between media violence and aggression." [380] Leonard Enron et al. conducted one of the pioneering causal-correlation studies by observing 8 years-old while they watched violence on the TV and then repeating the exercise *ten years later* when they turned 18 years old. Even though they observed a link between media violence and aggressiveness they also found out that there was not a *reverse correlation*—aggressiveness at age 8 did not prod them to watch violent TV at age 18.[381]

The meta-analyses are *refined summaries* of the empirical studies, namely the experimental and correlational variants. The researchers put all the previously collected data in their statistical programs to find out if there are any *statistically significant correlations* between two factors.

Valkenburg and Petrovski said: "the first large scale meta-analysis carried out by Haejunk Paik and George Comstock, encompassed 217 empirical studies. The researchers found a correlation of r+.31 between watching violent movies or television shows and aggressive behavior. Five meta-analyses published in the new millennium concerning the effects of video games on aggressive behavior have similarly shown a positive correlation between violent games and aggressive behavior, with effects sizes ranging from *r* = .08 to *r* = .20" [382]

In a recent paper about a meta-analysis of many peer-reviewed articles on this issue, Christopher Ferguson et al. found that, *once the data was corrected* for many publication biases, there *was not a statistically significant relationship* between the media violence and aggressive behavior. The corrected overall effect size was r = .08, which is not statistically significant [383] They said: "publication bias was a problem for studies of aggressive behavior, and methodological problems such as the use of poor aggression measures inflated effect size." [384]

In conclusion, although there might be a link between media violence and aggressiveness, it has not yet been proved to be *statistically significant*. There are other social, cultural, and personal factors that must be controlled in a valid study. If it does induce violence, then what came first? Did the media violence lead to individual aggressive behavior or did the societal one prod violence in the media? It is easy to blame the media in times of "alternative truths" (sic) as it has become a target of political pundits who sensationalize for spurious interests.

But ultimately, we, the citizens, must take responsibility for what we consume and honestly realize that a convenient scapegoat answer will not address the root of the problem. Mental Health is a *social concern neglected* in the USA, swept under the bottom rows of its complicated agenda. We often wait until it is rather too late and then try to scrabble, *searching for a villain,* at the margins of the room, while tiptoeing around the *giant elephant* lying dormant in its midst.

<u>That was the end of Gian Luca's participation in this book (the rest is all my fault)</u>

<u>Diary USS Awareness</u> – Speaking of violence, could you fix "that" problem? Were those radicals tossed out of the dinghy when we veered sharply sideways? Good. Did you throw a bucket of fish morsels and blood too? Fine. (*Deep sigh of relief*) As I said, there is a renewed hope…Hey, don't interrupt me, seaman. WHAT?!!! Sharks swim away… Leader yells they eat junk but not that *s****? Wants respect? Jesus…If we can't even use them as bait, we're *deep in that same stuff* ourselves.

Chapter IV – The cyber chantage

"It's not the foreign that draws us in, it's the familiar that mesmerizes us. Added to perfume in small quantities, skatole seems like a familiar person waving at us, like a hint of coming home." Parfum, a Netflix series.[385]

One of the most closely guarded secrets of the parfum industry is that a truly successful product must have, buried at the bottom of the bespoke combination of fragrances, *a residue of skatole—a* white crystalline organic compound that is a byproduct of the metabolism of tryptophan and is found in the human feces. In low concentrations, it has a *flowery smell* but at higher ones, it is *a malodorant*.[386]

Human beings are deeply attached to the smells and sounds of their first years of life; feces are the final product of the decomposition of organic material by bacteria in our gut, which allows the absorption of needed nutrients. All mammals have **a unique signature odor**, which is distinguishable from those of the other creatures and gives away our presence, even when others are present.[387]

Women, with a bigger sense of smell [388], build *an odor-based emotionality* by layering the impressions associated with events over a deep substratum whose information can be retrieved when a similar stimulus excites their olfactory bulbs. Like skatole, in extremely small dosages it can add an *attractive ingredient* to the combination of fragrances they collect. But in higher dosages, it can be *repulsive*.

What is the importance of their sense of smell in women's interactions?

In their book *The Neurobiology of Olfaction*, Anne-Marie Mouly and Regina Sullivan said: "One of the most characteristics features of odor memory in humans is the rather unique ability of odors to vividly trigger the evocation of experiences. This property might be sustained by the direct connections established by the olfactory bulb and piriform/olfactory cortex on two structures involved in emotion and memory, namely the amygdala and hippocampus. In animals, memory for environmental odors plays a vital role because it regulates many behaviors that are crucial for survival."[389] The *emotionality* associated with particular odors is of paramount importance for the **close bonding** of women with their sexual partners, children, and family members, which will shape their long-term social interactions.

The *olfactory bulb* is the first area of the Central Nervous System to receive the incoming signals transmitted from the human nostril's receptors. Researchers found gender differences for the *olfactory sensitivity, odorant identification* and *memory* as well as the tasks where the odors are rated for psychological features such as *familiarity, intensity,* and *pleasantness*. Ana V. Oliveira-Pinto et al. found that the total number of neurons in the olfactory bulb was much higher in women than in men—16.2 million in females compared to 9.2 million in males.[390] The senses of *sight*, *audition* and *smell* are closely intertwined in our brains, for which any stimulus in one of them has *a corresponding response* in the other two.[391]

To this day we still do not know who she really was and what she wanted.

Isabelle Marie was born on February 17, 1877, in Genève, Switzerland. She passed away on October 27, 1904, at Ain Sefra, Algeria, at age 27.[392]

Isabelle Wilhelmine Marie Eberhardt was the illegitimate child of Natalie Moerder—born with the name of Eberhardt, she was the out-of-wedlock child of a Lutheran pastor and a Russian Jew—and Alexandre Trophimovsky—an Anarchist, former Orthodox priest, and tutor of Natalie's children. After wandering with her children in tow through Turkey and Italy, Natalie settled down in Switzerland where she started to receive a stipend from her late husband, General de Moerder.

Isabelle was born four years after the general's death and some speculated that she might have been fathered by Arthur Rimbaud, the tortured French poet. She was home-schooled, learning French, Italian, German, and Russian; she was interested in Latin, Greek, and Arabic, which later became her lifelong passion. She read the works of many writers—Rousseau, Leo Tolstoy, Voltaire, Zola.[393]

Her brother Augustine fled the stultifying social atmosphere of the canton and joined *La Legion Étrangère*[394]; stationed in Algeria, he corresponded with his sister and instilled in her a longing for life in the desert. In 1895 she published her first work in a literary magazine with a pseudonym to camouflage her true gender. *Inphernalia* deals with a young medical student's attraction for a dead woman; she published *Vision du Maghreb*, based solely on her correspondence with him.[395]

In May 1897 she travelled with her mother to North Africa to start anew; from the beginning, they were both disdained by the colonial community as they were friendly with the local Arab population, spoke their language and eventually both converted to Islam. The unexpected death of her mother made her move back to Switzerland, but her stay was very brief as her brother had married a French woman that disliked her. She resettled again back in Africa—that time for good.

Liberated from any family attachments, she began to dress, talk, and behave like *a wild man*—drinking heavily, smoking cannabis, and sleeping around. She took the name of *Si Mahmoud Essadi* to do what women were not allowed to do by the equally oppressive patriarchal institutions of *the colonizer* and *the colonized*.

To travel alone. To discover new places. To write at ease. To feel alive.

Eventually both the French colonial authorities and their Algerian proxies resented her free-wheeling lifestyle and attempted to assassinate her. She survived. She fell in love with a charming but meek Algerian soldier called Slimane Ehni. After the battle of El Moungar in 1903, she was dragooned by the *Foreign Legion* to work as a translator in a military campaign in the Atlas Mountains. She fell sick and had to be transferred to the military hospital in Ain Sefra; against the medical advice, she moved out to a precarious house with Ehni on October 20, 1904. The next day, a cascading mud slide fell on it. Unlike her partner. she did not run away.

With a smile, the wandering mystic turned around to boldly face Fate.

The date of "October 1904"—when Isabelle died in "an accident"—might seem far away, but in terms of this planet's history, it has happened only yesterday. And to this day, most women with a restless spirit *must disguise themselves* with some kind of "socially sanctioned costume" in order not to alert reactionary foes.

When Isabelle became a cultural burden for the French colonial authorities and the Algerian religious leaders, they sent some goons to assassinate her. In our "modern times" rattled men still place *contracts on rebellious women*, but the enforcers travel, not on camels' back over the dunes, but astride the computer's mouse to post scurrilous slander, abetted by the ubiquity of the social media. If it does not bring the most defiant ones to keel, they will *finish them off* via *Twitter*.

We will start the discussion of how women who have chosen a different path that the traditional *maiden—married—mother—nurturer—moved aside course* fare by aiming at the center of the paradigm with consequences for them: **Motherhood**.

Patriarchal societies have emphasized the need for women to bear and take care of children in detriment of almost any other task, except their mate's support. It seems that the ovary, and not the brain, became the center of female anatomy, influencing each and every one of their moves since they start playing with dolls until the time when they take care of their grandchildren to help their parents out.

Respecting Nature's endowment, this is not a censure of Maternity itself.

It is a denunciation of its shameless manipulation to oppress women.

—"Doctor…When I buy gifts for my nephews, it's always the same story."

Karen X. is a wealthy middle-aged lawyer that, having chosen not to have children, feels uncomfortable when a salesperson asks her: *"is this for your kids?"* She joined the ranks of millions of women worldwide that have made that choice. Census figures in the USA showed that 47.6% of women between the ages of 15 and 44 did not have children in 2014, up from 46% in 2012.[396] It keeps growing.

Alina Tugend said: "despite these statistics, the majority of marketing talks to adult women like they are all moms or want to be mothers…"[397] Melanie Notkin—who wrote a book about the various alternate social pathways of modern women—wonders why the marketing companies irrationally ignore this large demographic group.[398] One reason for this *commercial inertia* is that marketing studies usually focus on "the woman in a household" making the buying decisions. They might also be *reluctant to survey* the childless women—political correctness. Besides spending a lot of resources on their nephews and pets, the **NotMoms** also spend more on beauty products, premium food, and foreign travel. Unburdened by rearing obligations—both in terms of time and resources—they spend more freely.

Our society still views *women without children* differently from those that have them: it is a mix of low-key prejudice, ignorance and curiosity that crosses all the socio-economic and ethnic boundaries—to the dismay of the affected ladies.

Like having children, "not having them" should be a respectable choice.

—"Doctor…When the *New Mom* returns, nobody cares who covered her."

Nilda X. is a successful career woman that has made the conscious choice of *not having children* many years ago, as she never contemplated starting a family. That decision has seared "her utility" in the shared Unconscious of her co-workers. If a rebellious woman does not want to fill a "socially accepted role"—like Isabelle did when she donned the attire of camel rider—she is expected to give "reasons" and atone for the "affront" by taking raw deals. **The taken-for-granted trooper**.

The fact of not being a mother does not mean she is bored. On the contrary. She likes to make artistic pottery and has an unusually stimulating social network. But when someone goes on maternity leave, she is invariably "asked" to pitch in. She *has* to handle more clients' requests. She *has* to prepare more memos. She *has* to take more calls. She *has* to sit in more boring meetings. She *has* to work longer hours. And many times she skips her lunch to finish the tasks. *It keeps piling up.*

When the novel mother comes back, they celebrate with pictures and stories. Besides a perfunctory acknowledgement of her sacrifice, nobody notices Nilda X. When a child is sick or has a soccer game or a school play, her boss has his fix. "Go on," the boss says with confidence. "Nilda will cover—she's a good trooper." By the time, the worker on leave returns, Nilda is already exhausted and depressed.

Despite her help, she does not get a raise from her boss. Not even a smile.

Neither by the woman who got her coverage. Talk about girls' solidarity.

Vanessa de Largie said: "childless women often run second in the workplace when it comes to rosters…Employers are more accommodating to mothers; early shifts are reserved for them. They are not reserved for actresses like me, who must schedule auditions around work. A childless woman's obligations are deemed meaningless outside of her day job compared to the martyr mother." [399] Mothers with a full-time employment *must juggle* the demands of both work and parenting. Without a good safety net, society is *shifting* the burden of child rearing to them.

And to conscripted helpers like Nilda, who were never asked their opinion.

A rehash of the "droit de seigneur" [400] *over a woman's right to choose.*

A nugget of Wisdom. You had the same routine on Friday afternoons: you summoned Mary, your secretary, to your office and asked if she could close shop. Unmarried, you assumed she did not have any urgency to go home. Even though she had to first hop in an overcrowded subway and then a tortoise-moving bus to reach her flat in the suburbs late at night, she always assented with a sweet smile.

When *a little bird* tells you that she has a new flame, *a little lamp* lights up in your limited manly brain. *Eureka.*[401] You plan a little surprise for next Friday. Handing her a nice voucher for a dinner for two, you say: "Leave early. Enjoy."

Secretary. Traffic cop. Fire marshal. Rescue commando. Confidante.
Quasi-wife. A tad smitten. That big little deed meant "the world" to her.

—"Doctor… Why should people assume that we're not a good family, eh?"

Bruna X. is an entrepreneurial and charming immigrant from Brazil who, after being abandoned without much explanation by her husband two years ago, has been able to raise her two children with the profits of a downtown cafeteria and the priceless help from her mother who did not hesitate to re-settle from Recife. She gets upset every time someone says: "don't have a man with you?" Really?

It seems that a woman must also don "a wifely disguise" to get some respect.

The experience of single parenting has a common denominator: *isolation*.

The **single parent**—most of them women, but men are more conspicuous — is questioning sur-le-champ the *fallacious message* from the patriarchal institutions that prop the "classic set-up"—father plus mother—to raise children. Woefully, that same parent in *subtle*—and *not so subtle—ways* is being insidiously socially shunned by some friends, colleagues and, worse of all, family members. The opportunities to mingle and meet new people in social gatherings and events often become *scarcer* for single working women that have small children at home.

Raising children *without a good partner's company*, especially in a modern society that has not yet a comprehensive safety net like the USA, could provoke nefarious Mental Health consequences for the isolated, overworked individuals.[402] Even in the progressive Nordic European societies with generous benefits, single parents may lack the social and family support to fully develop their potential.[403]

Child rearing entails *being attentive* at their minor and major developments, trying to prevent any and all potential harm. Parents cannot blink.... Not once.[404]

The *sole company* of a small child and the *lack of adult communication* are two alienating factors for millions of modern women (and a few men as well).[405]

To make matters worse, many of them are shunned by their family members. Our society provides tons of reading material and media discussions about self-parenting but not an iota of *real, practical empathy* for their challenging plight. Vanessa Martir, struggling as a single mom, said: "We can't say it's hard. We can't cry over the pressure. We are supposed to grin and bear. It's no wonder so many snap, so many are depressed, so many take this pent-up rage and resentment out on their kids. I'm not saying it's right. I'm saying I understand." [406]

A nugget of Wisdom. Finally, you found that girl you were looking for.

After a few dates, she invites you for dinner with her small son at her home. Keep in mind that she is a courageous woman that earned her place under the Sun. She does not need you as a "surrogate dad." She wants to share her life with you.

Remember that beneath all that polished and seductive layering, her mind has a thick coat of skatole—a stinking residue of her multiple sentimental failures. She is trying hard to get away from its pull. You must offer her some extra energy.

Be patient. Become her lavender tree. Make her Seventh Chakra vibrate.

The Life Force will blow through her other six chakras located below.[407]

—"Doctor...My two-years old wets the mattress again—what's wrong?"

Silvia X. is the young mother of a lovely girl called Camila, who was being trained how to use the potty and toilet for her physiological needs. But she had *a sudden regression* that set her physiological training way back. What happened? She found out that her mother was expecting a child. She is **jealous of the baby**.

Liliana Fois, a diplomate of Psycho-pedagogy in Buenos Aires, said: "it is not convenient to keep silent about the piece of news because children perceive changes in the daily household activities; therefore, it is best to handle the information from the beginning and watch how they are receiving it." [408] The arrival of the baby has focused Silvia's attention more into the physical needs of her gestation, which was duly perceived by her child. That attitude is the normal reaction of a defenseless human being that *fears losing* the motherly protection.

Parents should not freak out when they hear that one of their children utters horrible words like "I wish he would die" or "I hate you." Dr. Constanza Duhalde, a professor of Psychology in the *Universidad de Buenos Aires* (UBA) said: "when the adaptation is perfect, the eldest child does not show any signs, everything is perfect and there is a good adaptation. One should become suspicious that there might be a process hidden to our eyes, that it was internalized, and it could show up in more complicated ways at any moment." [409] The verbal outbursts should be considered as *an escape valve* for feelings corroding the child's confidence.

What should parents do? They should take the opportunity to explain to the child that the family is adding a valuable new member that will become the best buddy for playing inside and outside their home. "Know how much fun it will be?" "Finally, you can go to the playground and get all muddy with your little brother." "We will go together to the zoo and watch the chimpanzees and tigers." "If Mom asks us to clean the dishes, we'll have another pair of hands. Isn't that cool?"

Family members must be recruited to contribute their own to this process.

Grandparents provide *a critical support role* in these family conundrums.

A nugget of Wisdom. Hey, it is time to get off your butt and do some work. Yeah, we know that you had to get up to fetch a pizza in the middle of the night. But fulfilling an occasional caprice from your pregnant wife is not nearly enough. Tell your mother to come over to your home with a present for your jealous child. Her grandparents should make plans to take her to the zoo next Sunday afternoon. That way your wife will get a needed break to rest properly, and the child will be re-assured that the baby's arrival will not dislodge her from the center of attention.

What? Wanna go to the zoo too? Shouldn't you rather stay with your wife?

Oh, I see. You're seething with anger 'cause they took your sister. Not you?

Seriously? How could your own parents dis you in such a miserly way?

Such a shameful effrontery from our own stock should be squared up to.

<u>Diary USS Awareness</u> – Never face women's wrath without a good shield.

—"Doctor…Money is not bad….And I missed that sense of inclusiveness."

Deborah X. is a nice middle-aged lady that, after becoming a widow, has been living alone in a deserted mansion; her two children had left out for college. She decided to downsize by selling that house and buying an efficiency in Miami Beach. Being in a quarter with many retirees, she signed up to work part-time as *concierge help* instead of staying home to watch TV or sell goods. She rejected calls to become a "cosmetics lady" because she figured out that she would not be compensated fairly for her time, and she wanted a more exciting opportunity.

The job trend of **elderly concierge** occurs because the *semi* and *fully retired* can assist the steady stream of *baby boomers that need help* in their twilight years. Liz Moyer said: "some 43 million people already provide care to family members—either their own parents or children—according to the AARP, and half of them are 'sandwich generation' women, ages 40 to 60. All told, they contribute an estimated 470 billion a year in unpaid assistance." [410] These helpers cannot supplant the care professionals like nurses or assistants regularly perform for the elderly; they take care of necessities like *home errands*, *minor housekeeping* tasks or give *company* for those that want *to feel connected* but remain independent. [411]

For all the improvements in long-term care, nothing beats "staying at home."

Diary USS Awareness – You're homesick, eh? Miss your Mom's tuna melt? But did you ever notice how tired she ended up at the end of her long workday?

Deborah X. goes twice per week to the apartment of an eighty years-old retired teacher to help her prepare a nice meal, read the newspaper and answer the telephone calls. When the lady has a physician's appointment, she accompanies her, as her children are busy professionals. When they come back home, she calls her two daughters to give them updates about her medical follow-up. They also go together to see a movie with a pre-showing nice dinner. Deborah believes that she became *a surrogate daughter* for her client who corresponds with her affection.

<u>Diary USS Awareness</u> – Roll call. Only 7 left ? Like Kurosawa's *Seven Samurais?*

A nugget of Wisdom. Stop feeling sorry for yourself all the time. We get it. You are still mourning the loss of your kind, devoted wife of four decades. She made sure that nothing important was missing or in the wrong place in your life. Sadly, she did not prepare you for the cruelty of being alone in this valley of tears. Your daughter—who has a husband, two kids in primary school and a demanding profession—tries to pitch in but her time availability is limited. Do not push her.

What will you be doing until the Grim Reaper knocks on your door? TV binging? Believe it or not, there are people that actually need your precious help. Widowed individuals, much older than you, that cannot ambulate. Single working women with school-age children. Caregivers of the disabled that need a "holiday."

What are you waiting for? Pick up the phone and call an agency. When?

Right now.

Deborah de Robertis does not shy away from the boldest of statements. She likes to attach a personal touch to the curated artistic exhibitions.[412]

In 2014 she exposed her vagina to the audience admiring Gustave Courbet's *The origin of the world* [413], which depicts the organ where Life springs out from. Even though she was arrested, the museum's authorities did not press charges; she went back there to repeat that stunt in front of Manet's *Olympia*.[414] Incorrigible.

The progressive empowerment of women in society has encouraged some trendsetters *to take total control* of their public image—cavities included. Laren Stover said : "the V-selfie, though very much here, is perhaps less insistent (than the male counterpart). Shared on dating apps or in texts, it has been sent to create longing and a sense of intimacy; a missive of lust and promise to lovers, or would-be lovers, who are separated." [415] (*You've certainly come a long way, baby* [416])

The women that use that selfie consider it as a bold statement that they are in charge of their own sexuality and how it would be shared. As younger generations consider their sexuality as a centerpiece of *who they are*, they are ready to hold it aloft. There are new business ventures where the intimate parts get cosmetic make-up for photography, film, intimacy, etc.[417] Some women in love use those images to stay in touch with distant boyfriends to remind them what awaits them. They are also used in *cyber-infidelity*, which may or may not end up in an actual affair.

Emma Bovary would have gladly used it—except with dull Charles.[418]

—"Doctor…My ex-boyfriend won't go away—he's blackmailing me."

Thelma X. is a nice, smart young medical assistant that after a few failed romantic relationships has finally met what she considers as "the man of her life." Unwisely, she allowed her former boyfriend to take some *suggestive photo shots* during intercourse, which at the time seemed like an innocent prank. However, her Ex now wants to go in and out of her life as he pleases—the *ghosting* phenomenon; to coerce her into relenting to it, he is threatening her with the **digital chantage**.

For Millennials—meeting via *Tinder*, texting with *Twitter* and romancing through *Instagram*—the *V-selfie* might seem like a candid extension of their chat. If there is trust in both members of a loving couple, what should they worry about? Plenty, it seems. When we are smitten with someone, we naturally tend to overlook defects, but when the relationship falters, they usually re-surface with a vengeance.

Joni E. Johnston said: "for a minority of unstable individuals, the mutual infatuation stage morphs into something quite different—a one-sided obsession in which one partner increasingly attempts to mold and shape the other into an object with which he or she can play out their fantasy." [419] The objectification of Love.

A nugget of Wisdom. Your teenage daughter has introduced her boyfriend. The beau came for dinner and passed the vetting—your cursory visual inspection plus *the full psychological and physical battery of tests* administered by your wife.

-"Don't leave stains," you whisper to *your angel*. "His mom will find them."

—"Doctor…Only with him can I be 'my true self'—with defects included."

Kimberly X. is a divorced, attractive, middle-aged mother of two children who is **dating a much younger man** who seems to be pushing "her right buttons." While she enjoys his furious stamina in bed and his obsequious attention, there is much more at play than the mere physical attraction. She *feels different* with him.

More confident. Less defensive. Open to the world. Definitely happier.

Before she started that relationship, she used to show up in our office with a clean but slightly negligée look that included a way too frumpy long skirt; she spoke in short sentences, mostly avoiding our gaze and even stuttering. Sensing that she needed a radical change of lifestyle, we prodded her to attend happy hours.

In a casual Friday visit to a bar near her workplace, she finally met HIM.

After the event, she became a completely different woman with great looks and the relaxed confidence of someone who was in charge of her destiny. Her long years as *a serious spouse* had seared the need to spin all her stories, becoming *predictably polished and protective* of the image she provided to the outside world. Spontaneously showing one's emotions was frowned upon in her social circle and she chose not to make waves for his staid accountant-husband. When he dumped her for his young secretary, after a brief down period, she felt a sense of relief. Grinning like a schoolgirl, she said that she was experimenting with daring poses.

A mischievous glint in her blue eyes gave a peek at her Sea of Happiness.

Women of all ages have a stealthy foe on the prowl behind a screen.

"Doctor...I'm desperate. My husband fell in love with a web woman."

Did Claudia X. mean that he had met someone through an app? No.

Did she mean that he was pursuing someone in the social media? No.

Did she mean that he was registered in an online dating service? No.

She meant that he had designed **a virtual woman** of his total liking, like Joaquin Phoenix did in the film *Her* [420]. (*Never watched it... Chicken? You betcha*)

The daily travails of a relationship—marriage or other partnerships—mean that the members must tough it out. The fantasies of *a forbidden relationship* can help to endure that slogging in a clandestine way, without any lasting consequences.[421]

The *modern connectivity* has enabled many frustrated individuals to surpass the limits of their faltering sentimental life with secret, quasi-platonic relationships with persons they never met—and do not plan to... Clean. Fulfilling. Exhilarating.

Anita Rani discussed a weird demographic trend: "unless something happens to boost Japan's birth rate, its population will shrink by a third between now and 2060. One reason for the lack of babies is the emergence of a new breed of men—*the otaku*—who love manga, anime and computers—and sometimes show little interest in sex...A survey by the Ministry of Health, Labor and Welfare in 2010 found 36% of Japanese males aged 16 to 19 had no interest in sex." [422]

<u>Diary USS Awareness</u> – Why stop at a duty-free shop in Tokyo? Buy a doll?

—"Doctor…My husband does not want to have sex—I'm like so desperate."

Claudia X. is a good looking, intelligent, and charming lady in her early 40s that had decided to stay at home to take care of the couple's three children while her physician-husband toils with *Stakhanovite hours* [423] in his private practice. She said it to us, hoping to find out if there was an interloper that we might know of.

Her husband is not dating another gal. Her husband did not become gay.

Her husband still adores her. Something much more ominous is at play.

Her husband is part of a rising cohort of people that do not care for sex.

Women have complained about the unrestrained, savage lust of men for ages. The coin flipped. Now they look aghast at its other face… (*They are not that into you*)

The **hypoactive sexual desire** [424] is a dire clinical complaint that affects all genders and has become more common in the medical offices of modern nations. Physicians should first rule out metabolic or hormonal diseases that may affect libido with a good clinical examination and proper testing. However, many patients have normal results, but they still avoid sex; it could be *episodic* or *continuous*.

An *unusual degree of stress* can cause disturbing symptoms like fatigue, insomnia, and lack of sexual desire, but it usually has waning effects. The myth of *an-always-wanting-stud-like-male* might be valid only for younger individuals. But when the desire disappears in a middle-aged individual, the possibility of sexual monotony and/or a couple crisis must be addressed by health professionals.[425]

There are sex therapists that can discuss possible remedies like the following:

1. Techniques to foster contact with one's body and your companion's one.

2. Develop better foreplay and take more time to raise the Libido.

3. Relaxation techniques like Yoga, Aerobics, Meditation.

4. Changes in dietary and lifestyle habits.

5. Use of new intercourse figures, erotic material, toys, and lubricants. [426]

The most important thing is to *honestly discuss this touchy issue* with your partner before engaging in any long-term remedy to obtain the best outcomes.

A nugget of Wisdom. Yeah. Yeah. I heard you the first time. You're tired of your wife because she does not attract you. She smells of garlic all the time. Of course, it would be easier to take a younger lover. But how about you, eh? Look at you… I SAID: LOOK AT YOU. Always sporting that non-descript T-shirt and baggy Bermuda pants from your high school years. Ain't that sexy?

The first step to try to fix your couple's sex life is to start with the physical. Give up the six pack and TV binging on weekends. Sign up at the local gym. Plan a romantic escapade. Anywhere. Just the two of you. No kids. No worries. If you can't afford it, at least book a table in a cozy resto to drink champagne.

And if you want her to be enamored of you , try a drop of a time-tried elixir. When she arrives home, escort her to the sofa. *"Sit down and relax, dear."*

One of the most persistent misconceptions is that the progressive decline in marital passion of married couples is directly and almost solely related to the loss of libido and/or sexual interest for each other. Independently of erotic attraction, it is a common problem that *disproportionally affects* more women than men. [427] There are some tactics that might re-kindle the flame of passion. They are:

1 – **Watch the communication modes.**

In the beginning of every relationship, we often tend to be obsequious and mellifluous with our partners; unfortunately, the daily routine and the wear-off from labor and family obligations will ultimately sap our willingness to say nice things, progressively drifting into rudeness and worse, indifference. We must shake our torpor and see our partners *in a new light*. We must listen to their concerns. We must talk to them as adults, not talk them down like children. We must speak softly in their left ears. Why the left? Because the sensory input from the left side of the body goes to the Right Hemisphere, the center of affection—no Right or Wrong.

Never underestimate the soothing effect of the Right at the Right time.

2 – **Respect the differences.**

When a romance starts, we value the differences in *our significant other* as a nice, new challenge, which gives us some needed excitement *to feel alive again.*

However, that attitude might change over the years as we become less tolerant of previously accepted features. We believe that it is difficult *to change someone*, which is a *recurrent wish* that some young women harbor when they daringly *decide to tinker* with any jarring trait of "their men." Certainly, when we love someone, we are ready to mend "our evil ways." A little. Perhaps maybe more.

But do not vacuum the living room when I'm watching the final inning…

Or ask me for a pastrami sandwich when Gorgeous is about to propose…

3 – Encourage the individual initiatives.

Perhaps one of the least considered and at the same time easier recipes is the fact that, in order to keep a healthy couple relationship, both women and men must have *separate activities*, either in the labor or social spheres, including reserved times for personal hobbies, old friendships, new business ventures, education, etc. There are still couples that "do everything together" but that smacks of Antiquity. Moreover, after some time spent apart, the *yearning to reunite* gets even stronger.

4 – Surprise your partner regularly.

One of the more reliable ways to break the routine that might asphyxiate any kind of steady relationship is *to do something unexpected* to surprise your partner. One day you decide to stop by a florist shop and buy her a bouquet of red roses;

you dare, not to use a pre-printed card, but to write a few simple but affectionate lines. Or perhaps you wait for him with an exotic dish that you discovered in a TV program, including how to order all its ingredients from an app… Whatever works.

A pauper's garniture per day will sow the luxuriant fields of Imagination.

5 – Watch your personal hygiene.

This is one of the trickiest issues. Of course. we know that we should take a shower every morning to get ready for our interactions with the public at large. But how about at bedtime? We should *avoid late feasting* with any red meat tough to digest, carbohydrates that swell your belly, beans and broccoli that encourage the colon bacteria to produce malodorous flatulence. Before jumping into bed, swing silently by the toilet seat and then take a quick shower to become squeaky-clean.

Exuding of lavender, you might arise the Count Dracul hiding inside her.

6 – Maintain family and friendly relationships.

The *interaction with other people* brings a much-needed breeze of fresh air to the couple, besides cementing their attachment to their family members and friends. We know that it is sometimes tough to bear the relatives or fellow workers of our "significant other" but remember that he/she/sie might be feeling the same.

By going along with your partner, you ease her burden. Pour quoi pas?

—Doctor…My ex-boyfriend is dating a gorgeous girl—and so very young."

Paula X. is a nice lady *d'une certaine âge* [428] that had a relationship with a fellow co-worker for many years. They seemed to be a very stable couple but one day, out of the blue, she started to doubt whether he was indeed the Right One. Eventually she told him that "it was all over" and kicked him out of her apartment; however, she kept **orbiting** around him, occasionally checking his media updates.

Her social life got a tailwind. One evening she came across him in a bar.

Not only he looked better than in his posts, but he was dating a knockout.

The concrete containment she built for his image came crumbling down.

With an excruciating stomach pain, her girlfriend took her home in a taxi.

<u>Diary USS Awareness</u> – She loved him…Then she did not… Now she does.

BATTLE STATIONS…Turn the ship's wheel 180 degrees…STRAP IN.

That *Medusa-like reaction* can be framed within the frenzy inside the Right Hemisphere of feminine brains—where *Right and Wrong* do co-exist in harmony. Neuroscientists hypothesized that humans in fact have, not one, but **two brains**. Our *Left Hemisphere* is keen for language, writing, logic reasoning, mathematical sequencing, organization of ideas and actions—*the computer* powering us. The *Right Hemisphere* integrates the emotional undertones to our ideas, prodding us to be creative and seek transcendence—it is the seat of our *artistic inspiration*.[429]

Those two sides of our brain are inter-connected by a thick set of neuronal fibers that constitute the *Corpus Callosum*, which allows the efficient integration of stimuli to carry our complex tasks. In women, that structure is usually more developed than in men, which explains their fabulous prowess at multi-tasking. Neuroscientific data showed that in men the linkage via the Corpus Callosum is from the *anterior* part of the brain (where attention/awareness lies) to the *posterior* part of the same hemisphere that helps to *translate our ideas* into concrete, focused actions. In women there is a higher number of fibers that travel from the Right to the Left hemispheres—for a better *integration of* the emotionality with behavior.[430]

A nugget of Wisdom. Our dear father Mario learned this lesson the hard way. One of the most painfully seared memories in our consciences—my brother Gustavo's and mine—is when our father Mario told our mother Gladys that he was leaving her. We still remember that it was another anodyne Sunday morning when they started to discuss in our apartment's kitchen. Our lives would change forever.

When our father came back to make the alimony arrangements later, he had the indelicate idea of wearing an engagement ring that announced *l'autre femme*.[431] Our mother unceremoniously kicked him out, warning him to respect our feelings.

That piece of metal rubbed in her face aroused our Mom's open hostility.

She quickly grasped its emotional significance for our present and future.

—"Doctor…He's madly in love with me—he just doesn't know it yet."

Maggie X. is an attractive young secretary that was totally convinced that her dashing supervisor was sexually interested in her, even though he never gave her any basis for that supposition. Despite the dearth of any encouraging signals, she tracked his movements in the social media and spent hours on end dissecting even the finest of details, trying to find an edge to exploit. An exhausting stakeout.

The modern possibility of discreetly **stalking** other individuals from afar has created *privacy issues* for "the stalked" and *mental health issues* for "the stalkers": paranoia, loss of self-worth and delusional acts. It represents a *socially shared cost*. The stalking patterns run a gamut between a rather innocent interest in knowing "what the other person is up to" through intermediary stages up to the more morbid attitude of creating a **false internet personality**. The latter can include the use of insults and threats to coerce the recipient. The stalker picks bits of information and creates a *convenient collage* of the subject of desire that might not be accurate.[432]

Dr. Walter Ghedin said: "the imagination of the hurt person starts to fill up with a myriad data that meshes into a painful platform in the mind. And what in others produces just emotional pain, in others triggers a desire of vengeance…We all have psychological defense mechanisms to face an amorous deception, doubts about faithfulness, hurt feelings…But the permanent, voluntary exposure to images and texts that speak of *the other person's life* compromises any recoveries." [433]

In 1921 Gaétan Gatian de Clérambault, a French psychiatrist, described a new clinical syndrome that he dubbed as *le délire d'être aimé* [434] in his book titled *L'érotomanie* [435]. The **erotomania** is a rare variant of a delusional disorder [436] where the individual believes that another person is in love with him/her/ihr. It is often, but not exclusively, seen in *introverted* and *emotionally dependent* young women; the *object of delusion* is a person, imaginary or real, who is *unattainable* due to a higher social status; its onset is abrupt, and its course is chronic. [437]

The cause is not well determined yet, but some psychoanalytic schools have attributed it to an emotional void suffered during the childhood; sometimes it can be a secondary condition to *schizophreni*a, a *bipolar syndrome,* or a *brain disease*. It runs a checkered clinical course, with ups and downs. Dr. Nicolas Evrard said: "The symptoms of the erotomania have many presentations. More often, they are related to a series of interpretations, more or less delusional, of the facts and the gestures of another person. They can be associated to olfactory (odors) and tactile hallucinations, which reinforce the idea of being loved." [438]

In the *phase of hope* the individual will invest time and energies *to see* and *be seen* by the target, interpreting any small sign as evidence of correspondence. When the target cannot tolerate the harassment and pushes away , the patient enters into the *phase of deception*, provoking depression. The energies invested in loving will flip into hate in the *phase of grudge*, leading to aggression.

—"Doctor…He is convinced that I totally belong to him—so exhausting."

Sandra X. is a nice young professional who had met her partner weeks ago, which filled her heart with affection and her mind with beautiful possibilities. In the beginning she was so smitten that she overlooked a few "minor" details that might otherwise have puzzled her, like calling her many times during the daytime; as she had been alone for too long, she welcomed it and forced herself "to be nice." Slowly that attitude turned into an **obsessive control** of her time, her wardrobe, her conversation, etc. He censured anything in her that was "inconsistent with him." He started to vet her girlfriends until he tried that stunt with her mother. Too much.

Joni E. Johnston, a psychologist and author, said: "for a minority of unstable individuals, the mutual infatuation morphs into something quite different—a one sided obsession in which one partner increasingly attempts to mold and shape the other into an object with which he or she can play out their fantasy. Individuals who develop… obsessive interpersonal relationships often have psychological problems that prevent the normal progression of a romantic (one). Independence is seen as rejection; physical or emotional distance is viewed as a threat." [439]

The same author divided the evolution of this clinical entity into 3 stages:

a) **Absorbed stage**. Extreme attachment that suffocates the other partner.

b) **Agitated Stage**. The obsessive partner tries to control all the movements.

c) **Aggressive stage**. After the control attempts failed, they up the ante.[440]

—"Doctor…How could I not see it before? My husband is gay!"

Kathryn X. is an attractive middle-aged lady that has devoted her life to take care of her husband and three children with affection galore. When her partner suddenly decided to go to the gym three times per week after work, she accepted it as a needed step to lose his excess weight. However, when he started to return late at night or rush out to the patio to answer some phone calls, she became suspicious.

A rival? Yes… Turned out to be not a "she", but… Well, it's complicated.

In 1929, Marguerite Yourcenar published *Alexis or the treaty of the useless combat* [441], which basically consisted of a detailed letter from a famous musician to his wife in order to **confess that he is gay** and wants to leave her immediately. The sexual desire is hardly ever a single conscious decision but *a series* of subjective experiences that mold our needs; usually the choice of a partner is *aligned* with the sexual desire, but when there is *a mismatch,* an inner fight tears our very fabric.

Dr. Walter Ghedin said: "when the homosexual desire surfaces and settles in the emotional staple, thousands of images appear in the mind." They basically are:

1. What do I do?
2. How do I satisfy it?
3. Do I share it with someone?
4. Am I homosexual or bisexual?
5. How do I live with this burden? [442]

In young men there might be an *occasional brief imagery* of homosexual affinity that quickly fades away without ever being acted upon. For a minority, it comes during puberty, and it might be satisfied with a rare transgression. But for a few of them that same homosexual desire *becomes much stronger* as they grow.[443]

Dr. Walter Ghedin said: "when the desire and the homosexual orientation appear without any reprieve in a man 'apparently' heterosexual, the coming out of the closet is the healthiest attitude as you cannot live in the middle pulled apart by two opposing desires…The stronger sexual desire will prevail." [444] The "coming out of the closet" will disturb his heterosexual partner. She might ask herself:

1. How could I not notice it?
2. Why didn't he tell me before?
3. How am I going to tell the kids?
4. What will my family members say?
5. Should I have done more to retain him?
6. Was I too careless and distracted with the kids?

Dr. Ghedin said: "family members that go through the process of understanding the camouflaged sexual desire of loved ones are in fact burdening their psyches with useless dilemmas and assumptions. That need to understand must be replaced by a capacity to empathize."[445] The loss of *the-wife-of-social-label* might worsen it.

—"Doctor …I'm desperate. My husband is dating a travesty.... Imagine!"

Marilyn X. is a nice lady in her late 30s who, by virtue of her wits and wealth, is involved in Real Estate ventures and charity works in Dade County. Together with Orlando, her husband, we have shared many social events. Dragging the prominent belly of an unexpected third pregnancy, she came to our office with the crepuscular face, evasive looks, and parsimonious gestures of a frustrated lady.

Welling up, she told us that she had suspicions that he was having an affair because their relatively normal marital friction had suddenly disappeared one day. With a sunny mood in the morning, kissing her goodbye after breakfast, he did not show up again until the wee hours. Happy. Very. Too much. *Something was afoot.*

Dr. Ghedin, psychiatrist and sexologist, said that: "contrary to popular lore, those seeking the company of the Transgender *are not closeted homosexuals*, but heterosexuals attracted to their *feminized bodies*. They often reject any signs of masculinity, but the vestigial presence of a male sex organ might excite them." [446]

Men in couple relationships who are also **attracted to a Transgender**, are in a terrible *social bind*, much worse than if their clandestine lovers were women. They are trapped by rancid patriarchal conventions (reinforced by religious dogma) that dictate heterosexual men should only be attracted to women. At least formally.

How can they launder that relationship without caustic social censure?

How can they confront their family members with their difficult truth?

A nugget of Wisdom. Soon after his wife's visit, Orlando came to visit us.

-"She was here, wasn't she?" he asked. "Must have told you about Irene—"

-"You know I can't discuss that," we replied. "Besides, it's your life…"

-"Let me tell ya'," he shot back, irritated. "Instead of whining non-stop about her problems, like my f****** wife does, Irene listens to mine for a change. When I'm watching a Dolphins game, she doesn't plant herself smack right in front of the TV to give me a nasty tirade like she does…She brings me a cold beer and snuggles by my side in the sofa to watch it together…How can you beat that, eh?"

Demurring for a few seconds before responding, we took a deep breath.

-"Yeah, that's nice," we said. "But remember that she's pregnant—"

-"I know…Why is that relevant?"

-"Cause this ordeal might leave a lasting psychological mark in the child."

-"Nonsense…the baby is still in her womb—"

-"Precisely…If this goes on, her future well-being might be compromised."

-"What do you recommend, eh?"

-"Do you really love that Trans girl?"

-"Madly."

-"Then fight for your love. Come out clean with all your family members."

-"Easier said than done—"

-"Easy is to let her go…Grab her on the fly or be miserable."

—"Doctor…Carrying a vagina around does not entitle you to femininity."

Cristina X. is a determined, intelligent, and attractive Trans woman that had to fight long and hard against discrimination in the workplace and in her home. Initially her Hispanic parents criticized her transition, but they finally came around.

Paradoxically some of the radicalized feminists, who had fiercely fought for women's rights, have now turned their heavy artillery against the Transgender.[447] They made alliances with conservative circles to push an anti-Trans agenda. The **Trans-Exclusionary Radical Feminists** (TERFS) claim that Transgender women are *infringing* on their social rights and causing *emotional havoc* in their families.

Transgender women also face discrimination from *cis* lesbian women, even though the latter publicly proclaim that they are in favor of their sexual rights. The *cotton ceiling* phenomenon [448] refers to their stern refusal of having sex with them. nti-trans feminists argue that just equating, and conflating, womanhood with only the *cosmetic trappings of femininity* carries more water to the Patriarchate's wheel.

Andrea Long Chu, a Trans thinker, said: "the trans experience…expresses not the truth of an identity but the force of a desire." [449] She argued that becoming Transgender is all about *an individual's desire* and not just the social identity; she defends *ihr right* to aspire for the very same objects that have marked the women's oppression like red lipstick, racy lingerie, high heels and, *yes*, cheeky flirtation too.

Hubba Hubba [450]

Charles Robert Darwin was never a good match for our Gladys Josefa. Mommy [451] knew that we are molded by much more than evolution trends.

After the Darwinian revolutionary writings [452] enshrined the concept that *natural selection* and *evolution* were the major mechanisms to modify our bodies, some alternative hypotheses were summarily discarded. Jean Baptiste Lamarck, a French naturalist, had earlier proposed that all the living species strived to attain the *perfect state*, for which there were multiple variations; the living organisms not only evolved but they did it slowly, *little by little,* and *successively*.[453]

In 1800 Lamarck gave his first lecture in the *Musée National d'Histoire Naturelle* where he discussed the concept of *mutability of species*—later developed in a book.[454] According to Lamarck, life became *diversified* due to these factors:

a) The Power of Life: tends to make organizations more complex.

b) Effects of the Environment: modifying influence of circumstances.

When the molecular structure of the human DNA was discovered by Watson and Crick in 1953 [455], scientists determined that its *coded information* could not be altered in any significant way by the environment or the person's lifestyle choices.

In 1975 Robin Holliday and John Pugh, English biologists, and Arthur Riggs, an American, found that *methylation*—an inherited chemical change of the DNA—can be in fact modified by the environmental factors.[456] **Epigenetics**.[457]

Studying laboratory animals, they found that severe environmental stress can have long-term effects in the information stored in human genes, i.e. *epigenesis*. The genetic material stays untouched but its "expression" or "reading" is greatly altered; this biological alteration *can be transmitted* in some instances to future generations that have *not experienced* the initial triggering factor in their lifetimes. Rat or mouse pups were subjected to maternal separation and their behavior was studied for signs of depression; their genetic material was analyzed for alterations.

Rudolph and Adrian Bird published a paper in 2003 where they said: "stable alterations of this kind are 'epigenetic' because they are heritable in the short term but do not involve mutations of the DNA itself. Research over the past few years have focused on two molecular mechanisms that mediate epigenetic phenomena: DNA methylation and histones modifications." [458]

As part of our reaction to stress, we secrete a hormone called **glucocorticoid** that mediates certain immune mechanisms like *inflammation*; when the offending agent disappears, it *binds to some brain receptors* and its production in the adrenal cortex stops in a *feedback loop*.[459] In 2016 Gustavo Turecki and Michael Meaney published a paper where they showed that *the gene* that codified this glucocorticoid receptor was *inactive* in animals that had experienced great stress in their early days, thereby limiting their ability to shut off its production.[460] Even after the cause for stress had disappeared, they kept producing the stress hormone unabated.

The epigenetic mechanism consists of a physical barrier of methyl markers in the DNA, which prevents *the proper reading* of the stored information in genes. Can this epigenetic trait be transmitted from a mother to her children? Scientists are still debating this issue but there are indications that when the DNA replicates during the cell mitosis, the methyl markings can be *inserted* in the new material.[461]

Scientific studies have shown that when women experience undue stress during pregnancy, they give birth to children with *impaired responses to stress*. After the *Allied Armies' landing* in Normandy in August 1944, there was a stand-off between the opposing forces in the Lower countries—Belgium and Holland.[462] In order to force the local population not to collaborate with the advancing armies of Generals Montgomery and Patton, the German Army rationed food supplies.[463]

The women who were pregnant at the time of the *Dutch Hunger Winter*, eventually gave birth to offspring with a *higher rate of obesity* and *schizophrenia*. Nadine Burke Harris said that many of our societal problems may originate from the *exposure to undue stress* in our childhood that leaves a genetic marking.[464]

A nugget of Wisdom. Our mother Gladys counselled us to be more patient with our younger brother Gustavo because he had problems dealing with big stress. When she was pregnant, her marital problems started, which she felt affected him. With limited formal schooling but endowed with a great motherly intuition, she knew what was important for her kids. *Gracias Mamita querida.*[465]

Caroline Kitchener said: "all over the country, particularly in bright blue states like California, people are swapping the words 'boyfriend' and 'girlfriend'—and even 'husband' and 'wife'—for the word 'partner'…Originally used to describe a business relationship, 'partner' was slowly adopted by the gay community in the mid to late 80s…became the default word for much of the LGBT community until gay marriage was legalized in the United States in 2015." [466]

It comes as no surprise that *Gays, Lesbians* and *Transgender*—whitewashed by the mendacious semantics of discrimination to render them powerless—were in the vanguard of the search for *the right words* to signal their egalitarian approach.

Isabelle Eberhardt would be proud to watch the humongous progress we have witnessed in **gender equality** in our modern nations in the last few decades, including the acceptance of more than the *binary male-female* to define gender. Jean-Paul Sartre said: "whomever wants to be loved, must desire the freedom of the other person, because from that endowment love emerges; if I subjugate her, she becomes an object, and from an object, I cannot possibly receive any love." [467]

A nugget of Wisdom. You noticed that your wife acts kind of vague lately. Not that she has stopped doing her "wifely duties"…But it is as if she does not put the same enthusiasm…Know what I mean? Something bothers her… Did you ask?

Really? When? Yesterday? A week ago? A year ago? What did we tell you? *She wants her partner to insist up to the point of exasperation. Re-ask.*

The quasi-centennial woman had been living in the same humble shack with a loyal dog and some chickens in a clearing of one of the most forbidding sub-tropical forests of South America—El Impenetrable [468]. *It is a large expanse in the northwest of the Chaco province and part of southwest Formosa province in Argentina. One of her many grandchildren or great grandchildren, would come to check on her daily but preferred to live in a nearby urban settlement.*

She claimed that her social isolation in such natural habitat suited her. She woke up early to do her homely errands with enthusiasm, preparing her own meals based on a largely vegetarian diet with occasional poultry or fish. She continued to smoke moderately, and she sometimes drank a little alcohol. When the reporter asked what the secret of her unusual longevity was, she said:

"Because I don't have a man heating my head up with complaints." [469]

Singlehood by choice. The forced *social distancing and isolation* brought by the Coronavirus pandemic has obliged millions of people to stop working in public/ private institutions or attending educational ones with social estrangement. Individuals with *stable sex partnerships* have been traditionally considered as more apt to withstand the Mental Health consequences of this kind of social situation. However, there are countless persons who had expressly chosen *to remain single*.

In an article of the *Health* section of *The Washington Post*, Joan DelFattore reviewed the responses from several singles contacted by e-mail or found in the social media. "This is the moment I've been training for all my life!' an unnamed introvert asserts in a Facebook post...Edie Jarolim, a freelance writer and editor in Arizona, can relate to that sentiment—adults who have chosen to live alone may be better adapted than many to the stay-at-home restrictions in place in large parts of the USA." [470] Most of the respondents were nonetheless concerned that they could be *discriminated against* if rationing of the scarce health care resources, like access to the ventilators in ICUs, would eventually be instituted in hospitals.

A longstanding complaint of the *resisting singles* surfaced again: the lack of respect for their peculiar lifestyle choice from the mainstream citizenry. Many persons confound the fact of "being alone" with the sentiment of "being lonely." Especially because they disregard that many of these singles do have a *strong social support*. Moreover, the lack of sentimental strings prods them to seek a varied company for social and romantic interactions. Since Biblical times, humans have been encouraged to socialize and live-in partnership with the opposite sex. There has been a large pool of literature to buttress the need for *a stable sexual partner* to avoid anxiety/depression, insomnia, obesity due to unhealthy habits. [471]

Julie C. Bowker, Miriam T. Stotsky and Rebecca G. Ekin published [472] a seminal paper in 2017 where they examined the links between the *withdrawal subtypes* and some *psycho-behavioral variables*, finding challenging results for the avoidance models of withdrawal; they found that **unsociability** is associated positively with **creativity**. Julie Bowker said: "they are not antisocial…they don't initiate interaction, but also don't appear to turn down invitations from peers. Therefore they may get just enough peer interaction so that when they are alone, they are able to enjoy that solitude." [473] In order to study these *unsociable-by-choice* from the truly shy individuals or those who exhibit abnormal anti-social attitudes, they recruited 295 college students for a battery of psychological testing.

They found that those who were shy or antisocial scored *lower than average* on the creativity indicators; the participants who were "unsociable" *scored higher* on them. These authors proposed that unsociable persons "may be able to spend their time in solitude constructively, unlike shy and avoidant individuals who may be too distracted and/or preoccupied by their negative cognitions and distress."

If Vincent van Gogh would have been a blissfully married man, could he have been able to produce such beautiful tableaux of mundane situations?

Someone sated with domesticity's ambrosia cannot engage that kind of Id.

He channeled all his disgraces and frustrations to create exceptional art.

He firmly focused his maddening energies on the canvas for us to enjoy.

<u>Diary USS Awareness</u>– Watchkeeper, if you see a cozy cave for us, strike the bell.

Chapter V – The material girl

Why can't a girl change her mind twenty-six times when fixing her will?

Why can't she be so successful that she becomes the richest Brit subject?

Sarah Churchill, Duchess of Marlborough, was a cunning social climber.

The lovely nubile girl was chosen to stock the Court's fresh flesh pantry.

Unlike girls who, after their "tour of duty", were "married" to rich men,

she aimed higher and captured the eye—and clandestine love—of a royal.

In 1763, at the age of 13, she joined the household of Mary of Modena, the young second wife of the Duke of York, who would eventually become King James II. Later her services were required to accompany Anne, his youngest frail daughter; they became really close, feeding the court's gossip that they were secret lovers. They exchanged love pledges in a clandestine correspondence; Sarah made sure that her penned missives were destroyed but she kept Anne's. *En tout cas.*[474]

She wed John Churchill, son of the Duchess of Cleveland—a royal mistress. In 1688 James II, Catholic King of England and Scotland, tried to alter the line of succession—Mary, his Protestant daughter, was the rightful throne's heir—to place his newborn son; the noblemen and clergy rebelled, which lead to a civil war. Sarah wisely advised Anne to leave London for a countryside refuge, which seared their loving allegiance, even after Mary gained access to the British Crown.[475]

Working long hours for her ambition to consolidate her lineage, Sarah took advantage of her close relationship with Anne—she eventually accessed the throne in 1702—to secure multiple financial favors and privileges for her own family. She obtained a lifetime pension of 5,000 pounds, large land holdings, including a large parcel in Saint James Park to build the *Marlborough House*; she made sure that her descendants had nobiliary titles, including the right to be *Duke of Marlborough*.

When she saw an opportunity in the *South India Tea Company*—set up by one of her court rivals—she invested heavily in it. As she watched the shares rise, she astutely predicted that the stock bubble would burst, so she sold all her shares, tripling her investment; she then lent money to those eager to buy in, thus gaining a right for foreclosed assets when it failed. She was *the richest subject* in the Empire. Her lobbying for the Whig faction, against the Tories, finally alienated Mary.[476]

Her personal life was not particularly happy: her husband spent long years in the *Continental Wars* and was ultimately disabled by a stroke, she lost a son at birth and two more when they were infants, she was estranged from her daughters Marietta and Mary—she was a suffocating parent that wanted to control them. But she worked tirelessly to assure *the lineage of Marlborough* by finding suitable mates for her descendants who always married *the right person* at *the right time*.[477]

Sarah. Hated by contemporaries. Loved by feminists. Never forgotten.[478]

Her triumphs—and the inevitable envy—must serve as a cautionary tale.

—"Doctor...I may totally miserable—but at least I got a good provider."

Susan X. is a middle-aged wife and mother of three teenagers who, despite being blatantly unhappy in her loveless marriage, decided to *soldier on* anyway. Even though she has complained of multiple instances of *Emotional Frustration* to us in the office, she always opted to stay put in her drab yet well-off lifestyle.

Shanzez Khurram said: "the American dream is becoming more and more materialistic...I guess it was always a bit materialistic but when I look at it today, I see a nation obsessed with shopping... Shopping is not a problem on its own... It's the obsessive accumulation of unnecessary products, along with the hope that buying a Chanel bag will somehow make you happier that is problematic." [479]

Dr. Ryan T. Howell studied hundreds of individuals classified according to their relationship with material goods, ranging from *less materialistic* to *more materialistic*; the acquisitions were divided in purely "material" or "experiential" (experiences). The investigators asked: "how much has this contributed to your happiness?" The **more materialistic** study participants had *less happiness from experiential purchases*, which did not conform to their expectations; they did not get any happiness either from material goods. They were also burdened with a *negative social image* as they were perceived as narcissistic and shallow.[480]

<u>Diary USS Awareness</u> – We know that you feel guilty for your misdeeds... But every time we dock, do not buy a souvenir for your girls. Cargo hold is full.

—"Doctor... Just can't resist it. Got to buy lots, lots of stuff—all the time."

Claire X. is a nice middle-aged woman with a good job and a supportive family that visits the mall *a little too often* to browse and buy all kinds of goods. She suffers from a defined psychological condition: **compulsive buying**.[481] The psychological factors *at play* in this clinical condition are the following:

1. Desire for approval and recognition from others.
2. Bolstering of the self-esteem.
3. Escapism into a self-designed fantasy world.
4. Weak defenses against consumerist propaganda.
5. Social pressure "to have" instead of "to be".
6. Passive-aggressive expression of anger against someone. [482]

Helga Dittmar et al. studied *the link* between materialism and well-being. She said: "Materialism was associated with significantly lower well-being for the most widely used, multifaceted measures (materialist values and beliefs, $r = -.19$, $\rho = -.24$; relative importance of materialist goals, $r = -.16$, $\rho = -.21$), more than for measures assessing emphasis on money ($rs = -.08$ to $-.11$, $\rho s = -.09$ to $-.14$)." [483]

They said that there were two factors to explain this consumerism:

a) **Discrepancy** between the *perceived self* and the *desired one*.

b) **Attachment** to *material values* in contrast to the *spiritual ones*.

Like in Alcohol Abuse, Overeating and Sexual Promiscuity, the splurging on goods and services is needed by some individuals *to fill an existential gap*; some *prestige goods* might rank higher than others in their personal priority listing.[484]

The unrelenting peddling of *a vile consumerism* in the media disguise the publicized goods as needed objects for us "to be someone" and "express values". The *younger* and *more impressionable* individuals are willfully targeted as their "needs" might decisively influence the family's buying decisions; people marry later in life and have less children, which gives them more *disposable income*. This permissiveness with the young could be a psychological *compensation mechanism* for the parental guilt over the curtailed "family time" due to work schedules.[485]

It is much more common for women to use this **identity repair** than men. A concerned mother that works long hours outside her home, will rarely contradict her children when they chose to order a delivery pizza or eat sushi in a resto. That *lax attitude* also prevails at the time of buying clothes, shoes, software, electronics, vacations, etc.[486] A self-feeding, unsustainable frenzy to possess things only *per se*.

Roberta Paltrinieri, a professor in the *Università di Bologna*, has studied the impact of pure mercantilism in the *feeling of fulfillment* of individuals She said: "I propose a specific variant of happiness: the responsible happiness. A concept of happiness that makes us understand the issue of sustained development and geared at a shared social responsibility, based on responsible maturity of consumers." [487]

—"Doctor…My husband gambles way too much—he's destroying us."

Maria X. is an educated and charming middle-aged lady with a caring husband and three teenage daughters; unfortunately, her car dealer-husband likes to regularly drop by the various gambling venues of South Florida to try his luck. He has won big several times, but his losses are even greater. Unlike other conditions, there are *no overt signs* of this addiction as it is often hidden for social prudishness. Slowly *he has been eroding* their wealth—mortgaging their home to pay his debts.

For a woman concerned about the family's finances and her prospects in old age, a partnership with a man **addicted to gambling** is a discouraging proposition. *"Why would I bother to save a cent when he's blowing so many dollars away?"*

The act of repeated gambling stimulates the brain's *reward system* like drugs and alcohol do, being closely related to personality disorders of *highly competitive*, *restless,* or *easily bored* individuals. Sometimes it is a behavioral manifestation of Mental Health disorders like depression/anxiety, bipolar disorder, obsessive-compulsive disorder, attention deficit/hyperactivity disorder or substance abuse. It used to be much more common in men, but *emancipated women* are catching up; it often appears in middle age but when it does in later stages, it worsens rapidly.[488]

A report in *Scientific American* explained that: "In the 1980s, while updating the *Diagnostic and Statistical Manual of Mental Disorders* (*DSM*), the *American Psychiatric Association* (APA) officially classified pathological gambling as an impulse-control disorder—a fuzzy label for a group of somewhat related illnesses that (then) included kleptomania, pyromania and trichotillomania (hairpulling). In what has come to be regarded as a landmark decision, the association moved pathological gambling to the addictions chapter in the… *DSM-5 edition*." [489]

The gambling addiction—like the drug habit—stimulates the reward system in our CNS, prodding the *release of dopamine*. The addicted individual needs to increase the amount he/she/sie secretes to sustain the same level of satisfaction. Oftentimes it is *an escapist attitude* to cope with big personal problems that cannot be shared with an inner circle. When the addicted try to control this condition, they feel irritable with possible adverse social consequences, including violence. [490]

In a consumerist society like the USA with plenty of physical and virtual opportunities to wager on almost any kind of sports, this addiction is fast becoming not only a personal but also a *public problem*; many civic leaders are questioning the spread of state-sponsored lotteries with "the mission" of funding education.[491]

A nugget of Wisdom. You *had to stop* by the gas station for a Lotto ticket. With your filled card in one hand and a bill of U$20 in the other, you queue up. This week's jackpot looks too irresistible, with the possibility of becoming rich…

Rich? Really? Aren't you *already rich enough* with your lovely family?

Wouldn't it be better to pick up a gallon of milk? *Do the right thing*.

<u>Diary USS Awareness</u>– How many ships wrecked for this flaw did you see?

—"Doctor…Can't tell my husband how much I really earn—no way."

In the traditional marriages of yore, there was a clear-cut division of labor as men went out to *earn the daily bread* and *women stayed home* to care for children. The *asymmetry of power* often made men more powerful and women submissive. The massive entry of women in the workforce has changed that equation as they sought control of their monies, which opened the door to the **financial infidelity**.

Nowadays the couple's earnings usually go to *a common fund* that enables them to pay the expenses and save; when one of the couple's members earns more than the other, he/she/sie naturally assumes the *bigger expenses*—a good deal. But when women wield financial power, some men have a hard time accepting it.[492]

Women who earn more than their male partners tend to *hide their expenses* in order not to "offend them", if they are out of work or downgraded to lower jobs. But as many more of them *are wearing the pants*— not necessarily for fashion—a few insolently send a pictorial shot across the bow to men.[493] (*In your face, dude*)

Successful women might "downsize" to match their men in order to preserve their identity, virility, and image vis-à-vis their children's respect. The irony of it. When men were exclusively at the top of the pyramid, there was not a reciprocal coyness, as they assumed that bigger wages entitled them to more respect.[494]

<u>Diary USS Awareness</u> – Watch out for the deep currents of financial asymmetry! Wow…Only two left on the port side? Shift one from starboard for an even keel.

The financial infidelity of one of the couple's members could hide much more than mere coyness. When someone has an affair—a traditional escapade of men but women are "warming up" to it—all the *extra expenses* must be hidden. It implies *using cash instead of plastic* and a lot of creativity to cover for unusual activities at odd hours with "strangers.". It used to be only a "nasty manly habit." But some audacious women—who are not shy to leverage their financial clout—are engaging in fanciful *tours de force* [495] to derail the detection of their trysts.[496]

Sometimes the discretionary use of funds that belong to the whole family hides pathological conditions like *addiction to drugs*, *alcohol,* or *hard gambling*; it could be *a bipolar manifestation* of a neurotic patient in a serious maniacal cycle. Unfortunately, the rest of the family might suffer the consequences of this vice.[497]

Marianne Bertrand et al found that when in a marriage market a randomly chosen woman becomes *more likely to earn more* than a randomly chosen man, the nuptials' rate declines. Moreover, when women earn more than their husbands, the couples are less satisfied and more likely to enter into the divorce proceedings.[498]

A nugget of Wisdom. Right. She makes more money than you do. So what?

Instead of pouting to vent your frustration, consider the alternative. With all the "mola" she earns, she could be easily dating a young stud…Or two. But no. She hurries up at work to be with her family. Including you… The ungrateful one.

Get off the couch. Go to the kitchen to rattle some pots and pans. Now.

—"Doctor…It's so much easier than a real relationship—it's a transaction."

Carol X. is an entrepreneur that *might have mentioned* that she patronized the *suave services* of an escort agency (*Did she really say it? Can't remember* [499]) After meeting a male stripper in a bachelorette party that discreetly tendered her his phone number, she got hooked on his *sweet convenience*. **Paying for sex**.

When her insufferable marriage—with an indelicate man that only wanted to rush his orgasm through and left her wanting—ended in a bitter divorce once their children had left the nest, she swore never to return to the *gallows of monogamy*. She has experienced with several occasional partners, including a woman. But the *daily pressures* of tending to somebody else's needs is too much for her schedule.

The web has given that empowering opportunity to women who are not rich but have enough disposable income to *contract company* by the hour—or the night. Some professional and businesswomen appreciate that, once their adventure ends, they can return to their separate worlds, with no strings attached. They cynically branded it as "the perfect boyfriend experience." Without pesky follow-up calls.[500]

Women aspire for the perfect combo of sexual competence and affection—

a hybrid of both a gladiator shaking them with a wet nurse cuddling them.

Any feminine attachment to a man often transcends the pure desire in bed.

When she starts transgressing her own boundaries, real trouble occurs.

—"Doctor…I'm having the time of my life—my family just doesn't get it."

Sandra X. is a gorgeous-forty-something-recently-divorced lady that has a good job and a family of four—her mother and three children. But *no husband*. And therein lies the source of her *Emotional Frustration*, despite her successes. Her family cannot picture her without the "assuring company" of a man. Any man.

Not that long ago, any woman **without a formal partner** by the time she turned forty years old was dismissed as *only worthy of dressing up the saints* [501]; if she had lost her mate, she was still considered fit to take care of her grandchildren. But now "financially freed women" can *start anew* because there are many artistic, sports, travel options, etc., for those with enough leisure time and means.[502]

Our daring patient decided to make her dream come true: become a painter. She attended a college course given by experts, prepared a small atelier at home and mingled with friends interested in art. A thorough cleaning of the slate. As she felt a little bit uneasy to barhop like a co-ed to reboot her social life, she started to visit art galleries and watery holes with another lady who had become a widow.

Initially she dodged any compromise, but Apollo's arrow pierced her heart *at the first sight* of a painter 20 years younger that was sporting a too cute ponytail; coming from a Hispanic family, she has been reluctant to break the news to them.

She rented an apartment in the quarter of Wynwood to fix an atelier.

To drink champagne, eat sushi and make maddening love every night.

—"Doctor…Finally acted on my dear old fantasy—slept with two men."

Claudia X. is an attractive middle-aged divorced mother of two teenagers who has had a stellar career as a corporate lawyer. Her economic independence has spurred her to venture into hitherto fully forbidden territory for "serious people." After dating another lawyer for weeks, she mustered the inner strength to ask him:

-*"How about if we invite your bud Ted for a threesome? Like the idea?"*

Even though the idea of **group sex**, either hetero or homosexual, has always been a staple of the manly fantasizing, it has only recently emerged as a romantic possibility *for women as well*, usually with the help of a man's guiding hand.[503] The carried-out fantasies may include *a third player*: male, female, or transgender. The heterosexual fantasy of *one man plus two women* still gets priority attention but increasingly women are asking for *a quid pro quo* to their formal partners. If she wants to invite another man to their bed, she must first overcome her partner's reticence to watch "his woman" with another man and his own homosexual fears.

Dr. Walter Ghedin said: "the woman that dares to try erotic games with two or more men likes her sex intense and varied. No conventional poses. No romantic words. Far from a 'passive' role, she asks, does, and acts. She fulfills her fantasies. And more." [504] The well-off woman that dares to have sex with multiple partners does not want to worry about an unwanted pregnancy or any contagion diseases.

Totally avoiding strangers, she prefers the certitude of vetted players.

—"Doctor…Choosing ice cream flavors is a challenge—takes negotiation."

Maria X. is a middle-aged lady that has been married twice already. She has three teenage daughters from her first marriage and Victor, her partner, has two teenage sons from his first one too. They have a baby girl. They all live together.

Now the family relationships cannot be solely explained by the traditional tree as there is *crossed-over bonding* from remarried partners, adopted children and gay relationships. This social phenomenon called **family blending** is redefining the challenges of *our sense of togetherness* based on mutual respect and tolerance. [505]

In these new arrangements, the financial concerns appear early on for both partners as they must discuss and together decide *what to pay, to whom and when.* The archetypical image of the stepmother as *an ugly witch bent on mischief* is far from the reality sur le champ where young kids get oftentimes more attached to a *close mother figure* than their still remembered but more distant biological one.[506] Similarly, young children often revere more *a father figure* that helps them with their homework or plays baseball with them than the biological but absent one.

Children often have *a much better relationship* with the stepfathers than the stepmothers, especially when the combo includes young girls and stepmothers.[507] Adults tend to forget that their couple breakups often entail the *forced adaptation* of their children to a new hearth without them having "a real say" in those choices.

Children are often innocent by-standers of our successes and failures.

The assembly of these composite groupings occurs rather spontaneously as there is not a rational planification of "who will be who" in the final assemblage. There are often power disputes of *internal cliques* fighting for limited resources. There are *crossed friendships and allegiances* as their genetic similarities will not guarantee that they will automatically see eye to eye in their choices and dilemmas. Planning their daily chores, buying decisions, weekend activities, vacations, and something as mundane as "who gets the bathroom first" must be negotiated.[508]

The members must constantly develop varying grades of tolerance and trust. First of all, the parents must learn to love and show sincere affection for children who are not biologically related but share their same hearth and family objectives. The siblings must learn how to try to be *equitable in their dealings* with each other, avoiding the factionalism that might damage their will to live under the same roof.

According to Maria and Victor, occasionally they have had some rough moments, but they have been able to avoid intractable situations that build grudges.

A nugget of Wisdom. Your Mom will call to invite you for Thanksgiving. As it has been her custom for years, she is busy preparing food for four extra seats. However, the scenario has changed. Your new partner has two kids of her own.

Call your mother and advise her it is six or nothing. *No compromises.*

Still attached to your Ex, she'd love her presence at the table. *Say no.*

Got the work cut out for yourself. Wouldn't want to be in your pants.

—"Doctor…Another Valentine's Day has passed by—and I'm still single."

Veronica X. is an attractive, clever pharmaceutical representative who was sharing her frustration that the Right One was still evading her charmer's net. Even in our "liberated age" where most women pride themselves in developing their potential without the help of men, they often crave for the exhilarating experience of sharing life's vicissitudes with some **good company** of their own choosing.[509]

Mindful of their social status and careers' demands, they are paradoxically burdened by much more layers of *social sous-entendus* [510] than their parents were. Their financial clout—and plethora of good choices— only makes the dating game more difficult as there is a social urgency to *vet their prospects* right away. They must make sure that they find *the right choice* at *the right time* in their lives.[511]

Watching women in search of their *Knight in a Shining Armor* (sic), smart social observers identified *six major positioning strategies* to handle that task:

1. The hopeless romantic
2. The busy scavenger
3. The event-hopper
4. The perpetual denier
5. The married reader
6. The blasé activist [512]

The hopeless romantic. In our times of gender equality and often touted young people's disregard for an *über-passé etiquette*, this lady is paradoxically expecting a man to conform to *the ideal image* she is treasuring in her imagination. Obsessed with the pursuit of "an ideal", she unfortunately ignores *the more ordinary* but still worthy choices that are circling around her, sending her signals. *All that glitters…*

The busy scavenger. The tremendous expansion of all the social media's platforms has given individuals the possibility of *non-stop hunting* for a partner. This lady joins a few selective dating services and checks the available suitors; she always reviews *the latest profiles* to select new targets and update "her hit list."

But she might vacillate too much, which prolongs her exhausting search.

The event-hopper. An attractive lady usually gets invitations to many social events, private parties, inaugurations, expositions, etc., enabling her to spend the whole weekend *checking the scenery* while she has a good time with friends. After so much exposure, a good prospect might appear in her field of vision. But once she finds him, she is faced with a conundrum: slow down a little bit to try to make it work or continue her dizzying quest. *What is a girl in such demand to do?*

The perpetual denier. When the peddling of Saint Valentine's Day—the modern-day incarnation of the *village's wise woman* acting as a matchmaker—

erupts in our screens, most bachelorettes are possessed by a sudden hunting frenzy. Some ladies might ostensibly *turn their attention elsewhere* as they are supposedly not interested in that "frivolous quest." They often claim to prefer the company of girlfriends but when nobody is around, they stealthily peek at their horoscope. Who knows if there might be *a man willing to commit* out there? *En tout cas.* [513]

The married reader. Who says those in a couple should not check the goods? There are countless women who, hopelessly trapped in a loveless marriage, find *an escapist solace* in reading novels. They devour the saga of their heroines, including modern celebrities. As their husbands snore away, they fantasize in bed, craving for the company of Gorgeous. *When the opportunity to act comes, they hesitate.*

The blasé activist. As we are experiencing another wave of Feminism, this lady has an aggressive attitude against all the vestiges of the manly domination, including the *degradingly démodé* habitude of courtship. She screens the social interaction of her girlfriends and jumps at the occasion to criticize their choices for real and/or imagined flaws. She protests that she has their best interests at heart, but they might tire of her tirades. Listening to her , you might feel that, *if a man she likes* offers her a bunch of flowers, she would instantly melt. *Pour quoi pas?*

Reviewing this section, Noël Marie, our daughter, confessed to us that she had used two or three variants in her past…Women can be so practical.

—"Doctor…People stare at me all the time in the street—because I'm fat."

Rhonda X. is a charming young woman that just happens to be overweight. She has all the right attributes to be the perfect partner of someone, yet she is still stubbornly single, as she cannot meet a match of her liking. She attributes it to her *excess weight* and the *social stigma* attached to it. She is certain that she has been bypassed for a much-merited promotion at work due to her **obesity**, despite all the protestations to the contrary of her boss and the Human Resources Department.

For a woman with a career or full-time job, it does have consequences.

In modern nations there is *a rise of the obesity's indexes* due to many socio-economic factors that influence the diet—usually saturated with sugar and fat.[514] Even though there are laws that prohibit the discrimination against obese people, in fact there is *reluctance* to employ and house them.[515] Even the airlines joined the fray by charging extra to those customers that cannot fit snugly into their shrinking seats—a cynical diversion to pit one segment of the public against another one.[516]

Following the trend of EU nations, the French youth is eating less healthy dishes in favor of the processed and commercial junk food that provoke obesity. In the *ultra-mindful-about-silhouettes-Gaule*, a young, obese woman called Gabrielle Deydier wrote a book titled *On Ne Naît Pas Grosse*[517] where she narrated her daily travails and humiliations in the Hexagon.[518] She has urged the French citizens to overcome their barely concealed aversion for fat people . **La grossophobie.**[519]

A report published by the prestigious *Inserm* [520] showed that almost 16% of the population was obese in 2016 compared to 12% in 2008. In the USA, the *CDC* found that 36% of the population had a *body mass index* (BMI) of 30 or higher in a 2014 report. Another study said that the American States had an incidence of more than 20% of obesity and that in 22 of them, plus Guam and Puerto Rico, between 30 and 35% of the population had it. The South (32.4%) and the Midwest (32.3%) had the highest prevalence.[521] This worrying social trend has finally prompted a vibrant public discussion of the *dietary value* of foods in the USA and the need to limit the intake of noxious material and unhealthy additives of what we eat.[522]

A nugget of Wisdom. O.K. Let us get something straight. Up-front. Now.

She has the best qualifications for the job opening. She is smart. And smiles. Dresses correctly for your work environment. And seems to be blissfully discreet. What are you waiting for to give her an honest shot at it? Looks like a slam-dunk.

Well, there is a little detail… She is *like, like* thirty pounds or so overweight. She gracefully acknowledged her "defect" and told you she is in a dieting program; besides, she was excited to learn that you subsidize all the gym fees for employees.

There is another trump card. Her strong personality, professional demeanor, and a little less than fascinating figure will deter "occasional distractions." In order to manage a good business, you must assure a congenial workplace. *If you can , avoid risqué choices. L'occasione fa il ladrone.*[523] *Hire her.*

206

—"Doctor… So stressed out at work. But when I go home, I can't relax!"

The auspicious reality of more women enjoying the financial independence to fulfill their aspirations has *the mirror image* of millions more that live paycheck to paycheck, stuck with *low-paying, dead-end jobs* in public and private spheres. That complaint is heard again and again in our offices. After a grueling workday, women often must bear a disruptively uninvited guest at the family table: **Stress**.

In the 2012 *Annual Stress Survey* [524] done by the *American Psychological Association* (APA) 65% of the participants cited their *principal work* as a major source of stress in their lives; only 37% of the surveyed said they were doing an excellent or a good job managing their work-related stress. The most commonly mentioned stressors were *low salaries*, work that was *not engaging or challenging*, *few opportunities* for growth/advancement, and *not having enough control* over job-related decisions. Their 2012 survey of *Gender and Stress* [525] showed that:

1. Women are more likely than men (28% versus 20%) to report having a great deal of stress (8.9 on a 10-point scale)

2. Almost half of all women (49%) surveyed said that their stress has increased over the past 5 years compared to 4 in 10 (39%) in men.

3. Women are more likely to report that money (79% compared with 73% of men) and the economy (68% compared to 61% of men) are

sources of stress while men are far more likely to cite that work itself is a source of stress (76% compared with 65%)

4. Women are more likely to report physical and emotional symptoms of stress than men such as having had a headache (41% versus 30%), having felt as though they could cry (44% versus 15%) or having had an upset stomach or indigestion (32% versus 21%) in the past month.

Stress at work can produce *acute symptoms* like epigastric pain, headaches, sleep and mood disorders or *chronic diseases* like obesity, high blood pressure and depression. Stressed-out people tend to *eat unhealthily and/or too much*, abuse *alcohol or other substances*, and have *sleep disorders*, which curtails their rest.[526]

The critical issue of undue stress at work also involves the *Information Age industries* that offer more benefits to highly skilled workers. Dan Lyons claimed that the start-up techno companies' policy of treating their workers as if they were *disposable widgets* is spreading way beyond the companies of *Silicon Valley* to more traditional ones. He said that the much-touted model of "enlightenment" and "forward thinking" is nothing else than a rehash of an ancient capitalist axiom: *the exploitation of workers' labor.*[527] Is it an **aggiornamento**[528] of the appropriation of *surplus labor* from the working classes *as profit* by the ruling minority class?

Plus ça change, plus ça reste la même chose[529]

—"Doctor…when I get home, I can't help lashing out at the kids—so bad."

Verschiebung. This German term can be translated as "shift" or "move." It was used by Sigmund Freud to describe a psychological defense mechanism; it entails the *shifting* or *displacement* of an *aggressive emotion* from an *important person or object* into other ones that are less relevant and often lame. [530]

Our patient had many situations of *Emotional Frustration* in her blue-collar job with her despotic boss and his unreasonable demands but, being a single Mom, she hid her anger towards him and the system, fearful of losing her job in tough times. On many occasions, she scolded her children a little bit too much for not completing their homework or for just some obnoxious but inconsequential pranks.

This unconscious defense mechanism is an expression of what Freud dubbed as the *mortido*—our basic aggressive drive. There are three main mechanisms:

a) Displacement of object

b) Displacement of attribution

c) Bodily displacements

A – <u>Displacement of object</u>

Some acrid emotions are *displaced from one person* into another one. Our patient's *anger toward her boss*—who has authority and power to decide on her economic survival—had indeed been *transferred into her children*—who are innocent and unable to pose a serious threat as they are wholly dependent on her. This situation will sadly become much more common in our modern societies because the SARS-CoV-2 pandemic has furloughed millions of workers worldwide and many of them will not be able to return to their old jobs due to inevitable closure of businesses. In the much more genteel days of Freud's practice in nineteenth century Vienna, he put the example of *children's animal phobias*; in order "to sanitize" their fears towards parents, some children develop aversion to animals: dogs, cats, spiders.

B – **Displacement of attribution**

A *personality trait* that we might see in ourselves but that we consider as *socially unacceptable* or even *reprehensible* will be transferred to another person or entity. The typical example is a closeted homosexual who engages in unbecoming joking about gays or other LGBTQ individuals to perform a *psychological projection*. Or it could be someone that, feeling dishonest, will become paranoid, fearing that somebody else might try a trick to cause him/her/ihr damage by any means.

We can also find extreme examples in History like the horrific persecution of gays in Nazi Germany conducted by Ernst Röhm, co-founder with Adolf Hitler of the *Sturmabteilung* (SA); he was a barely hidden homosexual that was executed during an orgy by the German Army—fearful that his formations were gaining too much strength in the street—in the *Night of the Long Knives* in 1934. [531]

The epitome of the ideological hypocrisy of the Third Reich.

C – **Bodily Displacements**

It consists of the attribution of a *sensation experienced* by one part of the body to another one; a common instance is when an *oral sensation* "is experienced" as coming from the vagina. John Cleland wrote a book in 1748 titled *Fanny Hill* (*Memoirs of a Woman of Pleasure*) [532] where he used *funny euphemisms* for the body parts that were a taboo subject; he dubbed the vagina as *the nethermouth*.[533] He was a rebellious writer and some sources claimed that he finished it when he was serving a prison sentence for a bad debt. He printed it in two installments in November 1748 and February 1749; he was released from prison in March 1748.

"I picked two fights at work. One with a customer and one in a Slack [534] *queue with my colleagues, and I regret both terribly. They are possibly the first two fights I have ever instigated in my life. Wish I could have hashtagged those. #firstfightbearwithme."*

Ms. Chrissie, a lovely, clever, funny, fellow writer, and blogger [535], shared her unfortunate event at work in a recent posting, which elicited the commiseration of many of her loyal readers who understood why she had a *faux pas*. We wrote:

"The little anger that you inadvertently vented against two individuals is part of the humongous one building up in the street. It happened to almost all of us..."

Unfortunately, as we slowly come out of our forced *Social Distancing* and we interact much more with other human beings, we are **loaded up with stress** and, as a natural consequence, we will have *a shorter fuse*, easily snapping away. We will have a hard time containing ourselves, even with an act of *mea culpa* [536], if we allow our emotions to *get the best of ourselves* in the mad frenzy for survival.

Thousands upon thousands of small businesses in expensive cities like New York, Los Angeles or Chicago will not attract again the necessary customer traffic to at least recoup all the high expenses incurred by their rent leases, social charges, city, and county taxes, reposition of inventory, etc. An article in *The Washington Post* details the anguish of small business owners in the gentrified *D.C. corridor of 14th Street* as "Mayor Muriel E. Bowser extended the city's stay-at-home order until June 8, ordering nonessential businesses… to remain closed." [537]

Many independently owned and operated hair salons, dry cleaners, small stores, restos, bars, etc., will either not manage to re-open or bear decreasing sales. What we have to keep in mind is that we cannot bring that heightened state of alertness and aggressiveness to our families eagerly waiting at home for our return. Maybe we should go back to the old ways of our ancestors to vent off their stress.

Get the punching bag from the attic. Paste your boss's image up front.

Go for it. And do not pull any punches. Sweet.

—"Doctor…Can't go home with *so much mojo*—need to toss some away."

Audrey X. is a very gifted married business executive who has reached the top of the corporate ladder the old-fashioned way. She earned it. Fair and square. At the end of her workday she feels *unseasonably charged up*. Straight out of the office, she goes to the gym to stay in good shape. Not enough. Also once per week she has a clandestine date with **a casual lover** that she picks up in a dating app. [538]

The dating site *Ashley Madison* [539], which specializes in discreet match-up of adventurous hearts [540], made an informal canvass of the most common professions from the "players" regularly "scouting" their website. They found that for women, *the most unfaithful* professions were the following:

1. Business executives – 22%

2. Information technology – 12%

3. Technicians – 8%

4. Education – 7%

5. Medical personnel – 7%

6. Marketing – Communications – 7% [541]

In the men's section of most unfaithful trades (24%) the ones that ranked high had flexible and demanding schedules that offered a good cover to dupe their partners. *Diary USS Awareness* — Men's ranking: first, cops, second. docs. Keep mum. [542]

Neurophysiological studies have shown that women facing stressful events secrete more *Oxytocin*—the hormone of sexual desire—than men do. [543] Moreover, the presence of stress provokes the secretion of *testosterone* both in men and women as part of our ancestral biological defense mechanism. [544] The adrenal glands produce a small amount of that hormone in women that can increase if they are chronically exposed to challenging situations; women *are more sensitive* to its physiological effects, including **the sensory excitement** triggered by raw passion.

Feminine desire is based on *a mix* of visual, auditory, and skin stimuli, coupled with a hormonal rush that reach a CNS integrator—the Hypothalamus. Staying at the top of the food chain takes a lot of sweat. If women throw punches at work like a boxer in the ring, shouldn't they be allowed time off after to relax? The phonies that Maureen Dowd—a *most-impossibly-beautiful-NYTimes-writer*—has wittily dubbed as *Pharisaic Rollers* [545], would revile it as a sinful détente.

But, after a prize fight, did Jake LaMotta go home to knit a scarf? [546]

A nugget of Wisdom. You just found out that your wife is having an affair.

Not with an ex, a colleague, or a friend. The *swipe-to-the-right* kind of guy. What should you do? First try to *de-familiarize* and *de-institutionalize* your bond. If the issue is a waning flame, why not fire it up ? On the spur of the moment call the baby-sitter , make a dinner reservation, and pick her up at work with a bouquet.

Booking a kinky room with mirrors galore in a tawdry motel is optional.

—"Doctor…My boss has an affair with a guy in our office—hate her."

Alyssa X. is a nice, hard-working middle-aged agent of a Brickell real estate company who also juggles her marriage's demands. After toiling long hours in the office and outside it—she shows the units to customers—she feels neglected. She should have been promoted to a senior position with better benefits already but a *work issue unrelated to work itself* blocks her path : **a clandestine office romance**.

Discreetly, together with some of her colleagues, she has been fuming about the scandalous affair of her boss with a "cutie" employee that has recently arrived. Both are married and have children. They spend long hours in her corner office with the door tightly shut and she has given strict instructions to never interrupt them. They stay until late, with the false pretense of catching up with client's calls.

In fact that indiscretion is not the problem as society became more tolerant. The problem is that her attitude at work towards her subordinates has become *more insulting* as she has openly put down most of them while effusively praising him.

Her **sexual favoritism** is dislocating the well-honed process for promotions. Smitten, she has missed targets set by the main office—like a teen in love. When a top executive came to visit, Alyssa casually laid the latest sales chart on the table.

– "Holy s***." he said, blanching. "Didn't your boss see this plunging?'

-"Dunno know," she said, trailing her Os. "Seems SO distracted lately—"

Chapter VI – The bad negotiator

Eunice Kathleen despised the callously concocted conditioning of way.

On Saturdays she liked to walk along the railroad tracks near her home.

On one side, the Blacks like her dwelled. On the other one, the Whites did.

After studying at the Juilliard School, she applied to the Curtis School.

Bach? Black? Mix? How preposterous…Audition's result: not accepted.

The cowardly tracks ambushed her in the City of Brotherly Love. [547]

The sixth child of a preacher, Eunice Kathleen Waymon was born in a small North Carolina town in 1933 and showed such artistic aptitudes that her music teacher set a fund up *for her dream* of being the first black female concert pianist. After her failed attempt, she worked in "a very crummy bar" [548] of Atlantic City. To hide her job from her family, she took a *nom de guerre* [549]: **Nina Simone**.

She composed, played, and sung jazz themes, mixing some classical music's notes into her popular creations. The rise of the Civil Rights movement *radicalized her discourse*, which alienated the music industry's producers; eventually she had to flee the USA to live in Liberia. Ambassador Shabazz said: "Nina Simone was a free spirit in an era that didn't really appreciate a woman's genius." [550]

Female. Fierce. Feared.

On the night of September 12, 1912, Franz Kafka took refuge in his room.

At 6 A.M. in the following morning, the maid stepped inside to clean it.

He had been hopelessly stuck in the final words for "The Judgement." [551]

Dragooned into the text, Georg stumbled upon the maid on his way out.

Her "transfer" as a character gave Kafka a vital boost to finish his story.

When we were wondering how to continue this text, we heard the rising chant "Koulibaly, se a vita mi" [552] in the live TV broadcast from *Stadio San Paolo*; the fans of the *Napoli Football Club* [553] were chanting for their star black player.

Our Italian ancestors were *indentured servants* to absentee Roman landlords in the early 20th century, toiling tirelessly as destitute *braccianti* or *mezzadri*.[554] Desperate to improve their lot, they emigrated *en masse* to the Americas. Deep in the recesses of their guts, they had bacteria and minerals from the old country; our grandmother Yolanda said that they used to boil potatoes with dirt still attached. After we questioned its hygiene, she snapped: *"chancho limpio no engorda."* [555]

It is not just a coincidence that Viola Luzzo, an Italian American homemaker from Detroit, was *the martyr* of the US civic movement for Black Rights in 1965; shuttling demonstrators from Selma to Montgomery, she was killed by the KKK. Only after that brave citizen died, President Johnson signed the Civil Rights Act.[556]

The peninsular bugs in her gut leavened her volcanic desire for Justice.

—"Doctor…They wouldn't give me the job—whatever my qualifications."

Mireille X. is an extraordinarily gifted young black woman who has pursued a brilliant career as assistant chief of *Rehabilitation Medicine* in a big care facility. Born and raised in South Florida, she is the offspring of two hard-working Haitian immigrants; she studied in a local university, networking extensively with peers. Being second in command, she was considered as the natural successor when her boss retired. Feeling vindication for their family's untold sacrifices as newcomers that worked hard in the USA, her father kissed her, saying: *"Marché conclus."* [557]

Without much publicity, the corporate headquarters started a "talent search" for out-of-state applicants, including the *Jersey Boy* that was finally chosen. They went through the motion of a supposedly "impartial" selection process, a thinly disguised *charade* to give a patina of respectability to an ancient scourge: **Racism**. *The institutionalized racism saw her fit to work hard but not to reap its benefits.*

What really struck us was her sour yet stoic *esprit d'âme* [558] when she told it; it sounded as if she had to digest the revolting reality of *a fait accompli* [559] or quit. During our Internship in a big New York City hospital, we went through the tough apprenticeship in the hard-boiled, lightly rested world of post-graduate training.

One of the first things we learned is that Black people were invisible.

Except for those instances when they committed any crimes.

—"Doctor…Was only too happy to be accepted—but I was hoodwinked."

Allison X. is a promising *intellectual star* that got an acceptance letter from a prestigious college to join its faculty. After a few days. she was dismayed to find out that she would be *earning 20% less* than her similarly qualified male peers. On what grounds? (*A teeny-weeny detail…Oh, you're a woman?*) **The vagina penalty**.

Anupam B. Jenna et al. studied the *salary data* of public universities in 12 American states, including 24 medical schools, which are extremely competitive. The *physician database* had information on sex, age, years of experience, faculty rank, specialty, scientific tasks, official funding, participation in clinical trials, and reimbursements from Medicare, a public payor that is closely monitored. [560]

They said that: "among physicians with faculty appointments at 24 US public medical schools, significant sex differences in salaries exist even after accounting for age experience, specialty, faculty rank, and measures of research and productivity and clinical revenue." [561] The discrimination against women in Academia was not only limited to pay and benefits but also included *academic advancement*—the transition from non-tenured positions to the better-off tenured ones—that is facilitated by articles' authorship, receive funding from the *National Institute of Health*—a formal recognition akin to a *Papal benediction*—or conduct clinical trials. That career differential might be explained by different factors such as *childcare* issues, *inadequate mentoring* by bosses and lack of *peer recognition*.

Men and women do negotiate their way through life's travails differently.

We have seen the profusion of "sorries" from a distraught lady in a resto.

Not by the careless waiter that did not pay attention to the client's order.

Not by the busy cook that did not follow the kitchen slip's specifications.

They come from her when she sees an uninvited dressing on her salad.

Women refrain so adamantly to go against the grain that it hurts them. [562]

Whereas women are usually excited about new job prospects, which make them overlook and/or dismiss *important caveats* of their contracts, men have a useful narcissistic strain that *inflates their self-worth*, which toughens negotiations. Their initial assent is the first step in a long, winding road up to final acceptance.[563]

A nugget of Wisdom. Your "significant other" came back home excited. She was finally accepted for a teaching position in a prestigious university. Great. You should hug and kiss her. Share it with your kids. And her mother too… Once the celebratory dinner is finally over, you should sit down with a cup of tea.

–"OK, honey…What do they offer you? Is it a temporary or permanent post? What are the time and work obligations? What is the salary? And the benefits? Is this a tenured-track job or just a visiting professor position? Let's analyze it."

Playing the devil's advocate is the best help for her career prospects.

Screening for "the negative" is the first step in avoiding it altogether.

One of the most flagrant abuses of women involves a precious asset: **Time**. We all know that our mothers, grandmothers, wives, daughters, secretaries, etc., have the common trait of *efficiently administering time* to fulfill their various tasks. However, when the burdened women enter the workforce to carry out more tasks that are also time-consuming, the rest of society seems to ignore their limitations. T*ime-constrained* and *stressed-out*, they must juggle their various social demands.

Laureen Groff—an acclaimed novelist living in Florida—said: "no matter what people believe, American parenting remains a sexist enterprise. 'My husband is the primary parent, but my kids' teachers still call me first,' she says, which can lead to a complicated situation when Groff is travelling for author events." [564] She acknowledged that there were moments of tension when her role of writer collided with the one of mother. Her practical solution: **compartmentalization** of roles.

Successful men usually understand that their varied social roles could crash against each other and generate big friction, for which they build *separate spaces*. "From this time to that time, I am X… From this one to that one, I am Y." Simple. If a Primary School teacher usually understands that you cannot call a physician in the middle of the workday for some non-emergency notification about his child, why not extend the same courtesy when the professional happens to be a woman?

To create life, Mother Nature entrusted that task to a man and a woman.

Why does society stubbornly try to "apportion" all the blame only to her?

In early June 1940, Prime Minister Winston Churchill was in a bind.

His request for more RAF [565] squadrons to fight in France was rebuffed.

The Wehrmacht [566] chased the French Army into a pocket of resistance.

All the British Expeditionary Force had been evacuated from Dunkirk.[567]

He dreaded that the French would capitulate if he did not show support.

Despite the official propaganda, the Brits did not have stomach for a war.

Churchill had to be frank about the *military débâcle,* but at the same time he had to inject a much-needed *boost of optimism* for a victory against the Third Reich. On June 4, 1940, the world audience of the *BBC* [568] heard a hoarse voice saying: "we have before us an ordeal of the most grievous kind. We have before us many, many long months of struggle and of suffering. You ask, what is our policy? I will say it is to wage war, by sea, land, and air, with all our might and with all the strength that God can give us; to wage war against a monstrous tyranny never surpassed in the dark, lamentable catalogue of human crime. That is our policy." [569]

These lines galvanized the Brits and they started to support the war's effort. In an article reviewing Edward Stourton's book [570] about the BBC during World War II, Ian Jack questioned whether it had been Churchill who delivered them.[571] A circulating rumor attributed them to a famous actor who had impersonated him.

Did they pull such a cheeky stunt in the proud Brit's minds?

In a letter to the LRB [572] editor, Raymond Clayton said: "after reading Ian Jack's article I am now convinced that Churchill did not broadcast this speech. Its most defiant and inspiring passages were read during the nine o'clock news by the regular person. In the original speech Churchill referred to 'the odious apparatus of Nazi rule'. Did the BBC presenter read 'Nazi' with the German pronunciation, or copy Churchill's trademark, contemptuous 'Naarzi' (one)? It is easy to understand how, in that time of dread uncertainty, so many of us heard Churchill's own growling voice behind those words and felt a sense of reassurance and resolve." [573]

As pollster Frank Luntz said: "it's not what you say. It's what I hear." [574] Whether our *interpretation* is right or not is moot. Our *impression* is what counts.

A nugget of Wisdom. With a laptop's bag dangling sideways, you shudder. The company's obscurantist forces finally cornered you in a faraway beach. They cannot forgive you that you tried to use your brain and brawn at work. Giving you the howling fantods [575], the breeze fidgets with your ruffled hair. The incoming tide sways the corpses of sisters of all colors that had tried it before. Gazing into the horizon, you see a tiny little dot at sea, growing bigger and bigger. Your love is at the small boat's bow. He jumps into the surging surf to rescue you.

No, they do not get to eliminate you. Not today. You will fight them on.[576]

—"*Wake up, darling. Dinner's ready,*" says your hubby, caressing you.

Behind a great woman, there is always a great spouse.

—"Doctor…The bros don't invite me anymore—they're afraid of me."

Carol X. is a great lady that works in the Brickell financial district of Miami as a commercial insurance broker for a large house; she is a star associate as her expertise and affability easily win over the longtime trust of potential new clients. Her stellar performance does not assure her a place in the coveted *after-hours table* of her co-workers where they mingle with their customers and the affluent elite.

A few years ago, she was a regular in those impromptu gatherings where good business is always carried out *sotto il banco* [577], but they stopped inviting her. When she voiced her disagreement with the off-color jokes and rowdy antics of a few male colleagues that could not handle alcohol in style, she was progressively *dis-invited*. And, worse still, she was given an offensive little excuse the day after. Instead of reining in the *bad behavior* of the bros, the senior management let things run "its natural way" as they saw it as *a cheap way* for their subaltern staff to "let off steam" and return to the office the next day to carry on with their grind.

The **absence of women** in senior management posts makes this unfair *fait accompli* all too common but no less damaging to the careers of all those involved. A *Pew Research Center* article said: "the share of Fortune 500 who are female remains very small, reaching a record 5.4% in the first quarter of 2017…A recent study found that among the top 100 public companies by revenue, female CEOs are out-earning male CEOs, although there are only eight women on the list." [578]

Even though women constitute almost half of the workforce in the USA, they are still glaringly *under-represented* in most of the corporate boards where the significant administrative policies are being designed for the whole organization.

Erica Hersh said: "the percentage of women on boards overall in the United States is between 11 and 12% and has barely increased in the last decade. For health-related companies, the number of women in boards vary greatly, from 9.7 % for biotech companies with under 1,000 employees to 27% on hospital boards." [579]

Having much more women in positions of power will not only reflect more accurately our societies but it will add a necessary *feminine perspective* to business as they control 20 trillion U$ of *consumer spending* in the global economy.[580] The *more dynamic* companies in the Fortune 1000 index have a higher number of women in their boards; in 842 companies that compose that index, women hold 18.8% of the board seats. As a mirror image, more than 55% of *laggard companies*, have none. "When Fortune-500 companies were ranked by the number of women directors in their board, those in the highest quartile in 2009 reported a 42% greater return on sales and a 53% higher return on equity than the rest." [581] Women constitute a larger portion of college attendance and have caught up with men in the acquisition of graduate degrees in almost all the prestigious fields. [582]

If these corporations know that educated women make the buying choices, why does their top brass drag their feet at the time of promoting them?

One reason might be due to a human trait: we like to work *with people like us*. We all feel immediately comfortable with those that look, talk and act like we do; that feature harks back thousands of years to our solitary times in those dark caves. Adam Hampton et al. published a seminal social study where they discussed why "similarity with others" might increase *our liking*. The major reasons were:

a) **Consensual validation**: encountering people who share some of our opinions and/or interests might give us more confidence.

b) **Cognitive evaluation**: if we can recognize some familiar, common traits in other persons, we might instinctively like them—as we like ourselves.

c) **Certainty of being liked**: in general, we assume that people similar to us will like us; in turn, we tend to like those that like us too.

d) **Fun and enjoyable interactions**: usually we have more fun with those that have similar interests and perspectives in life.

e) **Opportunities for self-expansion**: we are enriched by new experiences and relationships when we share our lives with other people; people are prone to find opportunities of self-expansion with similar people. [583]

Gwendolyn Seidman said: "first there is a difference between *actually* having a lot of common with someone (*actual similarity*) and *believing* that we have a lot in common (*perceived similarity*) These two kinds of similarity are certainly related, but they are not exactly the same thing." [584] We might initially think that we share someone's interests and can work with them effortlessly, but we might be wrong.

In their study, Hampton et al. studied how the above-mentioned factors modified the *actual* and *perceived similarity* noticed by the participants; they liked their partner more if they were initially led to believe that there was a similarity. However, if the initial information was *false*, that impression eventually *waned*; the perceptions of similarity based on reality wiped off the initial effects of bogus information. After an actual interaction, the participants could have a consensual validation. The "certainty of being liked" and the prospect of "a joyful experience" were also important in the post-act validation of an *initial impression of likeability*. For young and older individuals, the *feelings of joy* seemed to be more important for them, overriding the *consensual validation* and *the certainty of being liked*. [585]

Unfortunately, the opportunity to participate in the solution of problems with persons that they initially like is limited for women in top management positions; considering that they are fewer of them *standing in the pipeline*, the lack of proper mentoring makes them feel isolated and vulnerable with the known consequences. In a show of spurious grandstanding to whitewash their inertia, many "masters of the universe" [586] say that they cannot find enough fit women to fill the board seats. If there are not enough **mentoring women** at the top, their promotion is arduous.

<u>*Diary USS Awareness*</u> — See how they must always climb the steepest cliff?

—"Doctor…Oh, they did call me—only when the s*** was hitting the fan."

Maggie X. is a feisty, savvy native of Georgia who has been working as a secretary in a Florida trucking company for many years; she was *the owners' right hand*, handling all their tough logistics, ever since he had founded the company. When he passed away, she rightly assumed that she would become his substitute; but the owner's family chose his eldest son who did not have an inkling of the task.

Despite that nepotism, the transition went fine as she stayed soldiering on. Until the moment when a few longtime clients—taking for granted that they could take advantage of the neophyte boss—demanded a draconian fees' re-negotiation. The owner's widow begged Maggie to personally intervene. She successfully did.

Everybody with at least one working ear has heard about **the glass ceiling**. The *Merriam-Webster Dictionary* stated: "an intangible barrier within a hierarchy that prevents women or minorities from obtaining upper-level positions." [587] However, much less known is the concept of **the glass cliff**, which refers to the *better chance of women* to reach the top executive positions in a time of crisis.[588]

Suzanne Bruckmuller and Nyla S. Braschombe designed a study [589] to find out if it existed. They recruited 119 college students and gave them *two articles* about an organic food company. The first article, which discussed the upcoming retirement of its CEO, had *two scripts;* in one of the versions, the company had been traditionally led by men and in the other one, it had been led by women.

Likewise, the second article had *two scripts*; in one version the company was prospering and in the other version it was in a catastrophic financial situation. They asked the students to identify *who might be the best choice* for CEO between a man or a woman with equally qualifying credentials. When the man-led company was in good standing, 62% of the participants *chose the male,* but when it was in dire straits 69% *chose the female* as the CEO. When the script said that the company was run by a female, there was not a significant difference between the versions.

They said: "we were especially struck by the finding that the phenomenon does not seem to apply to organizations with a history of female leaders. This suggests that as people become more used to seeing women at the highest levels of management, female leaders won't be selected primarily for risky turnarounds—and will get more chances to run organizations that have good odds of success." [590]

A nugget of Wisdom. Nicely seated, you attend the bank board's meeting. Saddled by his obligations, the President and CEO has quit, after months of being hounded by over-zealous regulators and the pestering press about his decisions.

To replace him, the board shortlisted two candidates: *a man and a woman*. Your colleagues at the table, which only has a token female *pour la gallerie* [591], are debating who would put up *the best defense* in an upcoming regulatory hearing.

The woman is a great candidate, but she does not check all the boxes.

So what? Neither does he…Take that leap. Audaces fortuna juvat. [592]

—"Doctor…The nicer I am, the more men try to take advantage of me."

Carol X. is a pleasant and attractive lawyer who regularly visits the South Florida courthouses to try tough criminal cases with potentially heavy sentencing. She strives *to be polite* to all the men and women alike—from the security guards at the metal detector in the entrance all the way up to the judges in the courtrooms. However, she has *the gut feeling* that some manly prosecutors had mischievously offered *raw deals* for her clients, which she had to bitterly fend off, because they foolishly *took for granted* that, being a woman, she could be "taken for a ride." Like Hamlet, she ponders: *"To be nice or not to be... That is the question."* [593]

The TV audience in the USA watched how, in the televised hearings of the Senate confirmation process of Judge Brett Kavanaugh for a vacant seat in the Supreme Court, there were *two different speaking styles*. He could afford to be arrogant while Dr, Christine Blasey Ford—who had dared to denounce him for a supposed sexual assault years ago—had to compose herself, even under strain. [594]

Maggie Haberman, a *The New York Times* correspondent, said: "regardless of whether Ford is right about what took place or Kavanaugh is, if any woman who is wrongly accused fought for her life by crying, yelling and being obstinate with senators, she would be eviscerated as crazy, hysterical and weak." [595]

<u>Diary USS Awareness</u> – Physical distances might be the same but coordinates act as gender-sensitive. There is a nautical chart for men and another one for women.

Solange X. is a young medical assistant who had a lovely baby girl. Besides juggling with labor's tough physical legacy and the sleep deprivation of parenting and the quaint social bias for breast-feeding in public and the delicate balance of work/family and her mother-in-law's prying (*Jesus…Got to catch my breath*) she must find **adequate daytime care** as her trusted family members live far away. Her monthly bill cuts almost a third of her salary. She feels badly short-changed.

In May 2018, the *Center for Diseases and Control* (CDC) released a report of the *fertility data* in the USA in 2017. The most salient features were these:

a) The provisional number of births was 3,853,472, down 2% from 2016, the lowest number in the 30 years-time period that it collected that data.

b) The general fertility rate was 60.2 births per 1,000 women aged 15-44, also down from 2016, which was another record low figure.

c) The provisional total fertility rate (TFR) was 1.764.births per 1,000 women, down 3% from the rate in 2016 (1.820.5), the lowest since 1978.

d) While the birth rates declined for nearly all age groups of women under 40 years, rates rose for women in the early 40s.

e) The birth rate for teenagers aged 15-19 was down 7% in 2017 to 18.8 births for 1,000 women; rates declined for younger and older ones. [596]

Women are having less babies at an even later stage of their lives.

In the USA, following a trend that started in Europe, women are having their first child at a later age, 26.4 years old on average, compared to 24 in the 80s. As women keep postponing motherhood, a statistical issue called *tempo effect* skews the predictive value of future fertility rates based on the current births by 25%. [597]

The *United States of America* is the only major industrialized nation that does not have a federally mandated and fully paid period for **maternity leave**. President Bill Clinton signed the *Family and Medical Leave Act* [598] in 1993, which guaranteed only a period of *12 weeks of unpaid leave* if the company had 50 employees or more. Raising a child in the USA is *financially onerous* and *labor-intensive*; often the mother must either reduce her working hours or quit her job.

Alexandra Stanczyk from *The Urban Institute* said: "I find that in the months when these new expenses hit, American families are likely to see drops in their households' income level. On average, American households (had) 10.4 percent declines in total household income from pre-pregnancy to the birth." [599]

After decades of states' under-funding, the *US Congress* enacted a law in 2014 that mandated a higher quality and minimum safety for the provided services. But they kept decreasing, reaching in 2016 the lowest number of eligible children for the *Child Care and Development Block Grant* (CCDBG) in 18 years.[600] Only the incoming wave of new female legislators is again discussing this critical issue.

And then we wonder why Jane and Dick fight for the Nintendo's joystick.

On July 5, 1948, a phalanx of physicians, nurses, pharmacists, clerks, and administrators entered the main ward of *Park Hospital* in Davyhulme, Manchester, led by the visionary Aneurin *Nye* Bevan— UK minister of Health—to inaugurate an emblematic British organization: The **National Health Service** (NHS) [601] That hospital—now named *Trafford General*—is the birthplace of that institution. The first patient he met was a thirteen-year-old girl called Sylvia Diggory who, in spite of suffering from an acute nephritis, grasped the epic value of that visit. She said: "Mr. Brevan asked me if I understood the significance of the occasion and told me it was a milestone in history—the most civilized step any country had ever taken. I had ear-wigged at adults' conversations and I knew this was a great change that was coming about and that most people could hardly believe it was happening." [602]

Despite three decades of economic and social transformation in the United Kingdom, the *NHS* still has the *widespread support* of its general population. A *King's Fund* survey that interviewed 1,151 persons aged 15 and over in England in August 2017 found that: "(on its 70th birthday) seventy percent of the public believe that the NHS should be maintained in its current form…around 90 per cent of people support the founding principles of the NHS, indicating that these principles are just as relevant today as when the NHS was established." [603] It has enjoyed a more solid public support than the scandal-riven Royals.

As a beacon of equitable access, the NHS should be egalitarian… Right?

In May 2018, the United Kingdom's *Department of Health and Social Care* did a study on **gender equality** in the NHS [604], led by Professor Dame Jane Acre; it used data from 10 years of electronic records of 16,000 general practitioners and 96,000 trust physicians. They found that the gender gap was 17% based on total pay, which contributed to the overall 23% NHS pay gap. "Male doctors are earning 1.17 pounds for every pound earned by female doctors in the NHS, and new data reveals that women are still not represented in equal proportions in senior medical grades, with nearly 32,000 male consultants to just 18,000 females. The General Practice gender gap is 33%, which is far higher than the average in medicine." [605]

Even though *half* of the physicians in training were female, only *a third* of the better consultants' positions were held by women—18,000 women in a total of 32,000. They were disproportionately present in the *lower-paying* specialties like Dermatology, compared to the *higher number* of men in *higher-paying* ones like Surgery. The same study showed that the demands of motherhood and the burden of irregular working hours seriously harmed their prospects for advancement. [606]

If this abject *pay scale disparity* for men and women can actually occur in a supposedly progressive society that had recognized the societal value of equitable access for Health Care, what can we expect of other less enlightened ones? We, the *XY-healers*, know that our female peers often work much harder than we do.

3 *Noblesse oblige.* [607]

—"Doctor…Don't want me to speak out —always f******interrupting me."

Carla X. is a young middle-level executive of an American corporation that due to her great expertise in targeting the *most dynamic segments* of the markets is destined to climb much higher in the corporate ladder. However, she resents the *not too subtle* attempts by her less endowed male colleagues to sideline her in meetings. She argued that, in the latter, men use an antediluvian tool to bring her to keel and sabotage her impact on the discussion: **the interruption of women's talk.**

The power dynamics in her job mimic the one prevailing in our society.

Christopher Karpovitz et al. studied data from several groups to find out if there really was gender inequality in *the deliberation process* and if improving the *feminine participation* would eventually raise their authority within those groups. They found a significant *gender gap* of the *social impact* from voice and authority in meetings that could be erased in two circumstances: when there is *unanimous rule* and *fewer women,* or when there is *majority rule* and *more women.*[608]

Lynn Smith-Lovin and Charles Brody studied *the speaker transitions* in task-oriented groups to determine if men do interrupt women often. They said that: "Gender inequality in these task-oriented discussions is created by a mixture of attempts to use power and of differential success…Men discriminate by sex in attempts and in yielding to interruptions by others. Women interrupt and yield the floor to males and females equally."[609] *Does their composition have an impact?*

The same authors found that in all-male groups, individuals often interrupted each other; but *when more women joined them*, the number of interruptions fell. [610] Another requisite for advancement is to get proper credit for our words and deeds in order to rank appropriately in the institution's formal evaluation for promotions.

Sean R. Martin et al. studied if there were gender differences in *speaking up* with data from cadets of the *US Military Academy* [611]. The first mailed survey collected *basic biographical information*; the second one was delivered prior to a *crucial two-day competition* of war games, at the end of their training period. In the latter they asked *to rate* each member's performance and standing to calculate individual scores. In the third survey, they measured *the leader emergence score* as members had to rank their *leadership potential*. They found that: "men who spoke up with ideas were seen as having higher status and were more likely to emerge as leaders. Women did not receive any benefits in status or leader emergence from speaking up, regardless of whether they did so promotively or prohibitively." [612]

—"Doctor...When I lead the way, men resent it—only because I'm a gal."

Marjorie X. is a very proficient management expert that works in a medical supplies company; whenever she opens her mouth to pinpoint a defective process or an outlier member, men often disparage her with gross epithets behind her back. Paradoxically a few women also join in the fray...Talk about a brave new world.

<u>*Diary USS Awareness*</u> – Is the *silence of the seas* teaching you the art of listening?

Ealy and Karay discussed a **role congruity of prejudice** toward all those women that dared to assume the pivotal leadership roles in our modern society. [613] These authors distinguished two major aspects in this generalized bad attitude:

a) Perceiving women less favorably than men if they are viewed as potential occupants of leadership roles.

b) Evaluating behavior that fulfills the needed attributes of a leader role less favorably when it is carried out by a woman.

Consequently, women are *perceived less favorably* in leadership roles, which can significantly gnaw at their real authority in times of crises of modern institutions. If women-leaders should become mentors for other women that are trying to emulate them, the camouflaged opinion of their co-workers will certainly have an impact. In every organization there is a *parallel structure of power* that must be reckoned.

According to women, what should be the major reforms in workplaces?

The *Price Waterhouse Coopers* [614] group, which provides tax preparation, assurance, and consultancy services in many countries, designed a survey in 2018 where they asked 3,627 professional women from around the world what should be done to advance *gender equality* in their workplaces. They found the following:

a) 58% of respondents considered that employers need to provide greater transparency to improve career opportunities.

b) 82% of women were confident in their ability to fulfill their aspirations.

c) 60% of women said their managers support their career aspirations.

d) 48% of new mothers felt overlooked for promotions and projects. [615]

The issue of **transparency** is of paramount importance for women with a career. Carol Stubbings said: "most organizations are still far too opaque in their processes, which means all involved, not only women, are left unsure exactly what they have to do to succeed." [616] Talking with career women, the issue of how the closed-door discussions of *old-boys networks* sabotage them always comes up.

If we are sincere about equality, these Tammany Hall [617] antics must stop.

Do women have to work much harder than men to prove their real worth?

A 2015 *Pew Research Center*'s online survey of 1,835 randomly selected adults between November 12-21, 2014, asked what stalled women's careers. They found that: "4 in 10 Americans point to a double standard for women seeking to climb to the highest levels of either politics or business, where they have to do more than their male counterparts to prove themselves." [618] Carol Stubbings said that women, once they feel ready for the next level, need *pushy mentors*. "At PWC we find that when women enter the process to become partners, for example, they succeed at a greater rate than men because they are much more prepared. The downside is that it takes them longer than men to put themselves forward." [619]

The same author pointed out that many recruiters do not quite grasp the needed skills to *access the higher level* rather than just staying at the same level. One of the most misunderstood—and misrepresented—concepts for a recruiting panel is the *technical requirements* of the job opening, which oftentimes *favors men* and *sidelines women*. In order to succeed, a new manager of an assembly line of an aircraft manufacturer does not need to be proficient in all its technical data. Rather the chosen individual must know *how to come up* with a competent team where everybody uses their best skills and feel that they share a higher mission.[620]

Henry Ford is famous for his T model-line, not how he tightened screws.

The guidance of **mentoring women** in the workplace can make a difference. When she was accepting the *VES* [621] *Visionary Award*, Victoria Alonso, producer at *Marvel Studios*, asked why there were only 40 women out of 400 nominees. She argued that if women in the upper echelons of companies do not help with their counselling and support other aspiring women, there will not be significant change. Being an ambitious woman in one of the most dynamic areas of the historically male-dominated *Entertainment* industry, her concerns carried an extra weight. But there was a new, portentous sign. In the 2017 *Siggraph* [622] conference, she waited a little bit too much to visit the ladies' room where she discovered a large queue.[623]

Women waiting? Something was afoot in that hitherto all manly reunion.

About time

Women are permanently subjected to an *anachronistic double standard* for grading their performance when they give a public message, especially in Politics. What works well for any man out there might not be necessarily true for a woman. In an article of the *Style* section in *The Washington Post*, Ellen McCarthy said: "the list of double standards women face on their path to public office is plenty long: they should be pretty, but not distractingly so. Assertive, but never aggressive. Maternal, yet devoted exclusively to their careers. And every word that passes their lips should be spoken in a tone, volume and cadence that is pleasing to the ever-alert ears of their audience." [624] *Their use of humor can be counterproductive.*

Jonathan Evans et al. studied the **use of humor** in the public speeches by asking *a man and a woman* to each give *two versions* of a presentation—one *with humor* and the other one *without it*. They found that when the manly participant used humor, his ratings for *social status, performance evaluation* and *potential for leadership* increased. However, when a feminine participant used the very same joke, her numbers *took a dive* in all these parameters. They argued that: "gender plays an important role in understanding when using humor at work can have costs for the humor source…gender stereotypes constrain the interpretation of observed humor such that humor expressed by males is likely to be interpreted as more functional and less disruptive compared to humor expressed by females." [625]

<u>*Diary USS Awareness*</u> – Still believe that women are *too serious*?

In the *We the People Summit*—an assembly of progressive activists in the USA, fired up in their fiery opposition to the Trump administration—there was a parade of many Democratic politicians that have expressed their intention to run for the US Presidency—supposedly the most coveted job of the land—in 2020. [626]

One of the most contentious issues in American Politics is the impact of what political pundits defined as **the likability factor** [627] at the time of voting. Jennifer Rubin, a *NYTimes* writer, compared the style of two contenders, one male and one female, that had similar policy stands but acted differently in public.

Senator Amy Klobuchar (Democrat- Minnesota), versed on policy topics, is one of the most productive members of her party's caucus. "She has put forward 69 pieces of legislation in the 115th Congress, eight of which passed the senate and four of which became law (compared to an average of 42 bills, 2 passing the Senate and less than one becoming law among other minority senators)" [628]

Beto O'Rourke—a former Texas congressman—is an aspirational politician that wants to bring back the flame of progressive politics.[629] "Sometimes he is imprecise on how he's going to accomplish things. He does not come armed with detailed policy proposals as does Sen. Elizabeth Warren (Dem-Mass.), but he can give a short discourse on the problem at hand, the history off addressing the issue and the impact of not solving our problems. In lieu of a long legislative record, you have to take it on faith that somehow he's going to (make us agree)" [630]

Beto O'Rourke had an *eclectic style* that shunned the policy wonks, savvy advisers, poll analysts and anything that smelled of "a party machine." He did not prepare his speeches and liked to brutally *crash on public sites* with no warning. "O'Rourke attracted overflowing crowds, record fundraising and tremendous media buzz for his inaugural tour as he raced across Iowa, New Hampshire, South Carolina and Nevada. He also irritated Democratic leaders with a seat-of-the-pants campaign approach that may… raise questions about his ability to govern."[631]

Mimicking *the thespian endowment* of successful politicians, Beto O'Rourke knew how to "work a crowd" and make people like him, from the first impression. He took advantage of his youthful energy to spontaneously hop on to a bar or patio table to deliver his impromptu stump speeches to a totally captivated crowd. [632]

Jon Krosnich found that *not all* voting behavior is rational. "What we know now from 50 years of psychology is that you can divide the brain in two parts. In fact, all decision-making is unconscious." We like other good-looking people.[633]

Claire Bond Potter said: "The idea that we should like our politicians predates women's suffrage, let alone women in politics. Pushed by Madison Avenue and preached by self-help gurus, likability is a standard that history shows us was created and sold by men. The bad news is that means it's a tricky fit for women. The good news is that what was invented once can be reinvented." [634] Monica Hesse criticized the *who-would-you-rather-have-a-beer-with* axiom.[635]

She said: "Plenty of women drink beer and hang out in bars. That's not the point here. The point is that certain questions seemed rigged to set up certain candidates to fail. The point is that women can be likable on entirely different terms… equally valid." [636] With the suggestive banner of *Policy vs. Persona*, Annie Linskey wrote about the political dilemma of Sen. Elizabeth Warren (D-Massachusetts) in her presidential bid. [637] The firebrand Senator has put forward interesting policy initiatives—subsidized housing, federally funded-child care, etc. "Warren, alone among the Democratic candidates, is betting voters… want someone whose strength is a mastery of detail and a meticulous road map for pitchfork-style change…The risk is that detailed initiatives may excite activists but not voters, fill the op-ed pages but not the front pages, and leave Warren with an effort that resembles a policy roadshow rather than a political campaign."[638]

Claire Bond Potter wrote that the *critical connection* in the social media between the voters' emotions and competing politicians emphasize their fantasies about "how they should be", not their record. She said that: "women disadvantaged by a dynamic that emphasizes fantasies over real achievements should perhaps come as no surprise. Popular fantasies about women, sadly, still don't tend to feature intelligence, expertise and toughness at the negotiating table." [639]

Beto quit the race in November. Klobuchar and Warren did it in March.

Diary USS Awareness – Some ride before the mast well into their 70s. [640]

Chapter VII – The Vegan Harta factor

"Madness is rare in individuals, but in groups it is the norm."

Friedrich Nietzsche

Out of her body's sandalwood paste, Lordess Parvati created Ganesha.

Delighted and curious with her own creation, she breathed life into it.

Eager for a bath, she told him to stand guard and not allow anyone in.

Lord Shiva came back and was determined to enter Parvati's quarters.

When Ganesha blocked him from entering, Shiva asked who he was.

He resolutely replied that he was Ganesha, the son of Maa Parvati.

Flustered, Lord Shiva sent his Ganas to teach a lesson to the child.

Created by the Shakti, Ganesha could rebuff this and other advances.

Totally infuriated, Shiva decided to deal with that upstart himself.

With a swift swing of his sword, he severed the head of Ganesha.

When Maa Parvati came out of her bath, she found her son's head.

Deeply enraged, she demanded that Shiva immediately fix his misdeed.

Lord Shiva promised her that he would quickly comply with her wish.

He sent the demigods in search of an animal head facing rightly North.

The only living being that could fit Shiva's request was an elephant.

Using his supernatural powers, Lord Shiva transplanted the head and infused life back into Ganesha's body, which duly pleased his mother. Ganesha became the symbol of good tidings—the remover of obstacles. On September the 13th, Hindus celebrate the Vegan Harta festival. [641]

One of the most joyous festivals in India is based on the legend of a little boy that stood steadfastly *loyal to a woman*, up to the point of defying a big deity. Parvati felt safe from the prying looks of strangers as long as Ganesha stood guard. He acted as a *wall of contention* for the threats that might endanger her well-being. Tired from her travels, she sought some privacy for a shower. (*Too much asking?*)

As the genders progressively share more time and opportunities together, the issue of **friendship between the sexes** has prodded scientific studies of it.[642] April L. Bleske and David M. Buss surveyed hundreds of college age participants to test "evolution-based hypotheses about (1) sex differences in perceived benefits and costs of opposite-sex friendships and (2) differences in perceived benefits of same-sex friendships and opposite-sex friendships." [643] They found that men considered there was *more utility* in their friendships with the opposite sex than women did; women valued more the *protective benefits* they receive from their male friends. Both genres enjoyed the *confidential information* gleaned about the opposite sex's behavior during conversations at dinner, the beach, or other social interactions.

<u>Diary USS Awareness</u> – Miss their *yada yada* [644] ?

—Doctor…At the end of the day, only my girlfriends are standing by me."

Kim X. is a married mother of two grownup sons and one daughter that still chats and meets regularly with her two former classmates from a Catholic School in New Jersey. Neither sanctioned by the church nor recognized by the state, female bonding *withstands the tough test of times* and keeps growing stronger.

By traditional standards women are supposed to find their kindred souls and marry them, enjoying their blissful mating until they ride together into the sunset. However, in our ever more complicated times—with work and family obligations, limited time and financial resources, lack of family support, the alienation of a social media-obsessed citizenry, the clash of generations regarding their work/life balances—the need for *feminine non-sexual foundational relationships* remains. Moreover, as educated women are marrying later in life, having children in their thirties and forties, divorcing more often than their parents, and oftentimes not even having a steady partner , **the female bonding** plays a critical social role. [645]

Marilyn Yalom chronicled the evolution of female friendship from the dark days when women were excluded from the community forum and relegated to a demeaning *gossiping circle* in a kitchen's corner by their domineering males. [646] Cloistered nuns were one of the first examples of kinship *without the sex burden*. Without leaving her convent, *Santa Teresita de Avila* had many correspondents; her written pleas to King Philip II of Spain annulled her Inquisition's charges.[647]

In the 17th and 18th centuries, women in France and England befriended their neighbors, regularly exchanged letters, and organized cultural parties in the salons. Many of the greatest writers and philosophers of that time received the patronage of ladies who did not hesitate to sponsor social events—away from the censoring eyes/ears of the state and the religious institutions—to freely discuss new ideas. [648]

Female bonding was the ignition spark of powerful social movements like the *Suffragettes*, who fought for an equal access to voting in Western societies. [649] Eleanor Roosevelt, wife of one of the greatest US presidents, sought to create a unique role as *the first lady*, wholly separate from her partner's achievements. [650] Its attraction did not wither with the feminine liberation of late. On the contrary.

As their social roles became more prominent and they acted independently, women appreciated a "caring ear" more than ever; even the most satisfying marital relationship could not replace the critical need for the *sex-free female bonding*.[651]

Rebecca Traister said: "for many women friends are our primary partners through life; they are the ones who move us into our new homes, out of bad relationships, through births and illnesses. Even for women who do marry, this is true at the beginning of our adult lives, and at the end—after divorce or the death of a spouse." [652] She said that in her youth her girlfriends, unlike many of her boyfriends, restocked her desire to *spiritedly seek a spiritual sense of satisfaction*.

Most men are voracious drainers of energy. Only a few are replenishers.

In 1959 Michael Balint wrote a book titled *Thrills and Regression* [653] where he claimed that there were two major ways to organize our human bonding:

a) **Dependency on objects**: persons who are strongly *attached to objects*, both material and spiritual, which gives them reassurance and comfort.

b) **Preference for open spaces**: persons that prefer *to experiment the new*, both material and spiritual, which gives them the thrill they are seeking.

These are two extremes of a fluid continuum that we engage with at different circumstances of our lives; we are often *a mixture* of different percentages. The *lebensraum* [654] of the first type is organized through the *physical proximity* and *tactile connection* with the necessary object(s); they feel safe when they cling to them and anxiety when they are separated. On the other hand the *lebensraum* of the second type is organized with *open, wide spaces* full of opportunities. And danger.

Care professionals that regularly sit down with patients to talk and offer comfort might one day become "an object", with different degrees of attachment. A stagecoach waystation to pass their thoughts and feelings through reason's sieve.

A bobbing buoy in the choppy seas of Incertitude that they can hold on to.

If they lean too hard on it, it may flip over and jolt them back in the sea.

Feminine relief might entail the sacrifice of our transitory objectification.

<u>Diary USS Awareness</u> – Mind all the little buoys along a woman's route.

Good company is essential. What occurs when we get too little or none?

The forced *social distancing* of the pandemic has had two major effects. On one hand it has distanced us from some close family members that we miss a lot. And on the other hand, it has prodded us to share our living quarters with a few.

In March 2020 we attended a webinar given by an academic expert in Mental Health about the *psychological consequences* of **forced social isolation**. After an initial good exposure of expected consequences of *loneliness* and *isolation* in human beings, the presenter started to wallow in a sea of tired platitudes, which were tagged by a cohort of naive attendees asking some inconsequential questions. Right away we knew that she *did not a have a clue* about brutal kinds of isolation.

For all the countless diplomas held by both the speaker and the attendees, they were evidently lacking *the most important one* to certify the needed expertise. Not a single one of them had attended the coursework of the *University of Life*. Not a single one had earned a full scholarship for the most brutal of isolations: **jailtime**. As scandalous as it seems, all those that had tasted "the can" have a leg up now.

In the seventies, the *brutal military dictatorships* of Uruguay and Argentina (where we were studying our medical career at the time) did not have any efficient methods to verify the *police records* of anyone they randomly stopped in the street during their "razzias" [655] to check documents and spot the political activists. When the officer in charge of the platoon decided that you could be "a suspect", you had to silently comply with the arrest order and ended up in a police station, waiting for their *request for records*. In one of those "stays", an ageing *pickpocket* told us:

-*"Listen, young man...I don't know how long they are going to keep you here. Most likely just a few days and then they'll let you go. But, just in case, you have to learn and use the two basic principles of survival in jail. It's mandatory —"*

-*"Oh, yeah,"* we replied with a touch of sassiness. *"What are they?"*

-*"The first one is to always keep track of time, with any possible means. If you do not have any idea of what day of the week and what hour of the day you are living, you will progressively deteriorate...Seen too many guys like you going downhill."*

-*"And the other one?"*

-*"Follow the leaders' instructions and respect our discipline ...It's the only way to survive without any lasting mental or physical consequences...Got it?"*

-*"Yeah...I guess so..."*

-*" Grab this,"* he said, handing us a broom.*" "Last arrival, sweeps the floor."*

Thus started our instruction in the only college that smothers or toughens.

Years later, we proudly show its graduating pin on our uniform. **Jail Bird**.

The two basic survival techniques in a situation of extreme isolation are:

a) Safeguard your circadian rhythm at all times.

b) Adhere to a strict discipline of basic social and personal tasks.

A – <u>Safeguard your circadian rhythm at all times</u>

A forced isolation from the rest of society will bring *extreme anxiety* and *clinical depression* to anybody but the well-trained soldiers or hardened criminals. With radically restricted mobility in small spaces where the *parameters of your life* are gone, you lose track of the hours or the period of the day. **The sense of Time**. Totally isolated in a confined space with no fresh air or sunshine, you cannot appreciate, and recall, the details of a changing weather. **The sense of Seasonality**.

The multiple *sensorial stimuli* that our body receptors catch during a normal day suddenly disappear or at least significantly diminish during a forced isolation. We will no longer feel the suave caress of the early dawn coming from the East. We will no longer smell the enticing aroma of a delicious dish signaling it is noon. We will no longer hear the throngs of people in the street marking rush hour time.

Like a mechanical *grandfatherly clock* that, in spite of all its splendor, needs the regular winding of a little knob in the back, our internal *biological clock* needs stimuli to regulate our bodily functions. We develop bespoke *eating, self-grooming* and *sleep routines* that keep our homeostasis. But, when you are in jail, you might spend too much time lounging in bed, skipping lunchtime, or hitting the toilet.

The first order of the day should be to *wake up at a reasonable time* daily; if you are used to working or studying at night, then you can revert the directive. The second order of the day should be to *fill your day* with meaningful tasks that are useful for those sharing your *compulsory confinement* or the society at large. The third order of the day is to always find a *glimmer of sunshine* or outside light. Even with a minor, brief stimulus of the temperature and vision receptors, our hormonal system (with the *hypophysis* above all) will better regulate our bodily functions.[656]

One of the most annoying side effects is an *unrelenting constipation*. You must *sit down at the throne regularly*, even though you might not feel the need. If the organic waste materials, which will continue to be produced even with a more meagre amount of food, keep accumulating in our bodies, they will poison us.

B – **Strict discipline for basic personal and social tasks**

One of the most disseminated fallacies is that prisons are places of constant chaos, of unbridled lawlessness, of unchecked release of passion. Quite on the contrary. The best run prisons are managed with a firm hand accepted by all. The only way to have a semblance of functionality with so many people with different interests in such a limited space is to prod everybody—prisoners, guards, and administrative cadres—to respect the basic rules of a peaceful co-existence. When a companion with a higher hierarchy is also confined with you, you will naturally follow the *informal power structure*. One of the more memorable film scenes shows the British Army's survivors of the *Fall of Singapore* [657], after a punishing forced march through malaria-ridden country, enter with a flawless formation into the Japanese prisoners of war's camp for the Allied, led by a starchily solemn Alec Guinness, all whistling the catchy tune of *The bridge in the River Kwai*.[658]

First of all , you must respect the *national guidelines*, which in our case are enforced by the police and first responders that are bravely exposing themselves. Then come the *county-specific guidelines* of where you reside, which are related to the unique sanitary and safety codes of buildings, apartments, neighborhoods, etc. Finally you must consider the *private guidelines* for all those living together.

If there is only one shower, you cannot drill your take of *Singing in the Rain*. If there is a communal use of the kitchen, you must always *clean up* after yourself. If there is a pet in the house, you must *take turns* to clean it, to exercise it, etc. If there are children, you must consider *their need for distraction* with games or TV. If you like to smoke, you must go out in the patio to avoid the *secondary smoking*. If you like to listen to music, you must *lower the volume*, especially at nighttime.

The methodical practice of studying and writing at home for many years has prepared us for a smooth transition of our life into this new constraint guidelines. The pandemic's *Social Distancing* has just tightened the screws already in place.

<u>Diary USS Awareness</u> – Do you want to make real friends in those stifling berths? When you want to break wind, rush to the deck to disguise it with swirling ones.

Rodolfo Guglielmi was born in a humble farm of Puglia in 1895.

Only thirty-one years later he died as a rich celebrity in New York.

In the flickering darkness of cinemas, ladies were charmed by him.

Lacking sound, they pasted their personalized dreams on the screen.

The combo of good looks and erotic dancing was irresistible.

Precisely for those reasons, he was deeply hated by most men.

In his lifetime he endured tons of slanderous discrimination. [659]

In an exposition of the *Museum of Modern Art* in New York, the organizers studied the *stereotypes of male and female roles* in Hollywood with film posters. Ron Magliozzi, a co-curator, said: "we selected works to make points about gender, the fact that there are many gazes on this work whether you're gay, queer, trans, a man or a woman. We wanted to represent the work in that context." [660]

For playing masculine characters that nonetheless had feminine traits—like a suave treatment of the ladies—Valentino was rabidly *demonized in the press* then; he was denigrated as a gay character that liked to use mascara, jewels, and fancy furs. Despite that *queer baiting*, the actors' roles began to blur in Hollywood, with more men showing feminine traits and women the manly ones. Valentino's legacy.

Eppur si muove [661]

As some of their bitter detractors claim, are women always whining?

We must reluctantly confess that in the beginning of our medical career, stoically listening to *the women's biblical tales* in the ward or the office caused us the worst *katzenjammer* [662] we have ever had—without even a whiff of alcohol. Overwhelmed by their multiple, varied obligations at home and work, coupled with a profound *Emotional Frustration* of not finding an empathic partner close to them, many patients literally "opened up their hearts" in a torrent of complaints when they came to the medical office for an ailment, which could be related or not to the latter; with patience, practitioners finally learned how to manage these interactions.

There was a brave man who first listened to women. And he lived to tell it.

Sigismund Schlomo Freud—born on May 6th, 1856, in Pribor, Moravia and passing away on September 23rd, 1939, in London, England—is one of the most *respected* and at the same time *repudiated* physicians in modern medicine. He was one of the earliest practitioners of **Psychoanalysis** [663] and his pioneering work in the intricacies of the *Unconscious Mind* still perturbs us. He was the first man who saw women *as individuals* with their own special concerns, desires, and fears. [664]

André Brouillet painted the details of one of the masterly ward classes by Jean-Martin Charcot in the Neurology ward of *La Pitié-Salpêtrière* hospital [665]; in that setting the medical pioneer showed to his students *the power of the hypnosis' techniques* to glean clinical information from "hysterical" women with symptoms.

Charcot dismissed their sex-related complaints —*la chose génitale* [666]—as not being relevant for the clinical outcomes. But there was an Austrian physician who, after his stay there , went back to Vienna to team up with **Joseph Breuer** in developping the technique of *free association* and *interpretation* of dreams. The exteriorization of women's psychological traumas typified the **Neuroses**.[667]

In the stultifying social atmosphere of early 20th century Vienna, Freud was viewed as a *dangerously rebel practitioner*—he had a hard time to make a living. Even today he still has many ardent detractors that view him as nothing more than an impostor who has been unfairly idealized in the public sphere. Frederick Crews said: "we must strip him of his image as a lone explorer possessing courageous perseverance, deductive brilliance, tragic insight, and healing power." [668]

Crews' claim that Freud had plagiarized the data of **Pierre Janet**, a French psychologist, is refuted by the fact that he had given him due credit in his early writings about the *origin of the neuroses*. Crews lambasted Freud's use of cocaine—a relatively novel drug at the time—his Victorian views of women and even his purported affair with his sister-in-law—never proven. He questioned his whining about being a "lone outcast" in his profession, dismissed because he was a Jew: as 20 % of the student body in his medical school class were Jewish (only 10% of the population professed that faith) he doubts that he was discriminated.

<u>Diary USS Awareness</u> — When jibing [669], be ready for winds slapping your face.

Crews said that Freud had no contact with patients, fabricating clinical data. Preserved in the *Library of Congress* [670], *Freud's 1886-1889 book of appointments* shows that he had treated almost 500 of them. There is no possible way that Freud could have written so exactly about women's profligate intimate ideation without patiently *listening* to all his patients and then *recording* his clinical findings. The *Sigmund Freud Collection* in that institution was digitized for online search.

We can read Freud's regular correspondence with his friends and colleagues, some of whom were openly critical of his methods; there are notes related to many of his patients, including the infamously one nicknamed as "the wolf-man." His plethora of *clinical data* and his *epistolary exchange* prove that he was engaged in patient care; an army of ghost writers could not have come up with all of it.

Deftly looting the Unconscious' vault, he spared us from plenty of penury.

Is the "whining of women" a symptom of their psychological malaise?

F. Diane Barth said there are three main reasons why people may whine:

a) They are *deeply distressed* by something that they feel powerless to change.

b) They feel both *angry and sad* and worry that it is their own fault.

c) They do not know *how to soothe* themselves. [671]

She said: "although whiners may ask for advice, what they really want is for someone to acknowledge that their feelings make sense and help them manage their sadness, anger, and guilt about the situation. Yet offering soothing or sympathy alone seldom helps them feel better, which is why therapists and friends eventually get fed up. A better way to deal with these situations is actually to combine empathy and limit-setting from the beginning." [672] It is critical to let the "whiner" know that he/she/sie is not to blame—fully at least—for the deed or situation that is hurting them. Women are prone to *owning the guilty feelings* as reactionary entities have seared the **culpability complex** in their minds—a hidden enforcement of their gallows by "internalizing" the blame. Miki Kashtan said: "The underlying principle of patriarchy…is separation and control. The separation is from self, other, life, and nature. The fundamental structures we have created over these millennia are based on dominance and submission, and the worldview we have inherited justifies them as necessary to overcome both our basic nature and 'Nature', seen as separate from us. We pride self-control and frown on 'emotionality'; we operate, organizationally, in command-and-control forms." [673]

The camouflaging of the *Emotional Frustration* in women first entails the **separation of their emotionality** to control them better, prying it out of their inner self as if it were an extraneous object. An utterly anti-natural repressive move. As Dr. López Rosetti, an Argentine physician, writer, and TV commentator, said : "we are emotional beings that have the capacity to reason…it's a choice." [674]

Who/what has been robbing women of their emotionality to coerce them?

The culprit (or rather, culprits) might not be that far away.

In the beginning of times, men and women roamed the Earth as equals.

They hunted, prepped the food, build shelters, and took care of children.

Until one day, just a few thousands of years ago, men changed the script.

Eschewing equality, they started to treat women as their subordinates.

Gerda Lerner, an American academic that pioneered the *gender studies*, argued that *there is nothing natural* about the taken for granted-male dominance in societies but it is rather the *historical result* of a socio-cultural phenomenon that might have started somewhere in the Near East in the Second Millennium B.C.[675]

The term **patriarchy** refers to *the rule of the father* [676] and derives from the Greek language; it is a mid-seventeen century term based on the Medieval Latin language that itself derived from *patriarches*, which means "ruling father." [677]

Even though it was originally used to refer to *the autocratic rule*, it begun to define the *exclusionary dominance of men* in the modern societies of the 20th century.[678]

Based on her *Columbia University*'s thesis, **Katherine Murray Millet** wrote a ground-breaking book titled *Sexual Politics* [679] in 1970, which argued that patriarchy is *any social system* where political and economic power is held by adult men; after the initial rebellion of the sixties, she started the *second wave* of feminism. Sylvia Walby defined it as: "a system of social structures and practices in which men dominate, oppress and exploit women." [680]

In 1792 **Mary Wollstonecraft** wrote *A Vindication of the Rights of Women* where she affirmed that women had a functioning brain and should be heard. [681] Bee Rowlat said: "she argued, apparently outrageously, that women were capable of reason—all they lacked was education. An early role model, she translated and reviewed essays on natural history, and she was speaking the language of human rights before the term existed. She didn't exclude men, or… anyone. Her… maxim is: 'I do not wish(women) to have power over men, but over themselves." [682]

In 1861, **Johann Jakob Bachofen**, a Swiss jurist, wrote *Das Mutterrecht* [683] where he argued that in Ancient Times, women (and the mother goddesses) had the upper hand while men had a secondary role in the society's governance. Charlotte Higgins said: "matriarchy and patriarchy were opposites: dark versus light, 'the bloody law of the earth' set against 'the pure celestial power of the sun.' His vision of the elementally opposed 'female' and 'male' has been… influential." [684]

Inspired by an annotation of the philosopher Karl Marx [685] in a book by the American anthropologist Lewis T. Morgan, **Friedrich Engels** wrote—in a single month in 1884—*The Origin of the Family, Private Property, and the State.* [686] He argued that the emergence of *the manly domination* was indissolubly related to the enshrinement of fatherhood and private property's supposedly "natural rights" in Capitalism's dawn, which had the collateral effect of women's subordination.

Wealth inheritance required a certificate of paternity. Suivez le fric.[687]

In 1938 **Virginia Woolf** wrote *Three Guineas* [688] where she pulled the debate of Patriarchy out of the high-minded realm of Political Science down to the more pedestrian one of the travails of a young woman in the rancid British society. She argued that there was a battle between "the victims of the patriarchal system and the patriarchs" who excluded them from education, professions, and politics; she argued that only through *a proper education* could women really become free.

The book's title referred to the *three money donations* she would support:

a) One guinea for a society that would end the suffering of wars.

b) One guinea to contribute to the rebuilding of a women's college.

c) One guinea for a society promoting women's insertion in the professions.

Virginia Woolf believed that there was a direct connection between the authoritarian education of men and *their aggressive capture* of public institutions with the real possibility of recurring to warfare to continue the political discussion. Given that women were usually educated with *better human values*, she believed that once they entered the civic sphere, they would renege from that moral flaw.

Silvia Walby said in *Theorizing Patriarchy* [689] : "the dual-systems theory is a synthesis of Marxist and radical feminist theory. Rather than being an exclusive focus on either capitalism or patriarchy this perspective argues that both systems are present and important in the structuring of contemporary gender relations."

Aside from the theoretic differences, most thinkers agree on the consequences.

Do the skewed power arrangements in our society affect sexual desire?

In 1952 **Frantz Fanon** [690], a psychiatrist, political philosopher and activist born in the French island of Martinique, published *Peau Noire, Masques Blanc—* one of his most important and still neglected works.[691] Based on his experience growing up as a black man in a largely white society, he exposed the *dehumanizing effects* of racism in the psyche of vulnerable communities like in colonial Algeria.

Fanon applied the *psychoanalytic theory* and *praxis* to explain the sense of *inferiority* and *dependency* that oppressed Blacks felt towards White supremacists.

In the chapter titled *Le Noir et la Psychopathologie,* he claimed that, given that Whites had seized all the socio-economic levers, Black people cannot fit into the *mold set up by the dominating classes*, which creates **a schizoid dissociation** in their psyches that equates their "blackness" with "wrongness." The perfidious association of "black" with "villainy" will be seared in the young blacks' minds, shaping their eroticism. In a parallel effect, the *social castration* of adult Blacks elicits a *compensatory fetishism* in the Whites' *alienated minds*—of all genders—who mendaciously fantasize about the "sexual prowess" of their Black victims.

When he was working in Algeria, Fanon joined the *Front de Libération National* (FLN), the anti-colonial clandestine army, and became its public figure; he contracted leukemia and died at only 37 years old in Bethesda, MD, in 1961.[692]

His critique showed the skewed rationalities to prop asymmetry of power.

A few years after Fanon's passing away, the *Feminist Movement*, influenced by the struggle of colonized people, demanded the end of the dominance of men *outside* and *inside the bedroom*. Oppressed women could not be expected to freely choose their own sexuality. The **politization of sexual desire** was inevitably afoot.

In the late 70s, **Catherine A. McKinnon** [693], professor at Harvard Law School, affirmed that the traditional psychoanalytic view of desire as *primal* and *apolitical* should be discarded to recognize its *violent nature*—pornography being its consequence. She claimed that the *sexual desire of men* (the oppressors) was tainted by the odd co-existence of *contempt* and also *arousal* of the master towards his slaves; likewise *the desire of women* (the oppressed) was tainted by a *sense of vulnerability*. At work they were judged by standards used for wives and friends; the asymmetry of power caused the subordination of female labor to male desire.[694]

For the **radical feminists** the *erotic experience* of sex was inexorably related to the imposition of *patriarchal rules of domination* on women, questioning the true value of the supposed "voluntary consent", which precluded any enjoyment. Discreetly they advocated for a *self-disciplining* of educated, emancipated women that led to a "political lesbianism" in practice, as men could not be trusted. The psychological and physical abuse of men over women in bed was reinforced by the surge of demand for pornography material in the 70s and 80s in our societies.

Would women's desire end up banished to a politically correct-Siberia?

In the late 80s and early 90s, some feminists reacted against the anti-sex view of the McKinnonites and revendicated the feminine right to enjoy sex. They said that women were *entitled to sexual desire*, including the heterosexual kind. In her book [695], **Ellen Willis** stated that the MacKinnonites not only denied the right of women to a physiological need, but they also buttressed the quaint prejudice that "men only want sex and women can only endure it." This supposedly "natural" dichotomy was used to enforce their exclusion. Willis said that *anti-porn feminism* "asked women to accept a spurious moral superiority as a substitute for sexual pleasure, and curbs on men's sexual freedom as a substitute for real power." [696]

In an excellent LRB review [697], Amia Srinivasan said that the case for the **pro-sex feminism** was helped by the concept of *intersectionality* of the defenders of women's rights. She said that: "thinking about how patriarchal oppression is inflected by race and class—patriarchy doesn't express uniformly and can't be understood independently of other systems of oppression—has made feminists reluctant to prescribe universal policies, including the universal sexual policies."

Race matters. The demand of white women for an *equal access* to the workplace might seem a little irrelevant for poor black women who have usually *worn the pants at home*, which implied toiling in a job *plus* doing the house chores. Similarly the *self-objectification* of women has a different meaning for them as the white women were considered a paradigm of beauty solely by virtue of skin color.

"La Gloria o Incoronazione di Maria Immacolata" [698], *painted in fifteen months by Giambattista Tiepolo* [699] *in 1755, glided above us.*

Distraught that the concerts of Le putte di Vivaldi [700] *were cancelled, we summoned the priest's presence in Santa Maria della Pietà* [701].

A small bald man, fully clad in black, approached us with a stern face.

-"Why did you cancel the concerts held for years ?" we politely asked.

-"Because it's not a theatre," he shot back. "It's a place of worship."

Unmasking his fallacy, the pews were set in a circle around a stage.

In the times of the Crusades, the *Venetian Senate* opened hostels where the pilgrims to the Holy Land could rest, eat, and sleep free of charge; after the Crusades ended, they turned them into refuges for the impoverished and sick. The *Ospedale di Santa Maria della Pietà* was inaugurated in the *Riva degli Schiavoni* in 1346 and later reconverted into *an orphanage for poor girls*—the city's loose sexual mores had the collateral effect of "producing" a lot of street beggars.

The teaching of the musical instruments was meant to foster their social re-insertion. The orphan girls were divided into *figlie di commun* [702] who were taught a basic curriculum and the *figlie di coro* [703] who had another one with more music. By the seventeenth century, its prestige rose to the level of a *Conservatorio* [704], formally instructing the bourgeoisie's children and offered public concerts. [705]

From 1703 to 1720, a young priest from the *Campo della Bragora* was hired as a music instructor due to his *debolezza di petto*. [706] **Antonio Vivaldi**. [707]

Irene Marone said: "The duty of *master of the concerts* in the church of the Ospedale gave him some peace of mind and the chance of composing, experiment and to create a following for his music. The fame of the Ospedale and *the putte* [708] attracted the presence of music teachers, academics, and curious persons from abroad…visitors to Venezia tell (about) the marvelous perfection of the execution, the sweetness of the voices and the harmony of the instrumentation. Amongst them, there were celebrities like De Brosses, Rousseau and Goethe." [709]

Antonio Vivaldi *premiered* many of his famous compositions in the church; after he left his post, his pupils were often hired by the royals and rich merchants who enjoyed the feminine interpretation in the safe intimacy of their salons. [710] Those concerts could not have been held without the Church hierarchy's approval, which was no less misogynist at the time—excluding women in society. Allowing the artistic expression of a few destitute girls was a "safe escape valve."

Why would then a petty-minded priest prohibit the same concerts nowadays?

What scares the likes of him at present that was not relevant in those times?

Oppressors could cloak their yoke with void gestures *pour la gallerie*.[711]

Only when women demanded control of their fates, did they freak out.

Feminism

The *Compact English Oxford Dictionary* defines **feminism** as: "a movement or theory supporting women's rights on the grounds of equality of the sexes." [712] It aims for their political, social, and economic *egalitarianism* by fighting the social stereotypes and conditioning that limit women's education and advancement. [713]

Amongst its broad range of historical presentations, we can distinguish:

a) **First wave of feminism**: it was a period of intense activism in the 19th and early 20th centuries that focused on *equal civic* and *property rights*.

b) **Second wave of feminism**: after the initial gains in civic rights, women fought for *specific issues* like family/inheritance laws, cultural access. etc.

c) **Third wave of feminism**: it was *a rebellion* against the "objectification" of women in the public sphere and it demanded more political representation.

d) **Fourth wave of feminism**: in the early 21st century, feminists' protests surged against their systematic *sexual harassment and physical abuse*. [714]

Besides the expected media vitriol and push-back of recalcitrant men, the feminist movement has been reviled for *focusing too much* on the plight of White educated middle/upper classes women in developed societies like the USA. The nefarious experiences of *poor Minority women* were effectively disregarded by women's activists until *third-wave feminists* started to use a post-structuralist interpretation of gender and sexuality, focusing more on *micropolitics*. [715]

The rich-poor divide surfaced into the open

Every day there is a newspaper or web article, a video footage in TV or a streaming piece or a live conference that deals with the dramatic issue of refugees hastily crossing national frontiers due to war, ethnic persecution, or famine. The tightening of border controls in the *European Community* did not stop the flow of migrants from Sub-Saharan Africa or Syria ready to cross the Mediterranean Sea; they are just lingering on in Libya, exposed to big harm in its protracted civil war.

We are *becoming inured to their plight* and oftentimes we do not want to see or hear any more tragic news as if the problem would magically go away someday. Sadly, that indifference extends to all those that we find in public spaces, carrying the signs of a shameful scourge, akin to the lepers of Middle Ages. **Poverty**.

In our modern societies we have developed a subconscious yet powerful *fear of the poor, of the disadvantaged, of the relegated* to the far fringes of society. It may be natural to fear poverty, but it should not "naturally" extend to its victims. We look at pictures of the destitute, but *we do not* actually see what they represent.

Almost twenty years ago, **Adela Cortina**, a Spanish philosopher that taught an Ethics Course at the *Universitat de València*, had the occurrence to create a new word to rightly identify our *dejection of the poor* in the public discourse and social media. She readily consulted a Greek dictionary and fused two different terms: *áporos* (the resourceless one) and *phobia (*aversion to*)*. **Aporophobia**. [716]

The trespassing scarecrow in the placid fields of our minds got a name.

She used it because she believed that our rejection of those refugees—often blamed on *xenophobia* and *racism* in the media—is not produced by their status of undocumented migrants but rather by their dire poverty. She said: "I believe that it's necessary to show the existence of this phenomenon, giving it a name. I find it noteworthy that we put a name to storms like hurricanes so people will take preventive measures in their presence. Therefore, the rejection of the poor, which socially relegates them, should be prevented in the same way, because it is contrary to the human dignity and a challenge to democratic institutions. It's unacceptable that a part of the population despises another one and considers it as inferior."

The *Fundación del Español Urgente*, sponsored by the *EFE* news agency and *Banco Bilbao Vizcaya* (BBVA), defined it as "the word of 2017." [717] In our modern societies—where economic opportunities abound for the well-educated and entrepreneurial segments—there is *a widening gap* in the pay scale. Richard Partington, an economist and contributor to *The Guardian*, said: "Since the 1980s, the gap between the wages for an average worker and the boss of their company has ballooned, as executive pay has boomed, and the average salaries grown by far less. The average pay ratio between FTSE 100 chief executives and their staff has gone from 20:1 in the 1980s to 129:1 in 2016. In the US, the situation is far more extreme. The bosses of the top 350 US firms earned 312 times more than their workers on average in 2017, up from around 50 to 1 in the 1980s." [718]

Has the Feminist movement fostered gender equality in our societies?

With our daughter we enjoyed watching the smartly written and better acted episodes of *Sex and the City* [719] where a gang of feisty and empowered Manhattan ladies *acted out* the more common vicissitudes of their lives in a big city. Carried over by the astutely staged narrative and filming, we laughed at the odd situations where they pulled "girl power" on social interactions. (*Samantha was our favorite*)

In her book *The Aftermath of Feminism* [720] **Angela McRobbie** had second thoughts about her previous enthusiasm for feminist symbols like that same show. She argued that unusually strong cultural forces in the social media *had undone* the progressive gains of the various feminist movements with basically two tools:

a) **Scaremongering**: the feminists are discreetly yet pervasively depicted as a bunch of radicals that are breaking the foundations of our society.

b) **Banalization**: using the rhetoric of feminism, the mendacious mandarins are claiming that women no longer need the activism of a movement.

McRobbie described the reactionary deployment of a **double entanglement** to limit the progression of Feminism: on one hand, it has been undermined through the multiple levers of popular culture and on the other hand some of its most notorious emblems were "pasteurized" to allow its digestion by the society at large. She referred to it as the *complexification of backlash* started in the 90s. [721]

Revising McRobbie's book, Natalee Tucker said: "Post-feminist ideology is an exchange process, where women gain symbolic equality as long as they do not push for full political equality. McRobbie argues that the potential of feminism to change society is great enough to cause anxiety in those (interested in) maintaining the status quo. Young women find that there are social and cultural rewards for rejecting feminism…rewards include educational and occupational gains that are exchanged for a rejection of meaningful political transformation." [722]

McRobbie said that, as a kind of *Faustian Pact* [723] between the reactionary social forces and the educated women, damaging chronic conditions like *Anxiety, Frustration and Depression* were "normalized" to pay the price of freedom. Pried out of their real social context, women's concerns were wickedly force-landed in some "individual realms" like the *personal choices* between a career and family. After listening to the feminine complaints like we have done in our career, can we believe that a good safety net is not critical for their advancement? Absolutely not.

As long as women are burdened by **the double task** of working inside and outside their homes without proper social support like affordable childcare, paid maternity leave and, foremost of all, equality in benefits and career advancement, there cannot be a real, sustained equality of the genders in our societies.

The slick Patriarchate has been playing the Great Pretender in our faces.

For the past few years, it has slyly pretended it does not exist anymore.

In 1990, **Silvia Walby** [724] exposed the critical areas of Patriarchy's yoke:

a) At home, women are still largely *doing most* of the household chores.

b) In the workplace, the right to *equal pay* has not closed the gender gap.

c) In the institutions, women are *under-represented* compared to the census.

d) Despite recent advances, there is still *physical and verbal abuse* of women.

e) In sexual matters, men and women are *judged differently* by society.

f) In the media, education and religion, the *patriarchal opinions* prevail.

A quick review of these areas shows how society is still failing our women. In 2010 Sheryl Sandberg, the then chief operating officer of *Facebook* , gave a TED about women in the boardroom, which eventually led to a book. [725] She said that women unintentionally *hold themselves back* in their professional careers and should develop more networking and mentoring options to advance in earnest.

Her approach has been criticized as *too individualistic* and not taking into account the structural rigidities sabotaging women at work; moreover, she seemed to only represent the *wealthy* and *educated* segments of society, ignoring the worse lot of much poorer women in general and Minorities like Blacks and Hispanics in particular. [726] Despite the great gains of the *Feminist* and *#MeToo* [727] movements in recent years, women are wondering if there really is not much more "in there." <u>Diary USS Awareness</u> – Like Magellan [728], we enter into the stormiest of straits.

—"Doctor...I chose to take care of the kids—it limited my career options."

Marlene X. is an intelligent and sociable middle-aged physician that made the choice several years ago to downsize her professional aspirations. She met her husband in their last year of medical school, but they took *different pathways*. He completed a tough training in Orthopedic Surgery, and she went into Dermatology. She still has second thoughts about the choice of a *more laid-back specialty*, with structured office hours and no emergencies that might collide with family time. However, she loves her family and is quite satisfied to *soldier on* for their sake; her partner's earnings far surpass hers, which funds a wealthy lifestyle for their family. Thanks to her sacrifice, her partner carries on with his *Stakhanovite* schedule [729].

In 1974 Lewis A. Coser coined the term **greedy professions** to designate those careers that entailed a *total commitment* of subordinates to work demands.[730] The unreasonable encroaching on the *time* and *availability* of workers has extended from traditional tough careers like Medicine and Law to more mundane ones in Accounting, Real Estate, and Information Technology. The digital economy has enabled many more people to *work from home* at odd hours and on weekends; as a collateral effect, employers and clients expect *quick answers*. Claire Cain Miller said: "The pressure of a round-the-clock work culture—in which people are expected to answer emails at 11 PM and take cellphone calls on Sunday morning—is particularly acute in highly skilled, highly paid (professions)."[731]

In 2015 Irene Padavic and Erin Reid studied a global consulting firm, which back then had a *majority of male partners* and a *60 hours per week-schedule*, to determine what could that institution do *to promote more women* to the top level and avoid early departure. They concluded that : "the problem was not women's competing demands but that *two orthodoxies* remain unchallenged: the necessity of long work hours and the inescapability of women's stalled advancement." [732]

Claire Miller said: "just as more women earned degrees, the jobs that require those degrees started paying disproportionately more to people with round-the-clock availability. At the same time, more highly educated women began to marry men with similar educations, and to have children. But parents can be on call at work only if someone is on call at home. Usually, that person is the mother." [733]

The **wage penalty** for combining a career and motherhood is getting bigger. Kim A. Weeden, Youngjoo Cha and Mauricio Bucca studied "how changes in the social organization and compensation of work hours over the last three decades are associated with changes in wages differentials among fathers, mothers, childless women and childless men." [734] They found that similar people with a 50 hours per week-schedule *earn 8% more per hour* than those working a 35-49 hours-schedule. In our modern economies, many workers are supposed to work long hours while they are in the office and then continue at home— a never ending on call schedule. <u>Diary USS Awareness</u> – In these waters, all hands must be on deck. Right now.

—"Doctor…It's tough out there…Got to hold the line and protect our kids."

Laura X. is an attractive, clever, and charming middle-aged lady that we had treated for Chronic Migraines, which was psychosomatic in origin; she confided to us her disappointment at her partner's many flings and her mounting resentment. She knew. And he knew that she did. Hypocrisy and conjugal distancing conflated.

He was a rich banker—first at a brokerage house and then at the bank that took over it in the financial crisis of 2007. She was ready to ask him for a divorce, but she stood down; they dug *opposite trenches* to wait their *war of attrition* out. Their bond based on **mutual Hate** turned out to be much *more stable* than when they dabbled with **romantic Love**. Transactional. Less efforts. Less unpredictable.

When you "use people", you are less exposed to their emotional vagaries.

In 1933, James Truslow Adams coined the term **American Dream** that he defined as: "the dream of a land in which life should be better and richer and fuller for everyone, with opportunity for each according to ability or achievement." [735] For all those like us—immigrants to this merit-based land of opportunities—that have toiled tirelessly to create a family and build a career here, *it still lives on*. However, many segments of the American society have been feeling progressively disenfranchised for cultural, social, and economic reasons, in the past few decades; increasingly we are seeing explicit signs of cynicism and disbelief in the street.

Is there a quantified parameter for this valetudinarian's general attitude?

Raj Chetty et al. studied the anonymous data from millions of tax records spanning five decades in the USA. They found that: "rates of absolute mobility have fallen from approximately 90% for children born in 1940 to 50% for children born in the 1980s. The result that absolute mobility has fallen sharply over the past half century is robust to the choice of price deflator, the definition of income, and accounting for taxes and transfers." [736] By solely raising the economic growth, as measured by the *Gross Domestic Product* (GDP), the *absolute mobility of the 1940s* might not be emulated; they said that the more equal distribution of the 1940s could only restore 70% of the lost social mobility. They also said that: "reviving the 'American Dream' of high rates of absolute mobility would require economic growth that is spread more broadly across the income distribution." [737]

This blatant **societal inequality** explains the ever-growing mistrust of the American population for their institutions, as duly expressed in recent polling. [738] In our digitalized economies, the admission to prestigious colleges in order to get a solid education constitutes a *reliable pathway* for good jobs and social standing. [739] Claire Cain Miller said: "Parenthood in the United States has become much more demanding than it used to be. Over just a couple of generations, parents have greatly increased the amount of time, attention, and money they put into raising children. Mothers who juggle jobs outside the home spend just as much time tending their children as stay-at-home mothers did in the 1970s." [740]

Educated working women are at a big crossroads in our modern societies.

Except for a few ones, they have competing demands at home and work.

At work, the need to clock in an unusual number of hours has skyrocketed.

At home, the demand of parenting entails spending more time and funds.

Except for the few financially endowed ones that can hire help or those who have a fully cooperating partner that shares the household tasks equally, they must juggle the *competing*—and oftentimes *opposing*—demands on their time. In the case of the USA, the lack of *proper childcare, maternity leave,* and *adequate benefits* for their families, can adversely influence women's performances.

The deployment of a galling **gatttopardismo** [741] by the mutating patriarchal institutions—tacitly allowing socio-political reforms that are more spurious than substantial—seeks to buffer the public backlash by *shifting the attention* elsewhere. Moreover, they often whip up the *natural friction* between the genders by solely ascribing the plight of women to a collateral effect from the acts of " just a few bad men (sic)." Francesco Borgonovo said that some exalted feminists have picked up that *faux message* focusing on purely individual misdeeds to demand the eviction of men from the civic space; he disparagingly said that the admirers of *the vagina monologues* [742] were promoting an elitist coup d'état for a women's elite. [743]

Some of that discourse's asperity has zeroed in on a troubling target.

Contrary to some entrenched prejudice, the **Transgender** population is not uniform, being varied in its socio-economic, cultural, and sexual features; their common denomination might be, alas, the *raw discrimination* they must face. [744] The Transgender community can be divided in the following major categories:

a) People that tolerate gender incongruence without transitioning.

b) Others transitioning without any gender-affirming healthcare.

c) Others that, without having gender identity disorders or gender dysphoria, do not accept a simple binary system to identify their identities. [745]

Oftentimes the Transgender also belong to a **Minority** like Blacks or Hispanics, which worsens their access to care services for a *safe transitioning*. A *NIH* report said: "Unlike the Europeans that invaded the North American continent, the Native peoples of what is now called the United States of America did not confound the 'gender identity' with the 'sexual orientation.' The presence of multiple-gender individuals was an accepted and even revered fact in their communities. They were respected as visionaries, healers, medicine people and caregivers." [746]

The Native American people divided the sexual genders into four categories: *feminine woman, masculine woman, feminine man,* and *masculine man.*[747] Individuals can have more than one tendency coexisting inside them. **Two-Spirit**.

The obtuse Patriarchal discourse strives to smudge that distinction.

Representative David Cicilline—Democrat, Rhode Island—et al. introduced a bill called *H.H.2282-Equality Act* in the *115ᵗʰ Congress* (2017-2018) [748] that would ban any kind of discrimination due to sexual orientation and gender identity.

On January 28, 2019, the *Heritage Foundation* [749]—the conservative think-thank based in Washington, D.C.—hosted a panel discussion titled "The Inequality of the Equality Act: Concerns from the Left", which had three women from the *Women's Liberation Front* (WoLF) [750], a radicalized feminist group. The four panelists—two were Trans—voiced their concerns that gender identification *might supplant* the sexual one as the legal basis, endangering women and children. [751]

The *Southern Poverty Law Center* issued a report of the 2017 meeting of the *Family Research Council* [752] that said: "a trend emerged during the session, as various speakers wrapped their opposition to nondiscrimination measures in rhetoric passing as progressive transgender rights were depicted as anti-feminist, hostile to minorities and even disrespectful to LGB individuals. This seems to be part of a larger strategy, meant to weaken (trans) rights advocates by attempting to separate them from the allies, feminists and LGBT rights advocates." [753]

On June 15, 2020, the United States Supreme Court ruled that the language of the Civil Rights Act of 1964, which prohibits sex discrimination, also applies to discrimination based on *sexual orientation and gender identity*. Protecting Gay and Transgender workers gave the movement for L.G.B.T rights a big victory. [754]

"When would I have written it, in what year, at what time of the day, in what house? I do not know anymore.

What is certain, evident, is that this paragraph, I do not have the impression of having it written during the waiting time for Robert L.

I do not know what day it was anymore—if it was a day in April or it was a day in May—but one morning at eleven the telephone rang."

"Listen carefully, Robert is alive." [755]

Marguerite Duras [756], a French writer that won the *Prix Goncourt* in 1984 for *L'Amant* [757]– a saucy tale of her liaison with an older married man as a teenager in Indochina—found two long forgotten notebooks in a drawer. It was some kind of *personal journal* she had used right before the end of World War II ; in it she had duly recorded her tumultuous personal feelings after her partner, Robert Antelme, had been arrested by the Gestapo in 1944. He was transferred as a political prisoner to Germany but was freed.[758] That text had been re-written several times as she tried to express the *basculages emotionnels* [759] she had to endure while anxiously waiting for his return.

The women in our lives often spend a lot of time waiting for us.

Alas, we are not always aware of it, let alone honor the devotion.

On Saturday nights, my brother Gustavo and I went to the IASA [760] dances. The action started at midnight and lasted until the next day's wee hours. On our way home we stopped at a bakery for freshly baked croissants. When our mother Gladys heard the noise of the front gate opening up, she got out of bed and rushed out to open the house door for us. Every time. She then skedaddled to the kitchen to fix a delicious café au lait for us. Still yawning, she stoically listened to our saucy tales, waiting for the end. Then we hit the bed and did not wake up until she summoned us for lunch.

We were blessed with parents and grandparents that patiently waited for us ; we have tried to bequeath that precious endowment to our children.

A nugget of Wisdom. After a long day at the office, you go home. Beware. Your wife had warned you that she would be cooking a nice pasta. As usual, you could not make it on time and her dish went impossibly cold.

Learning from past snafus, you showed up with an ace up your sleeve. -"Hi," you say, skimming her frigid left cheek. "Sorry, dear, but had to stop at *Giorgio's* for this fab *olive oil with herbs* to sauté the pasta on a skillet." (Jorge, the Puerto Rican bodega's owner, had been speedily re-christened)

-"Perfect," she blurts out, jumping to hug her hero. *Full hand.*

<u>Diary USS Awareness</u> – Snubbing her "little details" is foolish.

What kind of vilifying collective delirium has gripped Mankind for ages?

If there is a lesson that we might infer from Lord Ganesh's story is that there is nothing biological or natural—let alone inevitable—about the Patriarchate's rule. **Hinduism** is the *only major civilization* that has arrived almost unscathed through thousands of years of History to our times, despite many foreign occupations.[761] Anointed as his mother's protector, Ganesh stood firm against Lord Shiva; when Parvati found out about his slaying, she ordered Shiva to promptly redress his act. What better picture of a place where women had the upper hand? **A matriarchate**.

There cannot be real reform of society until we, men, stop being a hurdle in women's paths and become their **Vegan Harta factor**—*the remover of obstacles*. Despite the fact that women have made big strides in our civic spaces, there is still a reactionary clique of men that wants to absurdly turn back the wheels of History. Moreover, the *confused* and *confounding* discourse in the media, which seeks to dissipate the impetus of women's protest *by parceling* it into isolated complaints against individual misdeeds and *dismissing* them as passing flare-ups, must cease. Fed up with discrimination, a Transgender friend asked us what *sie* should do…

With arms inter-locked, bracing the winterly winds whipping our faces,

we advanced down General Flores Avenue [762] towards the Police line-up.

Taunting us with the tools of brute force, they were still at a disadvantage.

Right marched in our first row. ¡El pueblo unido jamás será vencido [763]!

Epilogue – What do women really want?

"La grande ambition des femmes c'est d'inspirer l'amour" [764]

Jean Baptiste de Poquelin (Molière)

Her father's alcoholism and bad decisions gave her a miserly childhood.

When she wrote her first poem at 12, it was centered on life's darkness.

When her mother read it, she strongly scolded her for her pessimism.

After years of financial penury, love deceptions and a cancer diagnosis,

she plunged into the cold waters of the South Atlantic. She was right.[765]

Alfonsina Storni was born in Sala Capriasca, Switzerland, on May 29th, 1892, and passed away in Mar del Plata, Argentina, on October 25th, 1938. Her parents were Swiss citizens of *Italian heritage* who temporarily relocated there to recover from her father's business failure in San Juan, Argentina. Her mother was a schoolteacher who saw such a potential in her that she decided to selectively, carefully school her, as opposed to her sons; she became a voracious reader. [766]

Eventually they re-settled back to Rosario, Argentina, where she had to toil hard in her father's bar; after he passed away in 1906, she moved to Coronda to study for a *rural teacher diploma*, working in odd jobs to finish her studies. [767]

After graduating from school, she briefly worked as a teacher in a rural school but had to quit her job due to a *nervous breakdown*; she published her first poems in *Mundo Rosarino* and *Monos y Monadas*.[768] Seeking anonymity, she moved to Buenos Aires in 1912, where she fell in love with a man 24 years older, married and a politician; at 20 years old, she gave birth to a son, Alejandro. [769]

Despite being **a poor single mother** without any contacts and not endowed with the attributes for *likeability* of the times, she published her first book in 1916. In her publications, she defiantly rebelled against the stereotyping of women that dismissed their intellectual capacity to ostracize and control them. Her poem *Tú me quieres blanca* [770] shows her disgust at the Hispanic men fondness for a fair skin color; her poem *Hombre pequeñito* [771] chastises men for women's angst. [772] With a pseudonym, she started to write articles for the daily *La Nación*; she joined a group of artists that met in the resto *La Peña* where she recited her poems. In 1920 she won the *first prize* of the *Premio Municipal de Poesía* [773] and obtained a teaching job in the prestigious *Colegio Nacional de Música y Declamación*.

When she was 46 years old, her solitude and the suicide of her writer-friend Horacio Quiroga [774], worsened her depression and turned her into a misanthrope. After an initial surgery for breast cancer, she refused another one for metastases. On October 20, 1938, she wrote *Me voy a dormir* [775] and sent it for publication.

In the wee hours of the 25th, she walked into the Sea and Posterity.

Alfonsina's tragic, short life epitomizes the drama for independent women. Early in childhood and adolescence, she had to *work hard* in her father's business, instead of enjoying the relaxed company of her playmates, nurtured by her family. However, she had the providential help of her mother who made sure she got a good education, despite *all the obstacles* thrown at her by her social environment.

As a young woman, she had to suffer the *societal opprobrium* due to her choice to carry an unwanted pregnancy to term without any kind of manly support. She worked in droning bureaucratic jobs *to sustain* her writing career in earnest. In spite of these odds, she was able to publish her uniquely fierce *feminist prose*. She never wavered from her commitment for women's equality in Argentine society.

Julieta Lanteri—another *brave Italian American woman* who immigrated to Argentina as a child—became *the first woman* to vote in a general election in South America; after getting a special court injunction, she cast her vote in the church of *San Juan* on November 28, 1911, watched by the hoodwinked men. [776] Like Alfonsina, Julieta was *demeaned* in her lifetime and afterwards *ignored* by the "official records" for having had the temerity of defying the power structure.[777]

Reneged by her family as *shameful*, dismissed by her men as *unattractive*, abandoned by her physicians as *terminal*, she had an *incrocio* [778] of EF causation. Before leaving, she tendered some sweet words that are still resonating in our ears.

She lived and died true to herself. An uncompromising Feminist.

Giuseppa Garbarino did not go footling around in our family's vineyard.

Waking up at dawn, the little woman took care of the winery's catering.

Precisely at noon, she struck a little bell at the entrance of the mess hall.

All those working in the field looked up and abruptly stopped their tasks.

Like ducklings, her husband, sons, and peons[779] lined up and marched on.

They sat at the table where the soups, entrées and desserts were laid out.

Resolutely she stepped up to the table and slammed a bottle of wine on it.

With her arms folded in front of her chest, she backtracked to watch them.

Nobody—not even her husband Beppe—ever dared to ask for more wine.

In a place filled with bottles of many varietals, they could only have one.

As a child, our mother Gladys [780] watched *la Nonna* [781] in her daily routine and she relayed that story to us to convey the fierce determination of that woman. In fact, considering that our mother had the middle name of *Josefa*[782] in her honor, every March the 19th—the day of Saint Joseph—her grandfather *Beppe* [783] hosted a gathering with hot chocolate made from imported Swiss Meunier bars and pastries. Longing for those times, our dear mother's voice was muffled by the emotion when she recalled them, often in the midst of hard times we went through later on. Precisely in that environment, we grew up happily safe from the menacing world.

A protective Matriarchate where Women were firmly in charge.

My first foray outside the Matriarchate did not go well—to say the least.

My mother neatly groomed me to start my first day in the Lycée Français.

In a sunny day of March 1960, we went down to the building's entrance.

With combed hair and a blue jacket with the school's insignia, I felt fine.

The bus was supposed to pick me up at noon sharp to take me to school.

After waiting in vain for more than hour, we gave up, totally frustrated.

My dear mother took my clothes off and readied me for a comforting nap.

Only later that day, our parents finally found out what had really happened.

The commercial drivers' union (run by men) decided to suddenly strike.

The school administration (run by men) did not bother to warn the parents.

TV and radio outlets (run by men) did not quickly inform the population.

The government watchdog agency (run by men) did not fine the culprits.

After spending the first years of our lives in that nurturing matriarchate, we were violently thrust into another world—cold, chaotic, competitive. The more we learned about a society imperviously run by men, the less we liked it. Moreover, we could not grasp why the creatures that gave us all dear life—our women—were often dismissively treated in public spaces as a bunch of dimwits and charlatans. We began to see how the *Emotional Frustration* heaped on them was hurting them.

In honor of the great women that molded us, we are writing this book.

The miserly young laborer had to cross a distant bridge in central China. On his way to his indentured job in a farm belonging to a rich mandarin, he often came across an old Kung Fu priest doing his morning exercises. One day he mustered the strength to ask: "Master, can you teach me?" Pitying his destitute looks, the priest said: "Fine. Come back tomorrow." The next morning, the young laborer walked up to the exercising priest.

-"No, it's too late," the old man said. "You have to come back earlier."

Disappointed but determined, he showed up at dawn the following day.

-"No, too late already," the cantankerous priest said. "Come tomorrow."

Befuddled but not scared by his pretense, the lad daringly doubled down. Before sunset he arrived at the bridge to set up a little tent to sleep inside. At early dawn, he was abruptly awakened by the priest's hoarse voice.

-"Fine. Now we can start. Let's have breakfast before our first class." [784]

One of the least discussed but greatly held beliefs of women is that men do not try hard enough to, not only to seduce them, but also to understand their angst. If we are seriously committed to making a difference in the life of a loved woman, we must try again… and again… and again. Without ever wavering in our resolve.

Go camp out in the bridge spanning from your reality into her spirituality.

We have discussed the causes of *Emotional Frustration* in these realms: the *sex life*, *family relationships*, *finances*, *workplace,* and *social interactions*. Each woman might feel *varying degrees* of serious frustration in any one of these dimensions, with a continuous reshaping via *expansion* or *shrinking* over time. Unwary actors might be tempted to, without trying hard, *throw the towel in.* [785]

If we are serious about helping a woman, we must become amateur sleuths. First *observe* her motion, *listen* to her words, and *try to feel* her inner frustration. Then slowly recreate **a composite holographic picture** of her *esprit d'âme*. Finally sit down with her to *tinker together around* various alternative screens. Previous experience is *not a must*, and it might be a hindrance for new discoveries. With her precious help—they are usually eager to offer you the info to succeed— you will build a dynamic view of the frustrating issue(s), including the coordinates. Invite her to *review your final cut* to make the last-minute revisions to the editing. Once you agree as to *the course of action*, do not procrastinate for a single second. Like Captain Kirk, commander of the *USS Enterprise* [786], press the intercom hard:

—"S*cotty, they're targeting the Enterprise…Give me more warp power."*

A nugget of Wisdom. You might not have the information for a full picture. You might commit one mistake or two by over or under-emphasizing a feature. However, what you cannot do, once you pinpoint why she suffers, is to waste time.

Make haste as if the whole Klingon armada were hot on your tail.

What piece of advice should we give to emotionally frustrated women?

We humbly believe that they should address the following major issues:

a) **Grant a little more patience to the men in your lives**. We hear you… If there is a common feature of the myriad stories we shared with you is the enormous amount of *patience* that most women have had with men. May we dare to respectfully remind you, ladies, that *Mother Nature* skimpily pasted our *limited* manly brains with much less *operating juice* than she dispensed on you. Please try to redress our bad deeds—except the most glaring cases of abuse—with *gentle coaching*. Do not overload our *bare minimum brain circuitry*, lest you risk a fatal burn-out.

<u>Diary USS Awareness</u> – Disclose your suzerainty [787] by flying her colors.

b) **Do not engage in spurious fights with strawman-woman targets**. One of the worst collateral effects of Radical Feminism has been the targeting of just individual men as the sole culprits of their social subordination. Aside from the most egregious cases of abuse, women must proselytize to enlighten manly minds; we should be fighting together for real justice. Moreover, they should not pay heed to the dubious calls to start irksome fights with the LGBT communities, wasting precious time and resources.

Deflecting the protest's thrust is a favorite ploy of any Tyranny.

c) **Do not delude yourselves about the demise of the Patriarchate**. One of the most perplexing residual effects of the spate of feminist rebuttal of the abuse of women in the public space has been the *Pyrrhic victory* [788] they ended up with, after the fickle media attention had turned elsewhere. Even though the treatment of women improved in workplaces and other public spaces, there has been *a discreet yet powerful sidelining* of them; many men, fearful that they might be unfairly accused, have stopped the necessary mentoring process of the young recruits in their companies.

Rachel Cooke said: "the #MeToo movement… has had a mixed effect on the world of advertising. People are certainly more aware and increasingly mobilized…But this doesn't mean that most sexual harassment has gone away—or that its victims are finding it any easier to report." [789] Warring men and women have retreated to separate bivouacs.

We remember one of our playmates from childhood's football matches. A stout little guy who could not run after the ball, let alone dribble others. If he wanted to play, he was always forcibly assigned to the goalpost. He brought along a good ball, as he seemed to be from a wealthy family. Everything went fine until they scored a goal past him, which he resented. Instead of protesting to the referee, he picked up the ball and went home.

Like that little boy, the Patriarchate acts as the final arbiter of the game.

Cloaking itself with hypocritical grandstanding, its act became refined.

Insidiously, it slices one pound of flesh off from the feminine frustration.

It "sanitizes" it out of its gaminess to make it palatable for the big public.

Then, it rolls it through the spicy batter of "politically correct" messages.

After a brief sautéing, it is callously promoted as the "healthier choice."

In our times of a growing citizenry's empowerment enabled by the digital media, we are becoming inured to *the duplicitous progression* of the social inequality. The arbiters of the social media present us with a skillfully skewed version of reality when we access our small screens—the ultimate deception of the *1984* [790] script.

Instead of tagging trends , why don't we welcome silence and meditation?

When women take their eyes off the screens, they find out that they are not alone. Their fathers, brothers, husbands, boyfriends, sons, friends, are looking at them; aware that something is terribly amiss in the lives of their dearest, most will help. Women and men must build *a more harmonious*, less confrontational society. By sharing their experiences and concerns, women will surely steel our wobbly wills. Critical issues like designing better and more equitable access to care services will need the cooperative work of many segments of our societies over the long-term.

In uncertain times, women can regal our pathways with their luminosity.

"Nothing happens. Nobody comes, nobody goes. It's awful."
En attendant Godot. Samuel Beckett

One of the most troubling plays in modern theatre centers around two "big losers" called Vladimir and Estragon waiting for the arrival of a mysterious Godot, who keeps sending messages that he will show up, but never actually does. They are two human beings that *do not know* why they are living in the first place; this is *a paining question* that has been popping up again and again during this pandemic.

Waiting for Godot [791] was initially published in French by Samuel Beckett in 1952 and became the first success of the *Theatre of the Absurd*; some critics have interpreted it as a product of *Existentialism* that proclaimed that life had no rational meaning and that we should not waste time trying to find any, even with religions. For all their miserable existence, the two central characters—usually represented as tramps—cling to the assumption that Godot—the *representation of God* or other altruistic meaning of life—will eventually appear and give answers. At the end of the play, dismissing its asphyxiatingly nihilistic message, many of us nonetheless can spiritually identify with the two hobos who finally rose above their banality.

In these times of *Social Isolation*, the hitherto boisterous venues of Life—the streets, the public transportation, the work offices—have *been deserted* of all the varied sounds from the human presence —their conversations, their laughs, their exclamations. Seizing the moment, **Silence** has abruptly filled those spaces.

However, there are interlopers from our past that dare to show up uninvited. Even though we might be busy during the "staying at home" mandate working at a distance, doing homely duties, parenting tasks, neglected tasks/repairs, etc., there is always a critical moment when the abetting "nothingness" invites **memories** that for some clear or even intriguing reasons, we often store in the back of our minds.

A few days ago, I suddenly stopped typing on this laptop because one of the memories from the most painful day of my life—when my mother Gladys had passed away and we were in her wake—brutally came crashing down on me. Right before the time to close her casket came, we were asked to leave the room. Being the last one to exit, I had a change of heart halfway down the hallway. I returned and gently leaned over my dear Mommy to kiss her saintly forehead. "Hasta luego, Mamá" [792]*, I murmured... No way was I saying goodbye to her.*

We had the feeling that she was rightfully, peacefully entering into another world, after working and, being a uniquely empathic person, suffering so much for us.

We must push back against the paralyzing inertia that may be poisoning our spirits with the renewed expressions of humanly endeavor filled with affection and hope.

Women have always been of paramount importance to carry out this task.

Let us recognize their past, present, and future help by respecting them.

"There is always some madness in love.

But there is also always some reason in love."

Thus spoke Zarathustra. Friedrich Nietzsche [793]

In Sweden—the land where citizens with generous social benefits enjoy the "best living standards" in the planet—there is a longstanding tradition of *labor flexibility* and *parental benefits* to allow for a work-life balance. But a report from the *Swedish Social Insurance Agency* [794] showed that the incidence of chronic stress-related conditions, including burnout, increased. Maddy Savage said: "Rates have shifted dramatically among young workers, with cases up by 144% for 25-29-year-olds since 2013. Women are more likely than men to be sick off exhaustion—experts say women still spend more time on household chores…and are over-represented in stressful, care-based jobs such as nursing and social work." [795]

Pia Webb, a Swedish *life and career coach*, said that their paradoxical stress, even though they work less, might be related to the fact that they are bad at "doing nothing"; there is a strong social pressure to dedicate time in "being fit, being busy and looking perfect", which has recently skyrocketed. [796] Dr. Marie Asberg, a Professor of Psychiatry at the *Karolinska Institute*, said: "failure to schedule proper relaxation time is the most crucial factor…the brain cannot differentiate between employment and other work-like tasks in your spare time, having a competitive hobby, or staying up late to ensure your social media profile is up-to-date." [797]

That *BBC Worklife* report said that Sweden is one of the more *individualistic* and *secular* societies in the whole Western Hemisphere—where young people are supposed to strike it on their own early and not expect any family support. The lack of family life means that young people are *isolated* in their homes, without family members to check on them and detect the early signs of stress/burnout.[798]

What is our parting piece of advice before we ride away into the sunset?

We believe that modern women should learn **how to relax** a little bit better. The compounding of systematic labor discrimination and political disenfranchising by the Patriarchal institutions understandably got them out *en pied de guerre*.[799]

Does the idea of pausing from the fixed fighting mode sound "insane"?

Of course it does, even bordering on the insult. But do not get us wrong.

There are many men ready to shoulder your burden of fighting for progress. You should be able *to differentiate* their honest support from any token flattering of the Johnny-come-lately "defenders" of women's rights that seek to mollify you.

Close that laptop. Silence that phone. Share a cup of tea with loved ones. Those who love you do not need to see you as "perfect." Just to see you around. You are the ones that console us, cheer us, heal us, love us, and finally, mourn us. <u>Diary USS Awareness</u> – You should enter the calm waters of the Pacific— What? The ship is capsizing with the TMI [800] storm? DROP A LIFEBOAT. MAYDAY.

—"Doctor…Never had so many fab orgasms—not going back to *same old*."

Wanda X. is a lovely middle-aged entrepreneur that had the misfortune of being surprised by the "staying at home" order in a business trip to a distant state. Fortunately, she had an old friend from college that gladly welcomed her to bunk. Unlike her, she was single and childless, which gave her a lot more sexual leeway.

One of the little perks of her friend's lifestyle is to unabashedly recur to the use of *a vibrator* when she felt the irrepressible urge to satisfy her sexual desire. Reluctant at first, Wanda X. eventually relented, after a month of seclusion. Slowly she learnt how to handle it and at the same time learn more about her sexuality. When she would be finally able to return to her home, she is planning to sit down for a serious discussion with her partner. She will tell him that she is tired of her culturally assigned role of a **passive giver of love** and that she wants the urgent addition of the role of **active demander of love**. *Clear as a spring brook can be.*

The emotional toss-up of Social Isolation has tumbled many certainties.

One of the most disregarded aspects of the *Social Isolation* that we have all been enduring for almost one year already is its *serious emotional toll* on us. Like the young women and men that went into isolation in a Florentine villa in the *Decameron*, those coming out of seclusion will not be the same ones that went in. There will be *multiple changes* in our societies, especially for labor opportunities.

Alea jacta est! [801]

The economic analysts are already predicting that, besides the contraction of consumer spending due to loss of jobs, there will be a **two-speed labor market**. On one hand there will be persons that can work at a distance, with little physical contact. But on the other hand, there will be those that will be dangerously exposed to contagion. This will bring a generalized **angry mood in the street** like we have never witnessed before. No longer will we be able to take for granted the barista's familiarity when we arrive at our *Starbucks*; she might be too worried about being infected while mulling about her son's day care. After her shift is over, she might be too stressed out to hang out with her girlfriends. A self-sustaining vicious circle.

"I'masinglemomworkinglongshiftsfortheminimunwagewithsofewbreaksthatsometimesialmostpeeinmypantsworriedthatmysonreturnshomewithoutabulletinhisbackcourtseyofacrazycopthatdunnolikehisskincolourandyouexpectmetosmileaboutwhatcom'ongrabyourlatteandtakeahikebusterbeforeigobananasnextcustomer."

On May 8, 2020, the U.S. Department of Labor issued its monthly report [802], which showed that the **unemployment rate** jumped to a staggering *14.7%* in April, its highest level since the Great Depression of the 1930s; it said that *20.5 million people* had suddenly lost their jobs due to the country's lockdown, wiping the past decade's gains. A detailed analysis of those that are *working part-time* and those *off the books* showed that the unemployment rate *might even be higher*; the coming tightening of federal/state budgets will *inevitably furlough* more people.

In the previous *recession of 2007-2009*, the majority of lost jobs belonged to men, as the *construction and manufacturing sectors* ground to a halt; but this time the real losers *are often women* as millions of their positions as clerks, secretaries, hairdressers, health care aides, travel consultants, stewardesses, airplane and ship chandlers, restaurant servers and cashiers, dry cleaning workers, etc., evaporate.

Once the lockdown is levied, many of the once thriving small businesses that *used to predominantly employ women* will be gone. And there will be hardly any credit for entrepreneurial initiatives as the banks will be reluctant to lend. Not only did women hold most of the jobs of *Education* and *Health Care* —the hardest hit economic sectors—but they were *also furloughed* in greater numbers than men.

In a *Washington Post* article [803], Heather Long and Andrew Van Dam said: "Before the pandemic, women held 77% of the jobs in education and health services, but they account for 83% of the jobs lost in those sectors…Women made up less than half of the retail trade workforce, but they experienced 61% of the retail job losses. Many of these women held some of the lowest-paid jobs." A large proportion of them are single parents of the **Latino** and **Black** Minority groups.

These disadvantaged single women, *lacking adequate social/family support*, rely on their children's school services for their care, instruction, and meals. If they cannot take their kids to school, they will not be able to resume their former duties.

The same *chronic anxieties* pervading the workplaces may foster a creeping *loss of libido and eroticism* in many blue collars' bedrooms. On the other hand, women with a "hot" privileged spot in the upcoming **New World Order** will be less amenable to passivity, demanding *equal rights* inside and outside the bedroom. Moreover, after months of this *pandemic* and its *Social Isolation*, our *nerves are so frayed* that we are seeing in our offices a rising number of patients sick with a *depression* associated with *high anxiety*—the **Post Covid 19 Anxiety Syndrome**.

Has my world become dangerous? Will I keep my job? Will I find a partner? Can I safely touch this person? Did I clean my groceries carefully enough?

Another major collateral effect is the increased *amount of time* we are spending with our families at home—a positive development. With the multiple distractions of modern life reduced to a minimum—save the necessary outings for grocery and meds shopping—we are sharing many more hours inside our homes, including *cooking together* with our children—a salutary development.

Preliminary data from a survey of 1060 American parents in mixed-gender marriages done in April 2020 showed that 45% of fathers *spent more time* taking care of children under 6 years of age than they did before. This study showed that 43% of fathers reported pitching in more with care of older children, and 42% reported an overall increase in housework time. Surveyed women claimed that the actual percentage of helping partners was much lower—between 20 and 34%. [804]

The misanthropic writer woke up well past four o'clock in the afternoon.

Precisely at that moment, he rang his bell twice and a woman stepped in.

She served him two large bowls of café au lait and two big croissants.

In his darkened room, Marcel Proust could count on his guardian angel.

She waited for him to return in the wee hours and opened the front door.

She became a "nocturnal animal" to match his bizarre circadian rhythm.

She picked up the special meals he ordered from the Ritz hotel's kitchen.

And if he fancied a beer at odd hours, she had the keys to enter the place.

If he wanted to talk, she would sit down and mutate into an "eager ear."

Proust wrote on school notebooks and stacked them up on his nightstand.

Every morning she picked up his nighttime production and delivered it.

He suggested Alexandre Dumas's books, but she refused to read Balzac.

Both devoid of family and friends in Paris, they were default soul mates.

He foretold that, at his final hour, she would be the one to close his eyes.

After he passed away, she guarded Proust's meshed memory and myth.

But disgusted with the rubbish written about him, she broke her silence.

In the 70s she dictated seventy hours to Georges Belmont, a journalist.[805]

Céleste Albaret protected Proust's reputation until the end of her days.[806]

In the program *Le mag de l'été* [807] of *Radio France Inter*, we casually heard a 1951 recording of Jean Cocteau, the French playwright [808], where he said that he visited Marcel Proust's apartment in Boulevard Hausmann after World War I. He confirmed that it was *always dark,* and that he *stayed in bed* most of the day, nursed by Céleste; as he had some bouts of *Bronchial Asthma*, the windows were tightly shut to block the entry of street allergens . He saw the huge pile of blank notebooks on the right hand-nightstand and the filled ones in the left hand-one. [809]

When we studied Proust's works in the *Alliance Française*, we pictured him as a fancy member of the landed gentry, leisurely lounging on a field of blooming flowers, sharing a picnic with delicately blushing ladies holding cute parasols; we would have never imagined him as a sickly recluse in that creepy dark dwelling.

How could the official story of this great writer miss that "little detail"?

The unyielding devotion of Céleste pulled that amazing *tour de force* on us. She protected him during his last years and afterwards shrouded herself in silence, only breaking it when she felt it was time to get the record straight. Total devotion.

A nugget of Wisdom. After decades of patiently listening to women's complaints , we advise you to take a long look at the great women in your life.

Then dive into your mind to recap bright and dark moments with them.

Diary USS Awareness – Any news from the search? What? Found those two "deplorables" [810] working as lifeguards in Sydney's *Bondi Beach* ? Shark-free.

« Séduire c'est distraire [811] » Michel Piccoli

On May 12th, 2020, Michel Piccoli—one of the greatest French film and theatre actors—passed away at 94 years old in the arms of Ludivine, his third wife, and accompanied by Inord and Missia, his young children. In an interview about his prolific and sophisticated acting career, Michel Piccoli reflected on it like this:

"*I'm a great professional, but I've kept an amateur, inquisitive heart.*" [812]

In a dedicated program of *L'heure Bleu*—a lush cultural space from *Radio France Inter*—we listened when a reporter asked him what his secret had been for seducing so *many beautiful women* personally and *a great audience* professionally. He responded that in order to seduce people, you must *first pay attention* to their little details and then use that information to launch *a diversionary movement* to derail their attention from their pre-ordained Conscious and Unconscious tracks.

We must remember that our women are usually extremely focused, not only on their personal problems, but also in all questions pertaining to their loved ones. That takes a lot of commitment, efforts, analyses, physical work, anxiety, and fear. Hardly ever will they be unable to see the whole forest by fixing on a single tree. Hardly ever will they give up looking for the solution to a challenging dilemma. Hardly ever will they lack the steely disposition to fight for their loved ones' sake.

How should we "distract" them, so they feel less Emotional Frustration?

In fact, to accomplish that feat, we must eliminate some bad distractions.

If we want them not to be distracted by their disgusting social stereotypes,

then we must fight on for a total reconsideration of our civic interactions.

If we want them not to be distracted by the gender inequality in benefits,

then we must demand a just compensation inside and outside their homes.

If we want them not to be distracted by the disgusting lack of childcare,

then we must mobilize for a much better re-distribution of social wealth.

If we want them not to be distracted by the appalling legacies of racism,

then we must override the toxic environmental primes and use better cues.

If we want them not to be distracted by the brutalizing family obligations,

then we must pick up more slack at home with child rearing and hygiene,

If we want them not to be distracted when we are ready for ardent love,

then we must sit down with them to discuss any aspect of our bonding.

If we want them not to be distracted by the foolishness of our tantrums,

then we must shoulder our fairer load at home and outside with a smile.

Woolley and Malone found that the more women a group has, the higher the group's *collective intelligence,* fostered by their much higher *social sensitivity.*[813] Alice Eagly proposed that women, relying on their much stronger *interdependence skills,* display a more *democratic and participatory* style of management, which she dubbed as **transformational**. In contrast men, relying on their stronger *independence skills*, have a more *command and control* style, which she called **transactional.** [814] Eagly et al. believe that, contrary to the punitive nature of men's transactional approach, the transformational leadership of women in the workplace inspire their subordinates to pay more attention to the system's functioning and to be more receptive to suggestions in order to obtain better and safer outcomes.

In our times of tremendous socio-economic upheaval due to the pandemic's consequences , more segments of our societies might be more receptive to the idea of a woman at the top of the power ladder. Are we ready for a *Madame President*? We need to diversify the top echelons of public and private spheres to ventilate the musty corridors of power as we are facing terrible social and economic challenges.

Women often love to discuss any major family, work, or study problem with the voluntary participation of all the concerned parties in their lives, eschewing solitary machinations and preferring solutions based on a final amiable consensus. In order to be ready for the critical all-genders collaboration, men must rejuvenate. If they do not have any clues about how to proceed, they must pause for reflection.

A nugget of Wisdom. Do not panic… Do not blink… Look her in the eye... When Emperor Tiberius felt cornered, he echoed Antipho's words: "I've got a wolf by the ears; for I neither know how to get rid of her, nor yet how to keep her." [815]

Auribus teneo lupum [816]

Post pandemic "feminine take-away"

A few days ago we were writing at our desk, casually listening to the program *Todo lo que pasa Edición Especial* [817] from Radio Mitre of Buenos Aires, when Gonzalo Sánchez, its smart presenter, started to discuss the *societal lessons* that we will gather after the pandemic eases off. He put forward three main ones:

a) The Sum – Up concept

b) The Trinity Effect

c) Democratization of Social Influencing

A – Sum – up concept

The obligatory rules of *Social Distancing* have swiftly re-written the rules of engagement at work, colleges, primary and secondary schools, associations etc. What was supposed to be a trend towards the *digitalization of human contacts* that would take years to materialize became a necessity that had to happen in just months. The *Webster Dictionary* defines the concept of "sum up" [818] like this:

a) In *transitive form*, it means "to be the sum of", or "to show succinctly."

b) In its *intransitive form*, it means "to present a summary or recapitulation."

The synonyms are "abstract", "brief", but also "digest", "epitome" and "recap." This rightfully describes the non-stop, obsessive **mental recap** we engage in when we face a choice between two or more options. *Our autopilot has been turned off.*

Before the pandemic, we never even gave a brief second thought when some higher up casually said: "tomorrow we have a meeting at 8 AM... Be there or be squared." We got up at 6 AM to prep the household (*if you were a wife/mother*) and our images (*got any idea, guys, how long it takes us, gals, to ready our bodies for your chauvinistic-cochonic scrutiny* [819] ?) before bracing traffic to be on time.

During and after the pandemic, *everybody will evaluate* if that meeting really needs our physical presence or it can be alternatively carried out via Zoom. Gary Shedlin, *Chief Financial Officer (CFO)* of the *Black Rock bank*, replied like this to a reporter's question about the *operational lessons* they gleaned from COVID: "I think the biggest lesson learned obviously was that we were able to very quickly migrate from 16,000 people in 60 offices to 16,000 people and 16,000 offices." [820]

When the time will come for our children to decide what career path they must choose, the possibility of working from the *safety of their homes*, full time or part-time, will weigh heavily in their consideration. For those that cannot avoid physical contact, like nurses and teachers, there will be *a raise in their salaries*.

In our long seclusion at our residences, we are again discovering the joy of *family cooking*, besides patronizing again *our local stores* for natural produce and healthier fare in a usually friendly environment that includes neighborly chit chat.

What can be more fitting for **the feminine ethos** than *keeping a watchful eye* on your family's needs while *working or creating efficiently* at your home office?

B – Trinity effect

-"Can you fly that thing?" Neo said, pointing at a parked helicopter.

-"Not yet" Trinity replied. She takes off her glasses and picks her Cel.

-"Operator...I need a pilot program for a B-21-2 helicopter...Hurry."

In the other end, the operator maniacally clicks his keyboard a few times.

She closes her eyes for a few seconds while her eyelashes suavely flutter.

Suddenly she opens her eyes and commands to Neo: "Let's go."

In that memorable scene of *The Matrix* [821], the central characters are quickly aided by **Artificial Intelligence** to flee the pounding pursuit of the malevolent Mr. Smith. In that vein, we can watch now that people who were barely able to send e-mails before are now turning experts in tele-conferencing and phone applications. The *tech vocabulary* is seeping into other socio-economic strata, including *the Old*. As Josh Brown, a CNBC anchor, said: "It is our vernacular...It is here to stay."

There might be empirical evidence that a **glaring gender gap** is spawning.

Recently *une femme d'une certaine âge* [822] told us that she had found solace from the forced distancing from family and friends by using *WhatsApp* chatgroups and *Zoom* conferences. "And your husband?" we asked. "Forget it," she shot back.

As distrait men yearn for the Past, their women are colonizing the Future.

C – Democratization of Social Influencing

After the Black Plague of 1348 eased, the European survivors came out to build much more *modern societies* based on mercantilism and progress, instead of the mysticism and religiosity of the Middle Ages. This process eventually led to the Industrial Revolution and blossoming of the scientific progress in the 19th century. Before that terrible pandemic, women were largely confined to the role of homemakers, mothers, and wives by the patriarchal institutions and the churches.

Slowly yet steadily, women started to come out of their residences and venture into many realms of society, including the burgeoning trades, care facilities and public education. In 1648 *Elena Cornaro Piscopia*, a Venetian philosopher of noble upbringing, became the first woman to graduate from a university when she received her *Doctor of Philosophy degree* (PhD) at the *Università di Padova*. Ever since then, millions of women in the world have been gaining a larger presence in the institutions of higher learning, the specialized technical schools and academia.

A Pew Research Center report claimed that the increased demand of skilled workers in the USA narrows **gender disparities**. They said: "Increasingly, U.S. employers are in pursuit of workers who are adept in social skills, like negotiation and persuasion, and who have a strong grounding in fundamental skills, such as critical thinking and writing. Jobs attaching greater importance to analytical skills, such as science and mathematics, are also adding workers at a brisk pace."

What is blocking the decisive consecration of women's achievements?

Aside from the disgusting discrimination of the patriarchal institutions and the unfair deals that many of them have had to grudgingly accept to carry on in our still misogynistic societies, we believe that there might be *reasons of their making*.

Even though most women are viewed as the "natural communicators", their impact in the labor realm may be blunted by little gaffes, which can be fixed. Ellie Williams said: "by understanding gender differences in communication, the impact of body language and the factors that attract and hold a listener's attention, women can learn to successfully communicate with even the toughest of crowds." [823] She recommends deploying *logical arguments* rather than any *emotional appeals* in a business environment, to *irradiate confidence* by keeping the discussion on topic at all times and to *avoid being interrupted* or derailed from their objectives.

(*Never show uncertainty by using disclaimers about your ideas. Stand firm*)

The obligatory distancing from the physical places where business, work and studies used to be conducted has had *the collateral effect* of giving most women a little bit "more space" to dodge the intimidating gaze of recalcitrant men and enjoy a more democratic access to the Internet resources to **become influencers**. We feel that progressively women will *master the use of novel resources*, out-pacing men in most realms, thus lifting their hitherto sabotaged public profiles in civic spaces.

The Web beckons tired, poor, huddled masses yearning to breathe free. [824]

What final piece of practical advice should we give the well-meant men?

If you are worried about the *Emotional Frustration* of a loved woman, you should:

Number One - Listen to her.

Number Two - Listen to her.

Number Three - Listen to her.

As difficult as understanding women seems to be (and often is) we are given a heads-up at the start of the race: they whisper in our ear where *the shortcuts are*. They want us, not only to win the race, but to do it with our full colors flying. As we are reaching the finish line, they turn around to exult over us. "*That's my man.*"

But it does take some dedicated training. Take the time to sit down with her. Do not talk. *Listen to her*. Do not intrude. *Listen to her*. Do not idle. *Listen to her*. *Masked by her routine's chaff, a small critical detail may go unnoticed by you.*

We might harbor certain certitudes about the women sharing our daily life. But we must remain *skeptical* as they might have been created with faux premises that layered a palimpsest of social prejudices and biased opinions in our minds. Watching the Cathedral of Agrigento's mass, an exquisite feminine voice warned:

Chi non dubbia, non cerca.

Chi non cerca, non vede

E chi non vede, rimane cieco.[825]

"Enivrez-vous...Il faut nous énivrer sans trêve,

Mais de quoi ? De vin, de poésie, de vertu,

A votre guise. Mais énivrez-vous « [826]

Charles Baudelaire

Thank you very much for taking the time and effort to read, and hopefully appreciate, our humble writings that were created with patient, dedicated affection. Let us turn this initial contact into an *active conversation* that we can continue at our medical, literary, cooking and travel web page to share ideas, fears, feelings.

https://drmolaplume.com

Due to the forced social isolation imposed by the terrible worldwide pandemic, we unexpectedly have more time to patiently research material and write more articles for the series that constitutes the scaffolding for our next book. What is the name?

Supernatural, Superstition and She

If you want to listen to our podcast, please go to **anchor.fm/dr-mario-o-laplume**. Please "come join us" at the seashore to watch the rainbow while IZ's suave music serenades us, becoming totally inebriated with red wine and poetry and each other.

See you later ! Hasta luego ! A bientôt! Arrivederci!

We were readying the manuscript for its final submission to the publisher when an odd twang interrupted us: "Howdy, Doc...Dunno close it yet."

- "Who— who are you?"

- "Joe Six Pack from Alabama, sir...the last survivor of the Awareness... When our ship went down in that storm of women's claims and concerns, we were thrown into the sea. We seized your lifeboat. Drifted for days."

- "Who rescued you?"

- "A US Navy plane spotted me and relayed the info to a cutter. Erika, a lovely Swedish nurse, cared for my wounds and made me good again."

- "Ain't you a lucky dog? What should we fix for the next cadets' class?"

- "Like Roy Schreider said after staring down at the size of that shark, 'You're going to need a bigger boat'...Women's waters are rough."

- "Indeed they are. And getting worse...But if someone like you...Don't take any offense....If you could make it, then anybody has a chance, bud."

- "None taken...Drop by my farm to celebrate with some baby back ribs."

- "Sure, we bring the beer... A round of applause for the first graduating midshipman of Emotional Frustration's circumnavigation...Bravo." [827]

References

[1] In Italian, it means "Whomever can, put something…Whomever needs it, take it."
[2] Can be translated as : "there are more things to be admired than disdained in men."
[3] Alber Camus, *La Peste*, Paris, 1947, Editions Gallimard.
[4] Term in the German language that means "find joy in the disgrace of others."
[5] Term in the French language that means "the never-ending defeat."
[6] André Malraux, *La Condition Humaine*, Paris, 1933, Editions Gallimard.
[7] Michele Bocci, "Coronavirus, medici strage infinita. I morti salgono a 107, 4 su 10 tra quelli di base" La Repubblica, 10 Aprile 2020. https://repubblica.it/cronaca/2020/04/10/news/medici_la_strage_infinita_i_morti_salgono_a_105_4_su_10_tra_quelli_di_bae/
[8] The *Via Crucis* or the *Via Dolorosa* is the path taken by Jesus Christ and his tormentors through the streets of Jerusalem to reach the Golgota, the infamous hill where he was crucified by the Romans.
[9] The name of the massive arena where the Romans had their games, ceremonies, and gladiators' encounters, located in the center of Rome.
[10] Term in the Italian language that means "courage."
[11] Black Death, History, Updated March 30, 2020. https://history.com/topics/middle-ages/black-death/
[12] Giovanni Bcaccio (autore), Luciano Corona (autore), "Decameron. Riscrittura integrale in italiano moderno:1 (italiano) Fermento editore, Roma, 2018.
[13] Introduction by Wayne A. Rebhorn, Giovanni Boccaccio, The Decameron, Norton Books.
[14] Sam McNeil, "China's virus pandemic epicenter Wuhan ends 76-day lockdown", The Washington Post, April 7. 2020. https://washingtonpost.com/world/asia_pacific/chinas-virus-pandemic-epicente-wuhan-ends-76-day-lockdown/2020/044/
[15] Glenn Kessler, "Timeline: how the Wuhan lab-leak theory suddenly became credible." The Washington Post, May 25, 2021. https://www.washingtonpost.com/politics/2021/05/25/timeline-how-wuhan-lab-leak-theory-suddenly-became-credible/
[16] https://franceinter.fr/direct/
[17] Acronym of the "Centers for Diseases Control."
[18] Tom Frieden, "I used to Run the C.D.C. Here's What It Can Do to Slow This Pandemic", opinion, The New York Times, April 12, 2020. https://nytimes.com/2020/04/12/opinion/cdc_coronavirus.html
[19] Can be translated as: "we have to re-invent ourselves, starting with me." Our translation.
[20] The words in the Castilian language were the following: "si no te quieren dar algo, tenes que salir a la calle a armar kilombo, siempre algo vas a sacar."
[21] Mario O. Laplume, "Madame D.C., Book I :Three voyages", https://amazon.com/Madame-D-C-Book-Three-voyages-ebook/dp/B01M715X63/
[22] Gustave Flaubert, "Madame Bovary", Frères Michel Levy, Paris, 1857.
[23] Name of the private institute based in Paris, France, that teaches the French language in many branches worldwide.
[24] After five years of writing more than 4500 pages, Gustave Flaubert, aged 35 years, published the 500 pages of "Madame Bovary" in the magazine directed by Maxime Du Camp, his companion in the trip to the Far East. There were six parts appearing on the first and fifteenth day of the months of October, November, and December 1856. He wrote to a friend that; 'you will know that I am presently being printed, I lose my virginity of non-published man in eight days as of Thursday, October 1st…I will for three consecutive months fill most of the pages of La Revue de Paris." Our translation.
Information was obtained from Yvan Leclerc, "Gustave Flaubert, Madame Bovary, pré-originale dans la Revue de Paris «, Recueil des Commémorations Nationales 2006. https://francearchives.fr/commemo/recueil-2006/39092/
[25] In the January 8, 2019, program "L'heure Bleu" of Radio France Inter, Laura Adler, the presenter, interviewed Vanessa Springora, author of the bestseller "Le Consentement". The subject of Madame Bovary and her frustrations came up for discussion. I believe it was Vanessa that suggested that Emma Bovary "devrait avoir pris la plume pour écrire" (she should have picked up the feather to write) Well, false modesty apart, let us inform these ladies that it is

never too late for Emma to at least voice her ideas, especially when she can recruit a submissive agent to take dictation like yours truly. Playing with the meaning of our last name, we dare to say: "je suis peut être Laplume qui manquait dans la vie de Madame Bovary" (I am perhaps the Laplume that was missing in Madame Bovary's life)

[26] Term in the Latin language that means: "in exactly the same words."

[27] Diccionario de la Lengua Española, Tomo 1, Real Academia Española, 2001, Espasa Calpe.

[28] https://www.britannica.com/biography/Sigmund-Freud/

[29] https://www.britannica.com/biography/Jean-Martin-Charcot/

[30] Can be translated as "the genital stuff."

[31] Name of the Paris hospital where Prof. Charcot directed a clinical ward of Neurology.

[32] https://www.britannica.com/biography/Anton-Chekhov/

[33] David A. Scola, "The Hemispheric Specialization of the Human Brain and its Application to Psychoanalytic Principles", Jefferson Journal of Psychiatry, Volume 2, Issue 1, January 1984.
https://jdc.jefferson.edu/cgi/viewcontent.cgi?referer/

[34] Babak A. Ardekani, Khadija Figarsky, John Sitdis, "Sexual Dimorphism in the Human Corpus Callosum: an MRI Study using the OASIS Brain database", Cerebral Cortex, 2013 Oct:23(10): 2514-2520.
https;/academic.coup.com/cercor/article/23/10/2514/29675/

[35] Word of the Hindi language that can be translated as "current of air."

[36] https://en.wikipedia.org/wiki/Jerzy_Grotowski/

[37] Many modern navies have extremely well preserved and updated *tall ships* that they use for Public Relations purposes and especially for *a long voyage* with their graduating classes of midshipmen and midshipwomen.

[38] In theatrical jargon the "fourth wall" refers to the space interposed between the actors and their spectators.

[39] https://www.goodreads.com/book/show/338798.Ulysses

[40] Mario Laplume Salguero was our dearest father and we prepared an article in his honor in our web page.
https://drmolaplume.com/2018/08/14/the-visionary-of-trinidad/

[41] https://www.britannica.com/biography/Mario-Benedetti/

[42] Can be translated as "The Impossible. It only takes a little bit longer." Mario Benedetti is one of the greatest modern Uruguayan writers who specialized in short stories and penned some of the most memorable romantic lines. Like James Joyce, he was interested in the vicissitudes of urban life and the multiple characters that inhabit—and suffer—them. "Montevideanos", his first major book published in 1959, has reminiscences of "Dubliners."

[43] Janus was the Roman god of the hearth and its dual representation was prominent in their homes with one ugly face towards the outside and a happy one towards the inside of a house. An antonym is a word that means the opposite of another one. An auto-antonym is a word that contains a meaning and its opposite one at the same time. "Compact Oxford Dictionary of Current English", Third Edition, Oxford University Press, Oxford, 2005.

[44] https://en.oxforddictihttps://definition/frustration

[45] According to a legend, when the Phrygians were left without a king, they recurred to an oracle at Telmissus that decreed that the next man to enter the city with an oxcart should be anointed as their king. A poor peasant called Gordias was the lucky winner and was immediately proclaimed as their king. Midas, his grateful son, tied his father's old cart to a post with an intricately arranged knot. Another oracle decreed that any man that could unravel the knot would be the ruler of Asia. When Alexander the Great arrived in that Persian satrapy, he was challenged to deal with the knot. Initially he tried to untie it, but he failed. Then he thought that the important thing was to unloose it and not the method to achieve it. He drew his sword and sliced in half. Thus the prophecy eventually came true.
https://en.wikipedia.org/wiki/Gordian_Knot

[46] https://drmolaplume.com/2016/05/11/49/

[47] https://drmolaplume.com/2016/06/04/emotional-frustration-the-trolling-toll-of-technology/

[48] https://drmolaplume.com/2018/07/28/the-cyber-chantage/

[49] https://drmolaplume.com/2016/11/12/the-material-girl/

[50] https://drmolaplume.com/2016/10/01/the-bad-negotiator/

[51] Word in the Italian language that can be translated as: "crossroads or junction."

[52] "Dizionario Garzanti di Italiano", Garzanti editore S.p.A., Roma, 1994; page 616.

[53] Anti-histaminic medication used to prevent the nausea and vomiting of Motion Sickness.

[54] Lord Ganesh is one of the major deities in the Hindu religion; he is the jolly guy with an elephant's head. We will thoroughly discuss him in that chapter.

[55] REM sleep is the second phase of the sleep cycle, the most profound one, that is critical for a good rest.
"Merritt's Neurology Twelfth Edition" by Lewis P. Rowland (editor) and Timothy A. Pedley (editor).

[56] Oxford textbook of Clinical Neurophysiology, edited by Kerry R. Mills; Oxford University press' ISBN-13:9780199688395 https://oxfordmedicine.com/
[57] Ibidem as above
[58] Ibidem as above
[59] Ibidem as above
[60] https://www.ncbi.nlm.nih.gov/pmc/articles/PMC3510904/
[61] Richard Howells, Joaquin Negreiros, "Visual Culture,3rd edition", Polity Press, Cambridge, 2019.
[62] https://www.scientificamerican.com/article/mirroring-behavior/
[63] http://www.talkingbrains.org/2010/03/mirror-neurons-unfalsifiable-theory.html
[64] https://www.ncbi.nlm.nih.gov/pmc/articles/PMC5023663/
[65] Yawei Cheng, Jean Decety, "Sex differences in the neuroanatomy of human mirror-neuron system: A voxel-based morphometric investigation", Neuroscience, 2009 Jan 23: 158 (2) :713-20. https://www.ncbi.nlm.nih.gov/pubmed/19010397
[66] Schulte-Ruther, M., Markowitsch, HJ., Shah NJ, "Gender differences in brain networks supporting empathy", Neuroimage, 2008 Aug 1:42 (1)393-403. https://www.ncbi.nlm.nih.gov/pubmed/18514546
[67] Anna M. Borgui, Lucia Riggio, "Stable and variable affordances are both automatic and flexible", Human Neuroscience, 2015; 9;351. Published online June 19, 2015. https://www.frontiersin.org/articles/10.3389/fnhum.2015.00351/full/
[68] Tanya Lewis, "How Men's Brains are wired differently than Women's" Scientific American, December 2,2013. https://www.scientificamerican.com/article/how-mens-brain-are-wired-differently-than-women/
[69] Italian term that means "thank you."
[70] *Tiger* is the cute tiger character in the *Winny-the-Pooh* series that hops around by bouncing on its tail.
[71] Jennifer Knudtson, "Female Reproductive Endocrinology", Merck Manual Professional version. https://www.merckmanuals.com/professional/gynecology-and-obstetrics/female-reproductive-endocrinology/
[72] Farage MA, Osborn TW, MacLean AB, "Cognitive, sensory and emotional changes associated with the menstrual cycle: a review", Archives of Gynecology and Obstetrics, 2008 Oct.278(4)299-307 https://www.ncbi.nlm.nih.gov/pubmed/18592262
[73] Annie Murphy Paul, "The Double Life of Women", Psychology Today, November 1, 2010. https://www.psychologytoday.com/us/articles/201011/the-double-life-women
[74] Karl Grammar, LeeAnn Renninger and Bettina Fischer, "Disco clothing, Female Sexual Motivation, and Relationships Status: is She Dressed to Impress?" The Journal of Sex Research, Vol.41, No.1, Evolutionary and Neurohormonal Perspectives on Human Sexuality (Feb.2004) pp.66-74. https://www.jstot.org/stable/3813404
[75] Nicholas Gueguen, "Gait and menstrual cycle: ovulating women use sexier gaits and walk slowly ahead of men", Gait Posture, 2012 Apr.35(4):621-4.
[76] Do Yup Lee, Eosu Kim, Man Ho Choi, "Technical aspects of cortisol as a biochemical marker of chronic stress", BMB Rep. 2015 Apr: 48(4) 209-216. https://www.ncbi.nlm.nih.gov/pmc/articles/PMC4436856
[77] Term that refers to the increased secretion of cortisol in women in the second half of the day.
[78] Lucy Rahim, "What to do if you argue before bed-and how to avoid it next time" Lifestyle, Women's Life. The Telegraph, January 11, 2017. https://www.telegraph.co.uk/women/life/do-argue-bed-avoid-next-time/
[79] The input from the peripheral sensory receptors of our body is carried up to the Central Nervous System through the anterior and lateral spinothalamic tracts, whose second-order neurons' axons decussate (cross over) at every segmental level of the spinal cord and travel up to the ventral posterolateral nucleus of the thalamus and then the somatosensory cortex of the postcentral gyrus. It means that eventually all the sensory information about crude touch and pain/temperature from the left side of the body will end up in the Right Hemisphere for processing.
Elan D. Louis, Stephan A. Mayer, Lewis P. Rowland, "Merritt's Neurology", Wolters Kluver, September 2015.
[80] Saint Paul was born as Saul in the city of Tarsus under Roman rule; he was a pharisaic Jew with Roman citizenship. His zeal for the Jewish law and traditions was so strong that he pursued all the Jews that were converting to the nascent Christina faith. Some accounts say that he oversaw the execution of Saint Stephen, the first Christian martyr; drawing his last breath, Saint Stephen implored God to forgive all those who were stoning him, including Saul. His conversion to Christianity happened when he was riding on horseback to Damascus for a commission to allow him to persecute more Christians. The book of Acts, chapter 9, says: "They heard a voice from heaven that said: 'Saul, Saul, why do you persecute Me?" And Saul said, "Who are you, Lord?" And He said, "I am Jesus, Whom you are persecuting; but rise and enter the city, and you will be told what you are to do."

Based on this religious anecdote, the term "Road-to-Damascus moment" describes a seminal moment in anyone's life when a higher truth is suddenly revealed, and it fosters meaningful change.
https://catholicexchange.com/the-conversion-of-st-paul

[81] "Anne Frank: The Collected Works", ISBN 9781472964915, Bloomsbury Continuum, 2019.
This quote was found in: Bart van Es, "Anne Frank: the real story of the girl behind the diary", The Guardian, May 25, 2019. https://www.theguardian.com/books/2019/may/25/anne-frank-full-story-bart-van-es/

[82] This term derives from the French term "collaborationiste" and refers to the local police and functionaries used by the Germans in World War II to enforce their occupation in France, Holland, Hungary, etc.

[83] Bart van Es, "The Cut-Out Girl: A Story of War and Family, Lost and Found :The Costa Book of the Year 2018", Penguin Books Ltd., January 10, 2019. ISBN 9780241978726.

[84] Bart van Es, "Anne Frank: the real story of the girl behind the diary", Books, The Guardian, May 25, 2019.
https://www.theguardian.com/books/2019/may/25/anne-frank-full-story-bart-van-es/

[85] Judith Orloff, "The Power of Being an Earth Empath", Psychology Today, April 17, 2017.
https://www.psychologytoday.com/us/blog/the-empathy-survival-guide/201704/the-power-being-earth-empath/

[86] https://en.historylapse.org/astronomy-in-the-ancient-times/

[87] https://en.wikipedia.org/wiki/Maya_calendar/

[88] Boyce Rensberger, "186 Top Scientists Dismiss Astrologers as Charlatans", The New York Times, Sept. 3, 1975.
https://www.nytimes.com/1975/09/03/archives/186-top-scientists-dismiss-astrologers-as-charlatans-scientists.html

[89] Expression in the Italian language that can be translated as: "just in case."

[90] Anne Prospère de Launay, the only surviving letter to the Marquis de Sade. Translated from the French by the author. Found in "Le who's who of Sade" in "Le mystère Sade", Hors-série Le Point, Paris, 2016.

[91] Donatien Alphonse Francois de Sade was born in Paris in 1740; he was the son of Jean Baptiste Joseph Francois, count of Sade and Marie-Eleonore de Maille de Carman, a relative of the Princess of Condé. Source : "Le Mystère Sade." Hors-Série Le Point, Paris, 2016.

[92] "Scandales en série" in "Le mystère Sade », Hors-série Le Point, Paris, 2016.

[93] Principal character of one of Sade's novels. "Histoire de Juliette, ou les Prospérités du Vice »
https://catalogue.bnf.fr/ark:/12148/cb12342211g

[94] Chantal Thomas, "Entretien" in "Le mystère Sade", Hors-série Le Point, Paris, 2016. Our translation.

[95] Peggy Drexler, "6 Ways Men and Women are (Mostly)Different", Psychology Today, Posted August 19, 2014.
https://www.psychologytodaay.com/us/blog/our-gender-ourselves/201408/6-ways-men-and-women-are-mostly-different/

[96] Sarah Ashton, Karolyn McDonald, Maggie Kirkman, « Women's Experiences of Pornography: A Systematic review of research Using Qualitative Methods". The Journal of Sex Research, Volume 55,2008 - Issue 3, published online Sep. 21, 2017. https://www.tandfonline.com/doi/abs/10.1080/

[97] Maria del Mar Sanchez-Fuentes, Pablo Santos-Iglesias, Juan Carlos Sierra, "A systematic review of sexual satisfaction", International Journal of Clinical and Health Psychology (2014) 14, 67-75.
https://www.academia.edu/15842933/a_systematic_review_of_sexual_satisfaction/

[98] Roy F. Baumeister, "The Reality of the Male Sex Drive", Psychology Today, December 8, 2010.
https://www.psychologytoday.com/us/blog/cultural-animal/201012/the-reality-the-male-sex-drive/

[99] Myrtle Wilhite, "Vaginal Dryness" in "Integrative Medicine", Fourth Edition, 2018.

[100] Kim Wallen, Elizabeth Lloyd, "Female Sexual Arousal: Genital Anatomy and Orgasm in Intercourse", Hormonal Behavior, 2011 May: 59(5):780-792. Published online 2010 Dec.30.
https://www.ncbi.nlm.nih.gov/pmc/articles/PMC3894744/

[101] Rodgers, Joann Ellison, "Sex: A Natural History", MacMillan Publishers, 2003, ISBN 978-81-89093-59-4.

[102] Term in the French language that means "cap" or "hood"

[103] Ian Kerner, "She Comes First: The Thinking Man's Guide to Pleasuring a Woman", Harper Collins, 2004.

[104] Annamaria Giraldi, AlessandraH. Rellini, James Pfaus, Ellen Laan, « Female Sexual Arousal Disorders », The Journal of Sexual Medicine, Online, September 13, 2012.
https://professionals.issm.info/news/research-summaries/female-sexual-arousal-disroders/

[105] Herbernick D., Reece M.Hensel D., Sanders S., Joskowski K., Fortenberry JD., "Association of lubricant use with women's sexual pleasure, sexual satisfaction, and genital symptoms: a prospective daily diary study", Journal of Sex Medicine, 2011 Jan:8(1)202-12. https://www.ncbi.nlm.nih.gov/pumed/21143591/

[106] "Algunos consejos. Hablar durante el sexo, la clave para gozar más." Buena Vida, Clarín, 22 Mayo 2019.
https://www.clarin.com/buena-vida/hablar-sexo-clave-gozar/

[107] Brewer G., Hendrie CA., "Evidence to suggest that copulatory vocalizations in women are not a reflexive consequence of orgasm", Archives of Sexual Behavior 2011 June; 40 (3) 559-64. https://www.ncbi.nlm.nih.gov/pumed/20480220

[108] Ibidem as above.

[109] https://www.britannica.com/biography/Niccolo-Machiavelli/

[110] Mihaela Pavlicev, "The evolutionary Origin of Female Orgasm" JEZ-B Molecular and Developmental Evolution, July 31, 2016. https://doi.org/10.1002/jez.b.2269

[111] This term was humorously invented by the author and used the French familiar term for the clitoris. In France, where the public is usually more relaxed about their sexuality, they created this moniker for it.

[112] Moniker for the French Resistance movement against the German Army and Police in World War II.

[113] Rieger G., Savin-Williams RC, Chivers ML, Bailey JM, "Sexual arousal and masculinity-femininity in women", Journal Pers. Soc. Psychology 2016 Aug:111(2):265-83. https://www.ncbi.nlm.nih.gov/pubmed/26501187

[114] Adriana Arias, "Vínculos y relaciones. ¿Eterno dilema…Se puede ser bisexual?" Entremujeres, Clarín, 13 Noviembre 2013. https://www.clarin.com/entremujeres/bisexual-bisexualidad-fantasias-adriana-arias-columnista/

[115] Slogan used by the protesters of the French May street insurrection of 1968; it can be translated as "the imagination to power."

[116] Das A."Masturbation in the United States", Journal of Sex and Marital Therapy 2007 Jul-Sep:33(4)301-17. https://www.ncbi.nlm.nih.gov/pubmed/17541849

[117] Yvonne K. Fulbright, "Touch me there. A hands-on Guide to your Orgasmic Hot Spots", Hunter House, Kindle edition. https://hunterhouse.com

[118] https://kinseyinstitute.org/pdf/womens%20orgasm%20annual%20review.pdf

[119] The Merriam-Webster Dictionary defines "sensual" as : relating to or consisting in the gratification of the senses or the indulgence of appetite". https://www.meriam-websteer.com/dictionary/sensual

[120] Acronym for "Make America Great Again", the *cri de guerre* of President Trump's election campaign.

[121] This in turn was the *cri de guerre* of the nationwide bus tour of Vice-President's Joe Biden campaign.

[122] Elizabeth A. Lloyd, "The case of the Female Orgasm: Bias in the Science of Evolution" Harvard University Press, ISBN -13: 978-0674022461.

[123] Pelletier G, Ren L., "Localization of sex steroid receptors in human skin", Histology and Histopathology 2004 Apr. 19 (2) : 629-36. https://www.ncbi.nlm.nih.gov/pubmed/15024720

[124] Randi Gunther, "Sex Actually", Psychology Today, Posted Feb. 15, 2019. https://www.psychologytoday.com/us/blog/rediscovering-love/201902/sex-actually

[125] The possessive article "ihr" from the German language is one of the alternative variants used for Transgender people. Considering that we love the German language, we will use it liberally, claiming "artistic license." https://lgbtrc.usc.edu/trans/transgender/pronoums/

[126] Jonathan Amos, BBC News, Monday, 25 July 2005.

[127] Jessica Wood, Sara Crann, Shannon Cunningham, Deborah Money, Kieran O'Doherty, "A cross-sectional survey of sex toy use, characteristics of sex toy use hygiene behaviors, and vulvovaginal health outcomes in Canada", The Canadian Journal of Human Sexuality, Volume 26, Issue3, December 2017, pp.196-204. https://utpjournals.press/doi/full/103138/cjhs.2017-0016

[128] "Las nuevas consumidoras de erotismo. Crece el mercado de juegos y juguetes sexuales para mujeres" Entremujeres, Clarín, 10 Diciembre, 2010. Our translation. https://www.clarin.com/pareja-y-sexo/juguetes-sexuales-erotismo-sexo-lacer-sexualidad

[129] Walter Hugo Ghedin, "Sexo y sexualidad: hacia dónde vamos", Ediciones LEA, Buenos Aires, 2014.

[130] https://www.trojanbrands.com/en-ca/sex-information/self-pleasure-and-self-care

[131] https://www.multivu.com/players/English/8528451-tenga-unveils-2019-self-pleasure-report/docs/Full2019Report_1557144644685-1929663640.pdf

[132] "Mica Viciconte usa un juguete sexual que era de Nicole Newman?" Temas del día, Revista Paparazzi, Buenos Aires, 31 de mayo de 2019. Our translation.

[133] https://www.britannica.com/topic/A-Dolls-House

[134] Gloria Steinem, "A Bunny's Tale", Show Magazine, New York, May 1,1963, pages 90-114.

[135] Alice Wright, "Should women wear makeup? Two writers argue for and against", Opinion, Metro, January 23, 2017. https://metro.co.uk/2017/01/23/should-women-wear-makeup-two-writers-argue-for-adn-against-6389837/

[136] Jennifer Weiner, "The pressure to look good", Opinion, Sunday Review, The New York Times, May 30, 2015. https://www.nytimes.com/2015/05/31/opinion/sunday/jennifer-weiner-the-pressure-to-look-good.html

[137] Audrey Nelson, "How Unconscious Bias Impacts Women and Men", Psychology Today, Posted June 25, 2018. https://www.psychologytoday.com/us/blog/he-speaks-she-speaks/201806/how-uncoscious-bias-impacts-women-and-men

[138] "Vaginal and Vulvar Comfort: Lubricants, Moisturizers, and Low-Dose Vaginal Estrogen", The North American Menopause Society. https://www.menopuse.org/for-women/sexual-health-menopause-online/effective-treatments-for-sexual-products

[139] "Vagina changes after childbirth" National Health Institute, United Kingdom. https://www.nhs.uk/live-well/sexual-health/vagina/-changes-after-chidbirth/

[140] https://drmolaplume.com/2016/08/20/guest-blogger-dr-walter-ghedin/

[141] Simon Romero, "Do Argentines Need Therapy? Pull up a couch", Americas., The New York Times, August 18, 2012. https://www.nytimes.com/2012/08/19/world/americas/do-argentines-need-therapy-pull-up-a-couch.html

[142] Walter H. Ghedin, "Listado. Miedos sexuales: ¿cuándo son normales y cuando patológicos?" Entremujeres, Clarín, 30 Mayo 2016. https://www.clarin.com/sexo/miedos-sexuales-normales-patologicos/

[143] Helen Singer Kaplan, "Sexual Aversion, Sexual Phobias, and Panic Disorder", First published in 1987, ISBN-13:978-0876304501.

[144] Sarah Hunter Murray, "The experiences of Highly Sexual Women", Psychology Today, March 31, 2019. https://www.psychologytoday.com/us/blog/myths-desire/201903/the-experiences-highly-sexual-women/

[145] Eric S. Blumberg, "The lives and voices of highly sexual women", The Journal of Sex Research, Volume 40, 2003- Issue 2. Published online: 11 Jan. 2010. https://www.tandfonline.com/doi/abs/10.1080/002224490309552176/

[146] George Orwell, "Animal Farm", Secker and Warburg, London, 17 August 1945.

[147] Dr. Amy Muise "What happens When Your Partner Wants to Do it and You're not in the Mood" Luvze, April 27, 2015. https://www.luvze.com/what-happens-when-your-parrtner-wants-to-do-it-and-youre-not

[148] Alexandra Katehakis, "Sex Addiction Beyond the DSM-V", Psychology Today, December 21, 2012. https://www.psychologytoday.com/us/blog/sex-lies-trauma/201212/sex-addiction-beyond-the-dsm-v

[149] Walter Hugo Ghedin. Ibidem as above.

[150] Belén Figueira, "Hipersexualidad y miedo a la intimidad, las paradojas que hoy rodean a los Millenials. ¿Por qué se retrasa la iniciación sexual?" Tendencias, Infobae, Lunes 3 de Junio de 2019. https://www.infobae.com/tendencias/2018/05/19/hipersexualidad-y-miedo-a-la-intimidad-las-paradojas-

[151] https://www.indb.com/title/tt1937390/

[152] Robert Weiss, "Nymphomaniac – A Realistic Look at Female Hypersexuality?" Psychology Today, April 04, 2014. https://www.psychologytoday.com/us/blog/love-and-sex-in-the-digital-age/201404/nymphomaniac-realistic-look-at-female-hypersexuality

[153] Can be translated as "a getaway going forward."

[154] Sternberg, Robert J. (2007). "Triangulating Love" In Oord, T.J. (ed). "The Altruism Reader: selections from writings on Love, Religion, and Science." West Conshohocken, PA: Templeton Foundation. P.332 ISBN 9781599471273.

[155] Ibidem as above.

[156] Human tendency to return to a stable level of happiness and fulfilment after events, good or bad, in their lives.

[157] Frank Bass, "Cheating Wives narrowed Infidelity Gap Over Two decades" Pursuit, Bloomberg, July 1, 2013. https://www.bloomberg.com/news/articles/2013-07-02/cheating-wives-narrowed-infidelity-gap

[158] Term of the Italian language that means: "discovered in the act of doing something."

[159] Term of the French language that means: "an irresistibly sudden feeling of love for someone or something"

[160] Dr. Jane Greer, "How Could You do This to Me? Learning to trust after Betrayal" Nov.1, 2010.

[161] Antoni Bolinches, "Amor al segon intent. Gia per superar el patient amoros i facilitat l'amor harmonic", Biblioteca Antoni Bolinches, num.43, Octubre del 2013. ISBN" 978-84-9034-162-9. https://www.cossetania.com/amor-al-segon-intent-1420

[162] "Vínculos. La infidelidad de la mujer es más peligrosa para la pareja" Entemujeres, Clarín, 11 Mayo 2013. https://www.clarin.com/pareja/pareja-sexo-parafilias-estimulos-rutina-amor-vinculo

[163] https://drmolaplume.com/2017/10/04/the-virtues-of-failure

[164] Charles Pepin, "Les vertus de l'échec », Allary Editions, 222 Septembre 2016. EAN : 978-2-37073-012-1. https://www.allary-editions-fr/publication/les-vertus-de-lechec

[165] Term in the French language that refers to " the reason for its existence."

[166] Charles Pepin. Ibidem as above.

[167] "Vínculos" Ibidem as above.

[168] "Vínculos" Ibidem as above.
[169] "Bajo Sospecha. 10 errores que cometen las mujeres infieles (y las delatan frente a sus maridos)" Entemujeres, Clarín, Buenos aires, 23 Enero 2015.
https://www.clarin.com/pareja/infidelidad-mujer-_infiel-engano-trampa-amantes-sitio-internet
[170] "Vinculos" Ibidem as above.
[171] Esther Perel "The State of Affairs: Rethinking Infidelity", Harper Collins, New York, 2017.
[172] "What's the meaning of the phrase 'Loose cannon'?" https://www.phrases.org.uk/meanings/loose-cannon.html
[173] Victor Hugo, "Quatre-vingt-treize" Michel Levy, Paris, 19 février 1874.
[174] https://www.phrases.org.uk/meanings/loose-cannon.html
[175] Kristen Houghton, "Affair survival: tips for dating a married man", Huffington Post, June 10, 2012.
https://www.huffpost.com/entry/affair_b_1408048
[176] Adriana Arias, "Vínculos: por que atraen los casados" Entremujeres, Clarín, Diciembre 27, 2013.
https://www.clarin.com/pareja-y-sexo/gustan-casados-0_SJO_MRYwXx.html
[177] Sandra Lustgarten, "En el diván. ¿Tu pareja te propuso un trio? Te puede pasar esto." Entremujeres, Clarín, Mayo 4, 2016. https://www.clarin.com/entremujeres/pareja-y-sexo/pareja/pareja-propuso-trio-puede-pasar
[178] Walter H. Ghedin "Revolución sexual. Parejas abiertas: cuando la infidelidad no existe." Entremujere, Clarín, 22 Setiembre 2015. https://www.clarin.com/entremujeres/pareja-y-sexo/pareja/pareja_abiertas-infidelidad-companeros-sexuales
[179] Ibidem as above.
[180] Clara Gualano "La sexóloga más famosa. Tríos, Swingers y BDSM: Alessandra Rampolla desarma los tabúes y fantasías sexuales de la monogamia", Entremujeres, Clarín, 18 Mayo 2018.
https://www.clarin.com/entremujeres/pareja/trios-swingers-bdsm-alessandra-rampolla-desarma-tabues
[181] Coumba Kane, "Au Sénégal, la polygamie ne rebute plus les femmes instruites », Le Monde,11 mai 2018.
https://www.lemonde.fr/afrique/article/2018/05/11/au-senegal-la-polygamie-ne-fait-plus-peur-aux-femmes
[182] Ibidem as above.
[183] "Banalisation du Mbarane et Dépravation des Mœurs. Les Séries Sénégalaises pointées du doigt. » Seneplus Société, 31 Mars 2015. https://www.seneplus.com/article/banalisation-du-mbarane-et-depravation-des-moeurs
[184] Term in the Latin language that means; " a total must."
[185] "Poliamor: Te presento a mi mujer, a su novio y a mi novia", Entremujeres, Clarín, April 10, 2019.
https://www.clarin.com/entremujeres/pareja/poliamor-presento-mujer-novio-novia
[186] Anthony F. Bogaert, "Understanding Asexuality", Rowman and Littlefield Publishers, August 2012.
https://rowman.com/ISBN/9781442201019
[187] Belén Figueira "Ansiedad, inseguridades y atracciones múltiples: las problemáticas sexuales más comunes entre los Millennials" Tendencias, Infobae, 8 Junio 2019. https://www.infobae.com/tendencias/2019/06/08
[188] This is the largest professional association of the Argentine psychoanalysts that treat a large proportion of the members of the middle and upper classes in Buenos Aires and other large cities in Argentina.
[189] Ibidem as above. Our translation.
[190] "The Anxious Generation: Causes and Consequences of Anxiety Disorder among Young Americans. Preliminary findings." Berkeley Institute for the Future of Young Americans, Policy Brief, July 2018.
https://gspp.berkeley.edu/assets/uploads/page/Policy_Brief_Final_071618.pdf
[191] Mike Pearl, "What did Porn do to Millennials?" VICE+, March 29, 2016.
https://www.vice.com/en_us/article/nne53b/what-did-porn-do-to-millennials
[192] Acronym for *Radio Televisione Italiana*, the public broadcaster in Italy that has several radio and TV outlets.
[193] https://www.raiplay.it/video/2018/09/Stanotte-a-Pompei-cec5883f-3ab6-4f56-8daa-7e2cd71c6a60.html
[194] Italian term that refers to "a whorehouse" and is derived from "lupa", i.e. a prostitute.
[195] This nickname most likely indicates that its owner was a former legionnaire that participated in the North African campaigns against the rival empire of Carthage.
[196] French term that means "great lady of pleasure"
[197] Sherry Turkle, "Reclaiming conversation: the power of talk in the digital age" Penguin Books, New York, 2015.
[198] https://www.emarketer.com
[199] Sherry Turkle. Ibidem as above.
[200] Nir Eyal, "Hooked: how to build Habit-forming products", Penguin Books, New York,2014.
[201] Alexis derives from the Greek word "lexis", i.e. text.

[202] Taylor GJ, Bagbt, M.R., Parker, J.D.A. "Disorders of Affect regulation: Alexithymia" in "Medical and Psychiatric Illness", Cambridge University Press, Cambridge,1999.

[203] Bar-On, Reuven; Parker, James DA (2000), "The Handbook of Emotional Intelligence: Theory, Development, Assessment and Application at Home, School and in the Workplace" San Francisco, California, Jossey-Bass.

[204] Walter Ghedin, commentary made in "Alexitimia, o la muerte de los sentimientos: porque algunas personas dejan de tener sentimientos", Infobae, Noviembre 6th 201. Our translation.

[205] Name of the Paris hospital where the great Neurology professor had a clinical ward.

[206] Bernard E. Harcourt "Desire and Disobedience in the Digital Age", Harvard University Press, Cambridge, USA, November 2105. http://www.hup.harvard.edu/catalog.php?isbn=9780674504578

[207] Wendy Hiu Kyong Chun "Updating to remain the same: habitual new media" The MIT Press, Boston, USA, May 2016. https://mitpress.mit.edu/books/updating-remain-same

[208] Antonio Meucci was the Italian immigrant to the USA that devised a form of voice-communication link in his Staten Island home in 1871; he filed a claim with the U.S. Patent Office, but he did not mention the electromagnetic transmission of voice sounds. In 1876, Alexander Graham Bell was granted another patent for that electromagnetic transmission of voice sounds by undulatory electric current. https://en.wikipedia.org/wiki/Antonio_Meucci

[209] In the French language, the verb "basculer" means to pivot, to swing from one position to another one.

[210] This term refers to the field next to a medieval castle where the jousting tournaments were usually held.

[211] Term in the French language that means: "field of honor." It usually referred to the open-air space where the chevaliers engaged in dueling confrontations.

[212] Virginia Satir, John Banmen, Jane Gerber, Maria Gomori, "The Satir Model: Family Therapy and Beyond", Science and Behavioral Books, Oct. 31, 2006. https://www.amazon.com/Satir-Model-Therapy-Virginia-published/

[213] Satir V., Bandler R., Grinder J., "Changing with families", Palo Alto, CA, Science and Behavior Books, 1976.

[214] Course syllabus, "Prescribing Controlled Drugs: Critical Issue and Common Pitfalls of Misprescribing", University of Florida Springhill Health Clinic, University of Florida College of Medicine, April 24, 25,26 2013. https://psychiatry.ufl.edu/education/addicition-medicine-cme-program

[215] Term in the French language that can be translated as "the main course."

[216] https://sociology.berkeley.edu/professor-emeritus.arlie-r-hochschild

[217] Arlie R, Hochschild, "So how's the family? And other essays" University of California Press, Berkeley, 2013.

[218] Judith Shulevitz "How to fix Feminism" The New York Times, June 10, 2016 https://www.nytimes.com/2016/06/12/opinion/sunday/how-to-fix-feminism.html?_r=0.

[219] Pamela Druckerman, "Bringing up bebe: one American woman discovers the wisdom of French Parenting" Penguin Books, New York, 2016.

[220] Name of the coalition of moderate and leftist political parties that came to power after the French general elections of 1936, which laid out the basis of the modern French welfare state.

[221] Elise Barthet, "L'économie française résiste bien au ralentissement européen «, Le Monde, 29 Mai 2019. https://www.lemonde.fr/economie/article/2019/05/29/l-economie-francaise-resiste-bine-au-ralentissement

[222] French term that means "taxation."

[223] French term that means "buying power."

[224] "Gilets Jaunes : Macron s'adressera à la nation, lundi à 20 heures » Le Monde, Dimanche Décembre 10, 2018.

[225] The Italian expression literally means "hunger for a piece of soil", which alludes to their profound desire to own a piece of land and work independently. Many of these impoverished immigrants were "mezzadri" in Italy, which meant tilling the land and sharing half (mezzo) of the produce with the landlord. They were grateful to their host countries, Uruguay, or Argentina, for offering them good tracts of fertile land to exploit for their financial gain. Even nowadays when you ride in the roads of rural Italy in the evening, you can see a lone peasant riding a bicycle with the right hand and holding an agricultural utensil on the left shoulder. The half-servitude of poor peasants continues.

[226] Spanish saying that means: "to malinger as a limping pig."

[227] Carmen Maganto, Maite Garaigorbodil "Empathy and conflict resolution in infancy and adolescence" Revista Latinoamericana de Psicologia, 43)2) :255-266, May 2011. https://www.researchgate.net/publication/262754974_Empatia_y_resolucion_de_conflictos_durante_la_infancia_y_la_adolescencia_Empathy_and_conflict_resolution_during_infancy_and_adolescence

[228] "Forgiveness: Your Health Depends on It" Health, Johns Hopkins Medicine. https://www.hopkinsmedicine.org/health/wellness-and-prevention/forgiveness-your-health-depends-on-it

[229] This word is shouted by the spectators when a matador swings the red cape and tricks a charging bull.

[230] https://www.nationalmssociety.org/What-is-MS
[231] A term of the French language that means "exacerbations."
[232] Gillian G. Leibach, MS, Marilyn Stern, PhD, Adriana Aguayo Arelis, MS, "Mental Health and Health-related quality of Life in Multiple Sclerosis caregivers in Mexico" International Journal of MS Care, January/February 2016, Vol.18, No.1, pages 19-26
https://doi.org/10.7224/1537-2073.2014-094
[233] Steven Petrow "Compassion fatigue hits not only professional caregivers. Other people get it too" Health, Perspective, The Washington Post, June 9, 2019. https://www.washingtonpost.com/health/compassion-fatigue
[234] Margo M.C. van Mol, Erwin J.O. Kompanje, Dominique D. Benoit, Jan Bakker, and Marjan D. Nijikamp, "The Prevalence of Compassion Fatigue and Burnout among Healthcare Professionals in Intensive Care Units: A Systematic Review", PLoS One 2015: 10(8): e0136955.
https://www.ncbi.nlm.nih.gov/pmc/aticles/PMC4554995/
[235] C. Daniel Batson "Altruism in Humans", Oxford Scholarship Online, May 2011.
[236] Sedipeh Poyana, Michelle Lobchuk, Wanda Chemomas and Ruth Anne Marrie, "Examining the relationship between caregivers. Emotional Status and Ability to empathize with patients with Multiple Sclerosis." A pilot study, International Journal of MS Care, May/June 2016, Vol. 18, No. 3, pages 122-128.
https://doi.org/10.7224/1537-2073.2015-023
[237] When my brother Gustavo and I were very young, my father Mario had some serious financial problems and was arbitrarily incarcerated to oblige him to pay up (a barbaric tactic that has long been banished by law in Uruguay) and he was only released after our dear mother sold some real estate properties to cover that default for him.
[238] Smith, SG, Chen, J, Basile, KC et al. « The National Intimate Partner and Sexual Violence survey (NISVS) 2015 Dated report" Updated release, Atlanta, GA. National Center of Injury Prevention and Control, Centers for Disease Prevention and Control, 2015.
[239] "Domestic Violence: the Florida Requirement" Continuing Medical education, Florida Physicians & Physicians Assistants, NetCE Continuing Education, Vol. 143 No.2, 2018.
[240] Ibidem as above.
[241] National Center for Injury Prevention and Control. Cost of Intimate Partner Violence against Women in the United States of America, Atlanta, GA; Center for Diseases Control and Prevention, 2013.
[242] Catalano S. "Intimate Partner Violence. Attributes of Victimization 1993-2011" Burau of Justice statistics, U.S. Department of Justice, Washington, D.C., 2013.
[243] https://www.dcf.state.fl.us/programs/domeasticviolence/publications/docs
[244] https://www.fcdav.org/sites/default/sites
[245] Bhandari M, Dosanjh S, Tornetta P 3rd, Matthews D, "Violence Against Women Health Research Collaborative. Musculoskeletal manifestations of physical abuse after intimate partner violence" J Trauma, 2006;61(6):1473-1479.
[246] Capaldi DM, Knoble NB, Shortt JW, Kim HK. A systematic review of risk factors for intimate partner violence. Partner Abuse. 2012;3(2):231-280.
[247] Bhandari et al. See above.
[248] Ibidem as above.
[249] Nancy Jo Sales "American Girls: Social Media and the Secret lives of Teenagers", Knopf, February 2016.
[250] https://www.pacer.org/bullying/resources/stats.asp
[251] Alvin Toffler, "Future Shock", Random House Publishing Group, 1984.
https://www.penguinrandomhouse.com/books/179096/future-shock-by-alvin-toffler/9780553277371/
[252] Hayley Brauer, "Personal Photo Retouching: Millennials Going to Great Lengths for Perfect Pictures Online", The Huffington Post Canada, January 22, 2013. https://www.huffingtonpost.ca/2013/01/21/personal-photo-retouching_n_2499220.html
[253] Peggy Orenstein, "Girls and Sex: navigating the complicated landscape", Harper and Row, March 2016.
[254] Recently the infamous painting was rescued from the dark vault where it had been hidden for many decades and given the pride of place in a new exhibition about Courbet in the Musée D' Orsay. Justice was finally done.
https://www.musee-orsay.fr/en/collections/works-in-focus/search/commentaire/commentaire_id/the-origin-of-the-world-3122.html
[255] Nicola Davis, "Artwork hidden under Picasso painting revealed by X-Ray", The Guardian, Feb. 17, 2018.
https://www.theguardian.com/science/2018/feb/17/artwork-hidden-under-picasso-painting-revealed-by-x-ray
[256] Brina Alseth "Sexting and the Law-Press Send to turn Teenagers into Registered Sex Offenders" ACLU, September 24, 2010. https://www.aclu-wa.org/blog/sexting-and-law

[257] Lauren Stover, "The selfie that goes there," The New York Times, July 7, 2018.
[258] Sadaf Ahsan, "Introducing the feminist selfie: Women using social media to challenge oppressive ideologies, researcher says" National Post, June 3, 2015. https://nationalpost.com/news/canada/introducing-the-feminist-selfie-women-using-social-media-to-challenge-oppressive-ideologies
[259] https://archive.org/details/traitdanatomie02test/page/n8
[260] Frank H, Netter "Atlas of Human Anatomy", Elsevier, ISBN-13:978-0323393225.
[261] https://britannica.com/biography/Mary-Cassatt/
[262] https://en.wikipedia.org/Impresionism
[263] https://www.ggoogle.com/search?=Marie+Cassatt+au+theatre/+edgar+degas
[264] Julian Barnes, "Not in a box," London Review of Books, Vo.40, No.8, pages 8-9.
[265] Term in the French language that means: "group spirit."
[266] John Naughton, "The evolution of the Internet: from military experiment to General Purpose Technology", Journal of Cyber Policy, Volume 1, 2016, Issue 1. https://doi.org/10.1080/23738871.2016.1157619?utm.
[267] This term defines a place or a state of oblivion to any kind of pain, suffering and the external reality, https://merriam-webster.com/dictionary/nirvana
[268] Ibidem as above.
[269] Stanley Fish, "Anonymity and the Dark Side of the Internet", The Opinion Pages, The New York Times, January 3, 2011. https://opinionator.blogs.nytimes.com/2011/01/03/anonymity-and-the-dard-side
[270] Maggie Doherty, "Jia Tolentino on the 'Unlivable Hell' of the Web and other Millennial Conundrums" The New York Times Book Review, August 4, 2019.
 https://www.nytimes.com/2019/08/04/books/review/jia-tolentino-trick-mirror/
[271] https://www.britannica.com/biography/Luigi-Pirandello
[272] Mark Thomas, "Six reasons why criticism is a good thing," The Guardian, Feb. 2, 2012. https://www.theguardian.com/culture-professionals-network/culture-professionals
[273] Josep Matali-Costa, Eduardo Serrano-Troncoso, Marta Pardo, Francisco Villar and Luis San, "Social Isolation and the 'sheltered' profile in Adolescents with Internet Addiction", Journal of Child and Adolescent Behavior, June 11, 2014, 2:139.doi: 10.4172/2375-4494.1000139
https://www.omicsonline.org/open-access/social-isolation-and-the-sheltered-profile
[274] https://www.imdb.com/title/tt0073195
[275] Monica Anderson, "Parents, Teens and Digital Monitoring", Internet and Technology, Pew Research Center, January 7, 2016. https://www.pewinternet.org/2016/01/07/parents-teens-and-digital-monitoring
[276] https://www.imdb.com/title/tt0084516/
[277] Title of the 1977 cult film from the brothers Paolo and Vittorio Taviani that depicts the harsh rearing of a Sardinian shepherd. In the Italian language, "padre" means "father" and "padrone" means a "mean boss." https://en.wikipedia.org/wiki/Padre-Padrone
[278] Margaret Paul « Emotional Dependency, Needing Space" The Blog, Huffington Post, May 2, 2012. https://www.huffpost.com/entry/emotionally-dependent_b_1469460
[279] "Separation Anxiety" Psychology Today.https://www.psychologytoday.com/us/conditions/separation-anxiety
[280] https://www.myfamilies.com/service-programs/domestic-violence/
[281] "Narcissistic Personality Disorder" in "DSM-IV and DSM-5 Criteria for the Personality Disorders". American Psychiatric Association. https://www.nyu.edu/gsas/dept/philo/courses/materials/Narc.Pers.DSM.pdf
[282] Jeffrey E. Young, Janet S. Klosko "Re-inventing your life: The Breakthrough program to end Negative Behaviour…and feel great again" Penguin Press, May 1994.
[283] In *The Odyssey*, after the fall of Troy, Ulysses took several years to return to his hometown of Ithaca. He had been warned that there were some dangerous sirens whose singing might make his crew mad to scuttle his ship. He prudently put wax in their eardrums so they could not listen to their enticing call.
https://ancient-literature.com/greece_homer-Odyssey.html
[284] The literal translation is "slow-cooking abuse." The term "au petit feu" means "a low simmering fire"; it is used as a metaphor for any human action or interaction that is carried out on purpose very slowly, almost parsimoniously.
[285] Jeff Kingston "Japan's Quiet Transformation : Social Change and Civil Society in 21st Century", Routledge Curzon, Oxford, 2004.
[286] Barry Bearak, "Dead Join the Living in a Family Celebration", The New York Times, September 5, 2000. https://www.nytimes.com/2010/09.06/world/africa/06madagascar.html

[287] Michael Biesecker, Michael Kunzelman, "Woman details sex accusation roiling Virginia politics", February 6,2019. https://www.washingtonpost.com/local/woman-details-sex-accusation-roiling-virginia-politics/2019/02/06/0f12acfe-2a5f-11e9-906e-9d55b6451eb4_story.html?utm_term=.aba3c6aaad73

[288] Italian expression that means purposefully "made by yourself" to perfectly match your personal needs.

[289] https://www.aa.org/

[290] https://www.niaaa.nih.gov/alcohol-health/overview-alcohol-consumption/alcohol-facts-and-statistics

[291] https://health.gov/dietaryguidelines/

[292] National Institute on Alcohol Abuse and Alcoholism, Video presentation "Alcohol and the Female Brain", presented by NIAAA Director Dr. George F. Koob, January 9, 2018. https://www.niaaa.nih.gov/alcohol-and-female-brain-presented-by-NIAAA-director-george-koob

[293] "Are women more vulnerable to alcohol effects?" National Institute on Alcohol Abuse and Alcoholism, No. 46, December 1999. https://pubs.niaaa.nih.gov/publications/aa46.htm

[294] Soon-Yeob Park, Mi-Kyyeong Oh, Bum-Soon Lee, "The effects of Alcohol on Quality of Sleep", Korean Journal of Family Medicine 2015 Nov; 36(6): 294-299

[295] Nigel Barber "Why Women Spend So Much Effort on their Appearance", Psychology Today, Dec. 22, 2016. https://www.psychologytoday.com/us/blog/the-human-beast/2011612/why-women-spend-so-much-effort-on-their-aapearance/

[296] https://www.thebodypositive.org/

[297] https://www.hbo.com/movies/fahrenheit-451

[298] "Sexo. Imagen corporal y autoestima. ¿Como influyen en el disfrute?' Entremujeres, Clarín, 29 Abril 2018. https://www.clarin.com/entremujeres/pareja/imagen-corporal-autoestima-influyen-disfrute-sexual_0_rk6qQ-03z.html

[299] Paul R. Albert, "Why is depression more prevalent in women?" Journal of Psychiatry and Neurosciences, 2015 July 40(4):219-221. https://www.ncbi.nlm.nih.gov/pmc/articles/PMC4478054/

[300] Expression in Latin that can be translated " Let us change things that can be changed."

[301] https://www.census.gov/

[302] Kochanek KD, Murphy SL, Xu J, Tejada-Vera B. Deaths: final data for 2014. *Natl Vital Stat Rep*. 2016;65(4):1-122.

[303] Murray, A., "Suicide in the Middle Ages" Volume 2, 2011, Oxford University Press.

[304] Emile Durkheim, "Le suicide", G.P. Ballin (editor), Paris, January 2016.

[305] Marzo Barzagli, "Congedarsi dal mondo. Il Suicidio in Occidente e in Oriente", Bologna, Il Mulino, 2009.

[306] "Chronic Illness and Mental Health", National Institute of Health. https://www.nimh.nih.gov/health/publications/chronic-illenss-mental-health/index.shtml

[307] Hayley C. Gorton, Roger T. Webb, Matthew J, Carr et al., "Risk of Unnatural Mortality in people with Epilepsy", JAMA Neurology 2018; 75 (8);929-938.

[308] Ibidem as above.

[309] Perri Klass, M.D., "Young Adults' Pandemic Mental Health Risks" The New York Times, August 24, 2020. https://www.nytimes.com/2020/08/24/well/family/young-adults-mental-health-pandemic.html

[310] https://www.who.int/mental_health/media/en/56.pdf

[311] Ibidem as above.

[312] Ibidem as above.

[313] Term in the French language that refers to the small dishes that precede the main course or constitute an informal meal for nibbling, typical of spontaneous gatherings of friends; they are similar to the Spanish *tapas*.

[314] Jinhui Joo, Seungyoung Hwang and Joseph J. Gallo, "Death Ideation and Suicidal Ideation in a Community Sample who do not meet Criteria for Major Depression", Crisis 2016 Mar:37(2): 161-165. https://www.ncbi.nhm.nih.gov/pmc/articlesPMC5116433

[315] This is not the whole story. That evening she asked me casually if I was willing to go through a test. As women are always testing you all the time, I said: "pour quoi pas?" She ceremoniously asked me: "If you were to give up one of your senses, which one would it be?" I immediately, resolutely said: "The sight." An embarrassing silence of a few seconds ensued where she stared mute and motionless at me. She finally said: "You are definitely special, as my friends told me. You are the first man I met that gives that answer. It is usually the smell or sound…" After recovering from than unexpected piece of flattery (yes, I have a very vain dimension) I responded: "I have seen a lot

already, maybe the equivalent of what 2 or 3 individuals do in their lifetimes. I can use my visual memory if I still have the excitation from my touch and above all, my smell" That statement gave my "feminine side" away.

[316] Expression in the Castilian language that means: "we write because we want to be loved."

[317] Friedrich Nietzsche, "Thus spoke Zarathustra", Ernst Schmeitzner, Berlin, 1885.

[318] Derrick Bryson Taylor, "Caroline Flack, Who Hosted 'Love Island,' Dies by Suicide at 40" Arts, the New York Times, February 15, 2020. https://nytimes.com/2010/02/15/arts/caroline-flack-dead.html?action

[319] *Top E.R. Doctor Who Treated Virus Patients Dies by Suicide*, The New York Times, April 27, 2020. https://nytimes.com/2020/04/27/nyregion/new-york-doctor-suicide-coronavirus/

[320] Donald M. Berwick, Thomas W. Nolan and John Whittington, *The Triple Aim: Care, Health and Cost*, Health Affairs, May/June 2008. https://doi.org/10.1377/hltaff.27.3.759

[321] Bodenheimer T., Sinsky C., *From triple to quadruple aim: care of the patient requires care of the provider*, Annals of Family Medicine, 2014, November-December; 12(6)573-6. Doi:10.1370/afm.1713. https://ncbi.nlm.nih.gov/pubmed/25384822

[322] West CP, Dyrbye LN, Shanafelt TD, *Physician burnout: contributors, consequences and solutions,* Journal of Internal Medicine 2018 June 283 (6) 516-529 doi 10.1111/joim. 12752. Epub 2018 March 24. https://ncbi.nlm.nih.gov/pubmed/29505159/

[323] Douglas A. Mata, Amarco A. Ramos, Narinder Bansal, *Prevalence of depression and Depressive Symptoms among resident physicians. A Systematic review and Meta-analysis,* Journal of the American Medical Association, 2015, December 8: 314(22) 2373-2383. Doi: 10.1001/jama 2015.15845. https://ncbi.nlm.nih.gov/pmc/sticles/PMC4866499

[324] Lisa S. Rotenstein, Marco A. Ramos, Matthew Torre, *Prevalence of Depression, Depressive Symptoms, and Suicidal Ideation among Medical Students*, Journal of the American Medical Association. 2016 Dec.6:316 (21); 2214-2236. Doi: 10.1001/jama 2016.17324. https://ncbi.nlm.nih.gov/pubmed/27923088

[325] Amy M. Fahrenkopf, Theodore C. Sectish, Laura K. Barger, *Rates of medication errors among depressed and burn out residents: prospective cohort study*. British Medical Journal. 2008 March 1: 336 (7642) ; 488-491. Doi: 10.1136/bmj. 39469.763218 BE.

https://ncbi.nlm.nih.gov/pmc/articles/PMC2258399

[326] Term in the French language that characterizes a sworn, relentless enemy that haunts you.

[327] https://www.srisriravishankar.or

[328] Term of Political Science that described the practical yet tense relationship of the United States of America and the Soviet Union during the Cold War.

[329] George F. Parker, "DSM-5 and Psychotic and Mood disorders", Journal of the American Academy of Psychiatry and the Law, Online, June 2014, 42 (2) 182-190.

[330] https://icd10cmtool.cdc.goc/

[331] https://www.britannica.com/biography/Bonnie-and-Clyde-american-criminals

[332] These paragraphs were excerpted from two separate papers he had written as class assignments in the outstanding *Creative Writing* program of the venerable *Florida State University* (FSU) in Tallahassee, Florida.

[333] https://www.psychiatry.org/psychiatrists/practice/dsm

[335] Ibidem as above.

[336] Ibidem as above.

[337] https://www.psychiatry.org/psychiatrists/practice/dsm

[338] Emily Dogwillo, Kim Menard, Robert Krueger and Aaaron Pincus, "DSM- 5 Pathological Personality Traits and Intimate Partner Violence among Male and Female College Students" Violence and Victims, Vol.31, issue 3, DOI:10.1891/0886-6708. W-D-14-00109. https://connect.springerpub.com/content/sgrvv/31/3/416

[339] www.courses.washington.edu

[340] Sigmund Freud, *Civilization and its Discontents*, James Strachey (translator) ISBN-13:978-0393304510.

[341341] The *Id* is the embodiment of our basic instincts, which usually lay in the Subconscious.

[342] The *Suoer-Ego* is the assemblage of all the educational precepts that mold our daily behavior in society and prods us to compete with other human beings.

[343] Fyodor Dostoyesky, *Crime and Punishment*, Cover Thrift editions, 2001.

[344] Kaplan, Arline, Violence in the Media: what effects on Behavior ?, Psychiatric Times, 5 Oct. 2012. https://psychiatrictimes.com/child-adolescetn-psychiatry/violence-media-waht-effects-beahvior/

[345] Christopher J. Ferguson, Eugene Beresin, *Social Science's Curious war with Pop Culture and How It Was Lost: The Media Violence Debate and the Risks it Holds for Social Science,* Preventive Medicine, 99, 69-76, June 2017. https://pubmed.ncbi.nlm.gov/28212816

[346] Committee on Public Education, *Media Violence*, American Academy of Pediatrics, 1, November 2001. https://pediatrics.aappublications.org/content/108/5/1222/

[347] Christopher J. Ferguson. See above.

[348] Schipiani, Vanessa, *The Facts on Media Violence*, Factcheckorg, 5 august 2019. https://factcheck.org/2018/03/facts-media-violence/

[349] *What role might video game addiction have played in the Columbine shootings?* , Addictions and Answers, New York Daily News, April 23, 2009. https://nydailynews.com/life-style/health/role-video-game-addiction-plaed-columbine-shootings-article-1.361104

[350] Johnnie Allen, Craig A. Anderson, Brad Bushman, *The General Aggression Model*, Current Opinions in Psychology, 19, 75-80 February 2018. https://pubmed.ncbi.nlm.nih.gov/29279227

[351] Baron, Robert A., Richardson, Deborah R., *Human Aggression*, 2nd edition, Plenum Press.

[352] Craig A. Anderson and Brad J. Bushman, *Human Aggression*, Annual Review of Psychology 20001 53:27-51 https://annualreviews.org/doi/abs/10.1146/annurev.psych.53.1000901.135231

[353] Ibidem as above.

[354] Ibidem as above.

[355] Ibidem as above.

[356] Ibidem as above.

[357] Ibidem as above.

[358] Anderson, Craig A., *Media Violence Effects on Children, Adolescents and Young Adults.* https://chausa.org/publications/health-progress/article/July-August2016

[359] Craig A. Anderson, Brad J. Bushman et al., *Screen Violence and Youth Behavior*, Pediatrics 140 (Suppl 2), S142-147 November 201. https://pubmed.ncbi.nlm.nih.gov/29093050

[360] Ibidem as above.

[361] https://britannica.com/biography/Bertolt-Brecht

[362] Anderson, Craig A. Media Violence Effects on Children, adolescents, and Young Adults. See above.

[363] Douglas A. Gentile, Craig A. Anderson, Shintaro Yukawa, Nobuko Ihori, Muniba Saleem, *The Effects of Prosocial Video Games on Prosocial Behaviors: International Evidence from Correlational, Longitudinal, and experimental Studies, Perspectives in Sociology and Psychology Bulletin*, 35(6), 752-63 June 2009. https://pubmed.ncbi.nlm.nih.gov/19321812

[364] Patrick K. Bender, Courtney Plante, Douglas Gentile *The effects of Violent Media Content on Aggression*, Current Opinions on Psychology, 19, 104-108, February 2018. https://pubmed.ncbi.nlm.nih.gov/29279205/

[365] https://britannica.com/biography/Sigmund-Freud

[366] https://britannica.com/biography/Albert-Bandura

[367] Jeannette L. Nolen, Bobo doll experiment Psychology, Encyclopedia Britannica, https://britannica.com/event/Bobo-doll.experiment

[369] Ibidem as above.

[370] Ibidem as above.

[371] Ibidem as above

[372] Mary E. Reuve, MD, and Randon S. Walton, MD, *Violence and Mental Illness*, Psychiatry (Edgemont) 2008 May 5 (5):34-48. Published online May 2008. https://ncbi.nlm.nih.gov/pmc/articles/PMC2686644

[373] Emmons, Sasha, *Is Media Violence damaging to kids?* Cable News Network (CNN), 21 February 2013. www.cnn.com/2013/02/21/living/parenting-kids.media-violence/index.html

[374] Patti M. Walkenburg and Jessica Taylor Pietrovski, *Plugged in: how Media attract and affect* Youth, page 96, Yale University Press, 2017. https://jstor.org/stable/j.ctt1n2tvjd.10

[375] Ibidem as above.

[376] Ibidem as above.

[377] Ibidem as above.

[378] Lauren A. Reed, Richard M. Tolman, L. Monique Ward, *Snooping and sexting: Digital Media as a Context for Dating Aggression and abuse among College Students,* Violence against Women, 22 (13), 1556-1576 November 2016. https://pubmed.ncbi.nlm.nih.gov/26912297/

[379] Naira Delgado, Amanda Rodriguez-perez, Jeroen Vars, Jacques-Philippe Leyten, Veronica Betancor, *Primary Effects on Infra-Humanization*, Project Infra-humanization and De- Humanization, December 2008. https://researchgate.net/publication/234542784

[380] Walkenburg and Pietrovski, see above. Page 100.

[381] L. Rowell Huesman, Jessica Moise-Titus, Cheryl Lynn and Leonard Eron, *Longitudinal Relations between Children's exposure to TV violence and their Aggressive and Violent behavior in Young Adulthood 1977-1992,* Developmental Psychology, Mar. 2003, Vol.39, no.2, p.201-221. https://pubmed.ncbi.nlm.nih.gov/12661882/

[382] Walkenburg and Pietrovski, see above. Page 102.

[383] Christopher J. Ferguson, John Kilburn, *The Public Health risks of Media Violence, a Meta-Analytic Review*, The Journal of Pediatrics, Volume 154, issue 5, May 2009, pages 759-763. https://pubmed.ncbi.nlm.nih.gov/19230901

[384] Ibidem as above.

[385] Parfum, second episode, 1st season, a Netflix series, Creators: Eva Kronenberg, Philip Kadelbach, Oliver Berber.

[386] Nelson, David L.; Cox, Michael M. (2005), Principles of Biochemistry (4th ed.), New York: W. H. Freeman.

[387] Andrea Thompson, "Your odor: Unique as Fingerprint", Live Science, November 5, 2008. https://www.livescience.com/5188-odor-unique-fingerprint.html

[388] Ana V. Oliveira-Pinto, Raquel M. Santos, Renan A, Coutinho, "Sexual dimorphism in the Human Olfactory Bulb: Females have more Neurons and Glial Cells than Males", Published: November 5,2014. https://doi.org/10.1371/journal.pone.0111733

[389] Anne-Marie Mouly, Regina Sullivan, Chapter 15 "Memory and plasticity in the Olfactory System: From Infancy to Adulthood" in "The Neurobiology of Olfaction", Menini A. editor, Boca Raton, USA: CRC Press/Taylor &Francis, 2010. https://www.ncbi.nlm.nih.gov/books/NBK55967

[390] Ana V. Oliveira-Pinto, Raquel M. Santos, Renan A, Coutinho, "Sexual Dimorphism in the Human Olfactory Bulb" Ibidem as above.

[391] Matthew Fulkerson, "Rethinking the senses and their interactions: the case for sensory pluralism" Frontiers in Psychology, Published online Dec. 10, 2014. https://www.frontiersin.org/articles/10.3389/fpsyg.2014.01426/full

[392] https://en.wikipedia.org/wiki/Isabelle_Eberhardt

[393] Mackworth, Cecily, "The Destiny of Isabelle Eberhardt", Harper Collins Publishers, September 1986.

[394] Official name of the *French Foreign Legion*, an all-volunteer military corps with many nationalities.

[395] https://fr.wikipedia.org/wiki/Isabelle_Eberhardt

[396] https://www.census.gov/programs-surveys/decennial-census/2020-census.html

[397] Alina Tugend, "Childless women to marketers: we buy things too," The New York Times, July 6th 2016 https://www.nytimes.com/2016/07/10/business/childless-women-to-marketers-we-buy-things-too.html

[398] Melanie Notkin, « Otherhood: Modern Women finding a new kind of happiness", February 2014, Seal Press. https://www.goodreads.com/book/show/18249396-otherhood

[399] Vanessa de Largie, "Miss Childless-by-Choice", The Huffington Post, July 24, 2015. Updated Dec.6, 2017. https://huffpost.com/entry/miss-childlessbychoice_b_7864162

[400] This French term described the abusive and widely despised right of the feudal lord to summarily seize a bride residing in his land to have a carnal relationship with her in her betrothal day .

[401] Supposedly it was the expression of joy that Archimedes used when, after finding that his body displaced the same amount of water in a public bath, he jumped out and ran home naked through the streets of Athens. https://www.merriam-webster.com/dictionary/eureka

[402] Dhruv Khullar, "How Social isolation is Killing Us". The Upshot, The New York Times, Dec. 22, 2016. https://www.m\nytimes.com/2016/12/22/upshot/how-social-solation-is-killing-us.html

[403] Michael Booth "Stop the Scandimania: Nordic nations aren't the utopias they're made out to be", Opinions, The Washington Post, January 16, 2015. https://www.washingtonpost.com/opinions/sto-the-scandimania

[404] This line was taken from the script of "Wind River", a 2017 Neo-Western movie directed by Taylor Sheridan. It was uttered by Jeremy Renner, who was playing an Alaska Department of Wildlife tracker, to Elizabeth Olsen, playing an FBI agent that is investigating a girl's murder. https://www.imdb.com/title/tt5362988

[405] Jen Hogan "Loneliness in parenthood – a modern day reality" Irish Examiner, May 10, 2018. https://www.irishexaminer.com/breakingnews/lifestyle/features/loneliness-in-parenthood-a-modern-day-reality

[406] Vanessa Martir "I'm a single Mom, and This Shit is Hard" Huffington Post, October 22, 2014. https://www.huffpost.com/entry/in-a-single-mom-and-this-s-is-hard_b_6023856

[407] https://en.wikipedia.org/wiki/Chakra

[408] Alda Palavecino, "La llegada del hermanito", Convivimos, No. 311, Buenos Aires, May 2018.

[409] Ibidem as above.

[410] "Baby boomers look to senior concierge services to raise income", Liz Moyer, The New York Times, May 19, 2017. https://www.ntimes.com/2017/05/19/business/retirement/boomers-retiring-concierge.html

[411] Ibidem as above.

[412] "Deborah de Robertis: shocking for a purpose" Stephen Heyman, The New York Times, September 29,2016. https://www.nytimes.com/2016/09/29/arts/international/deborah-de-robertis-shocking-for-a-purpose.html?module=inline

[413] https://commons.wikimedia.org/wiki/File:Gustave_Courbet_-_The_Origin_of_the_World_-_WGA05503.jpg

[414] Deborah de Robertis. Ibidem as above.

[415] Laren Stover, "The selfie that dares to go there", The New York Times, July 7, 2018 https://www.nytimes.com/2018/07/07/style/vagina-selfies.html

[416] A few decades ago, there were a series of famous ads for the *Virginia Slims* cigarettes that featured women in positions of power with the legend: "you've come a long way, baby)

[417] "Vagina grooming: brightenin'up down there' is big business" Hillary Fanum, The Irish Times, Sept. 21, 2018. https://www.irishtimes.com/life-and-style/people/vagina-grooming-brightening-up-down-there-is-big-business-1.3634463

[418] Name of Madame Bovary's husband in the homonymous novel.

[419] Joni E. Johnston, "The 3 Stages of a Dangerously Obsessive Ex," Psychology Today, August 14, 2017. https://www.psychologytoday.com/us/blog/the-human-equation/201708/the-3-stages-dangerous-obsession

[420] https://www.imdb.com/title/tt798709

[421] Daisy Buchanan, "Virtual girlfriends are a thing now. Sad or sweet?" Women. The Telegraph ,Feb. 26,2014. https://www.telegraph.co.uk/women/sex/10660472/Virtual-girlfriends-are-a-thing-now

[422] Anita Rani, "The Japanese men who prefer virtual girlfriends to sex" In "Magazine", BBC, October 24, 2013. https://www.bbc.com/news/magazine-24614830

[423] This term derives from the name of a worker in the former Soviet Union that supposedly worked for exceptional hours and was extremely productive; this myth was used in the propaganda posters of the USSR. https://www.merriam-webster.com/dictionary/Stakhanovite

[424] "Sexual Desire Disorder" Psychology Today, online edition. Reviewed on March 6, 2018. https://www.psychologytoday.com/us/conditions/sexual-desire-disorder

[425] Keith A. Montgomery, "Sexual Desire Disorders", Psychiatry (Edgmont) 2008 Jun: 5(6): 50-55. https://www.ncbi.nlm.nih.gov/pmc/articles/PMC2695750

[426] "Sexo. Estos seis consejos te ayudaran a recuperar el deseo sexual", Entremujeres, Clarín, 13 Marzo 2019. https://www.clarin.com/buena-vida/consejos-ayudaran-recuperar-deseo-sexual_0_BRzOZ1416.html

[427] Cynthia A. Graham, Catherine H. Mercer, Clare Tanton "What factors are associated with reporting lacking interest in sex and how do these vary by gender? Findings from the third British National Survey of sexual attitudes and lifestyles", British Medical Journal, Open access, Volume 7, issue 9. https://bmjopen.bmj.com/content/7/9/e016942

[428] This is a gentle euphemism of the French language delicately used to refer to "an elderly lady."

[429] Andrew Scull, "Left brain, Right brain; One brain, two brains", Brain, Volume 133, Issue 10, October 1, 2010.

[430] Madura Ingalhalikar, Alex smith, Drew Carter, "Sex differences in the structural connectome of the human brain" Proceedings of the National Academy of Sciences of the United States of America, January 14, 2014, 111 (2) 823-828. https://doi.org/10.1073/pnas.1316909110

[431] Term in the French language that means "the other woman."

[432] Esteban Bustillos, "How Technology plays a major role in modern-day abuse and stalking", Domestic Violence, Dallas News, August 2017. https://www.dallasnews.com/news/domestic-violence/2017/08/24/technology-plays-major-role-modern-stalking

[433] "Redes y control; ¿yo stalkeo, tu stalkeas…Curiosidad o Masoquismo?" Entremujeres, Clarín, Octubre 4, 2017. https://www.clarin.com/entremujeres/pareja-y-sexo/pareja/stalkeo-stalkeas-curiosidad-masoquismo_0_SJs1e7Kpx.html

[434] Term in the French language that means: "the delusion of being loved."

[435] Gaétan Gatian de Clérambault, "L'érotomanie", Empêcheurs de Penser en Rond, Paris, 1993.
[436] Kennedy N., McDonough M., Kelly B., Berrios GE "Erotomania revisited: clinical course and treatment" Comparative Psychiatry 2002 Jan-Feb:43 (1):1-6. https://ncbi.nlm.nih.gov/PubMed/11788912
[437] Oliveira, C; Alves, S, Ferreira C. , Agostinho, C. (2016) "Erotomania – A review of de Clerambault's Syndrome" The Journal of the European Psychiatric Association. 33 :664. https://doi.org/10.1016/eurpsy.2016.01.72
[438] Dr. Nicolas Evrard, "Erotomanie : les symptômes » Onmeda, 01, Aout 2014. Our translation. https://onmeda.fr/maladies/erotomanie-symptomes-3202.3.html//
[439] Joni E. Johnston, "The 3 stages of a dangerously Obsessive Ex" Psychology Today, posted August 14, 2017. https://psychologytoday.com/us/blog/the-human-equation/201708/the-3-stages-dangerously-obsessive-ex/
[440] Ibidem as above.
[441] Marguerite Yourcenar, "Alexis ou le traité du vain combat ; le coup de grâce » Gallimard, Paris, 1971.
[442] Walter H. Ghedin, "Me enteré que mi marido es gay," Entremujeres, Clarín, 22 Marzo 2017. https://www.clarin.com/entremujeres/pareja-y-sexo/pareja/enter-marido-gay_0_H1bxdSe3l.html
[443] Ibidem as above.
[444] Ibidem as above.
[445] Ibidem as above.
[446] Walter H. Ghedin, "Oferta sexual: ¿Que buscan los hombres en las travestis?" Entremujeres, Clarín, 25 Febrero 2013. https://www.clarin.com/entremujeres/pareja-y-sexo/hombres/travestis-transexuales-infidelidad-oferta_sexual-columinista-hombres-deseo-sexo_0_Sk6kNaKDQl.html
[447] https://vox.com/identities/2019/9/5/208401011/terfs-radical-feminists-gender-critical
[448] This term derives from the propensity of some Trans women, who have not had a change of sex operation already, to hide their penis under a tight wrap of cotton in their panties. Many consider it too derogatory.
[449] Eric Newman, "Andrea Long Chu on Desire, Weak Love, and Modern trans Identity" Literary Hub, October 29, 2019. https://lithub.com/andrea-long-chu-on-desire--weak-love-and-modern-trans-identity/
[450] American slang expression that is meant to celebrate the looks of a beautiful girl when you see her.
[451] If you want to have a glimpse of what a great woman our dear mother Gladys was, please read this blog. https://drmolaplume.com/2017/05/20/born-into-disobedience/
[452] Charles Darwin, "On the origin of species", Mass Market Paperback, New York, 2003. https://www.amazon.com/Origin-Species-150th-Anniversary/dp/0451529065
[453] Encyclopedia Britannica, "Jean-Baptiste Lamarck", https://www.britannica.com/biography/Jean-Baptiste-Lamarck
[454] Jean Baptiste de Monet de Lamarck, « Recherche sur l'organisation des corps vivants : précédé du discours d'ouverture du cours de zoologie donné dans le Musée d'Histoire Naturelle » Fayard, Paris, 1986. https://www.amazon.com/Recherches-sur-lorganisation-corps-vivants/dp/2213017018
[455] Leslie A. Pray, "Discovery of DNA structure and function: Watson and Crick" Nature Education, 1(1):100, 2008.
[456] Nelson Cabej, "Building the most complex structure on Earth: an epigenetic narrative of Development and Evolution of Animals", Elsevier, February 2013. https://www.elsevier.com/books/building-the-most-complex-structure-on-earth/cabej/978-0-12-401667-5
[457] Israel Rosenfield, Edward Ziff. "Epigenetics: The Evolution Revolution", The New York Review of Books, June 7, 2018. https://www.nybooks.com/articles/2018/06/07/epigenetics-the-evolution-revolution/
[458] Jaenisch R., Bird A., "Epigenetic regulation of gene expression: how the genome integrates intrinsic and environmental signals" Natural Genetics, 2003 March, Supplement 245-54.1 https://www.ncbi.nlm.nih.gov/pubmed/12610534
[459] Robert M. Sapolsky, L. Michael Romero, Allan U. Munck, "How do Glucocorticoids Influence Stress responses? Integrating Permissive, Suppressive, Stimulatory, and Preparative Actions" Endocrine Reviews, Volume 21, Issue 1, February 2000, pages 55-89. https://doi.org/10.1210/edrv.21.1.0389
[460] https://www.utsc.utoronto.ca/~pmcgowan/documents/McGowanBrainRes08.pdf
[461] Lisa D. Moore, Thuc Le, Guoping Fan "DNA Methylation and its Basic Function", Neuropsychopharmacology 2013 Jan:38(1): 23-38. Published Online 2012 Jul 11 doi:10.1038/npp.2012.112. https://ncbi.nlm.nih.gov/pmc/articles/PMC3521964/
[462] William Shirer, "The Rise and Fall of the Third Reich, Fiftieth Anniversary edition", Barnes and Noble, 2018. https://www.barnesandnoble.com/w/rise-and-fall-of-the-third-reich-william-l-shirer/1100214065#/

[463] Ibidem as above.
[464] Nadine Burke Harris, "The deepest well: healing the long-term effects of childhood adversity" January 2018. https://www.amazon.com/Deepest-Well-Long-Term-Childhood-Adversity/dp/0544828704/ref=tmm_hrd_swatch_0?_encoding=UTF8&qid=&sr=
[465] The translation from Spanish is: "Thank you, Mommy dearest."
[466] Caroline Kitchener, "Boyfriend and Girlfriend are out. 'Partners' are in. Here's why more Millennials are changing how they define their relationship" The Lily, January 18, 2109. https://www.thelily.com/boyfriend-and-girlfriend-are-out-partners-are-in-heres-why-more-millennials-changing-how-they-define-their-relationships/
[467] Jean Paul Sartre, "L'être et le néant. Essai d'ontologie phénoménologique », First Edition 1943, New Edition 1994, Gallimard, Paris. Our translation. http://www.gallimard.fr/Catalogue/GALLIMARD/Tel/L-etre-et-le-neant
[468] https://en.wikipedia.org/wiki/El_Impenetrable_National_Park/
[469] Her exact words in Castillian language were: "porque no tengo un hombre que me caliente la cabeza."
[470] Joan DelFattore, "Singles say they're better prepared to self-quarantine, but many fear getting shortchanged in medical treatment", Health, The Washington Post, April 11, 2020. https://washingtonpost.com/health/singles-say-theyre-better-prepared-to-self-quarantine-bu-may-fear-gettting-shortchanged-medical-treatment
[471] Aida Faber, Laurette Dube, Barbel Knauper, "Attachment and eating: a Meta-Analytic Review of the Relevance of Attachment for Unhealthy and Healthy Eating Behaviors in the General Population", Review, Appetite, 2018 April 1:123;410-438.doi:10.1016. https://pubmed.ncbi.nlm.nih.gov/29183700/
[472] Julie C. Bowker, Miriam T. Stotsky and Rebecca G. Etkin, "How BIS/BAS and psycho-behavioral variables distinguish between Social Withdrawal subtypes during emerging adulthood", Personality and Individual Differences, Volume 119, 1 December 2107. Pages 283-288. https://doi.org/10.1016/j.paid.2017.07.043/
[473] Ibidem as above.
[474] Ophelia Field Hodder, "The favorite: Sarah, Duchess of Marlborough", Saint Martin's Press, July 2003. https://www.goodreads.com/book/show/1243559.Sarah_Churchill_Duchess_of_Marlborough
[475] https://en.wikipedia.org/wiki/James_II_of_England
[476] Ophelia Field Hodder, ibidem as above.
[477] Ophelia Field Hodder, ibidem as above.
[478] Mark Kishlansky, "Why the richest woman in Britain changed her will 26 times", London Review of Books, Vol.24, No.22, November 14, 2018; pages 301-31.https://www.lrb.co.uk/v24/n22/mark-kishlansky/why-the-richest-woman-in-britain-changed-her-will-26-times?utm_source=LRB+icymi&utm_medium=email&utm_campaign=20180112+icymi&utm_content=usca_nonsubs_icymi
[479] Shanzez Khurram, "Is the American Dream becoming too materialistic?," The Huffington Post, February 17, 2013, Updated 5/19/13 https://www.huffingtonpost.com/shanzeh-khurram/is-the-american-dream-bec_b_2702164.html
[480] Ryan T. Howell, "The preference for experiences over possessions. Measurement and construct validation of the experimental Buying Tendency Scale", The Journal of Positive Psychology, Vol.7, No.1, January 2012, 57-71. https://www.psychologytoday.com/files/attachments/2557/howellpcheliniyer2012the-preference-experiences-over-possessions.pdf
[481] Roser Granero, Fernando Fernandez-Aranda, Gemma Mestre-Bach, "Compulsive Buying Behavior: Clinical Comparison with Other Behavioral Addictions" Frontiers in Psychology 2016; 7;914. Published Online June 15, 2016. https://www.ncbi.nlm.nih.gov/pmc/articles/PMC4908125/
[482] Ibidem as above.
[483] Dittmar, Helga, Bond, Red, Hurst, Megan, and Karen, "The relationship between materialism and personal well-being: a meta-analysis" Journal of Personality and Social Psychology, 107(5) pp.879-924. https://psycnet.apa.org/doiLanding?doi=10.1037%2Fa0037409
[484] "Do Prestige Goods Enhance Self-Esteem and Professionalism? A study on Users of Luxury-Branded shirts" Marketing Review St. Gallen 29(1):17-23. February 2012. https://www.researchgate.net/pubication/271660340/271660340
[485] http://mediasmarts.ca/digital-media-literacy/media-issues/marketing-consumerism/how-marketers-target-kids
[486] "Parents lavished gifts on children to compensate for lack of quality time" Daily Mail, Sunday, June 16, 2019. https://www.dailymail.co.uk/news/aticle-445381/parents-lavish-gifts-children-compensate-lack-quality-time
[487] "Cambiar nuestros hábitos de consumo nos hace más felices" Entremujeres, Clarín, Oct.8,2018. https://www.clarin.com/entremujers/bienestar/cambiar-habitos-consumo-hace-felices

[488] https://www.ncpgambling.org/wp-content/uploads/2014/08/DSM-5-Diagnostic-Criteria-Gambling-Disorder.pdf
[489] https://www.scientificamerican.com/article/how-the-brain-gets-addicted-to-gambling/#googDisableSync
[490] Seyed Amir Jaezeri, Mohammad Hussain Bin Habil "Reviewing Two Types of Addiction-Pathological Gambling and Substance Use" Indian Journal of Psychological Medicine. 2012 Jan-Mar; 34(1):5-11. https://www.ncbi.nlm.nih.gov/pmc/articles/PMC3361844/
[491] "The States' role in Gambling Addiction", Consults, The New York Times blog, November 4, 2010. https://consults.blogs.nytimes.com/2010/11/04/the-states-role-in-gambling-addiction/
[492] Casey Bond, "Marriages with female breadwinners still struggle" Huffington Post, July 12, 2018. https://www.huffpost.com/entry/female-breadwinners-marriage_n_5b3ef51fe4b09e4a8b2b780c
[493] Alexandra Mondalek, '"The History of Women wearing Pants as Power Symbol" Life, The Huffington Post, March 2, 2018. https://www.huffpost.com/entry/the-history-of-women-wearing-pants-as-power-symbol_n_5a99bb95e40a
[494] "Finanzas en casa. Infidelidad financiera. ¿Ocultar gastos es traicionar?", Entremujeres, Clarín, 25 Abril 2014. https://www.clarin.com/pareja/pareja-finanzas-dinero-convivencia-gastos-infidelidad-mentir-ocultar-compras-plata_0_Ske5tAYwXe.html
[495] Term in the French language that means: "impressive performance or achievement with great skill."
[496] Kelli B. Grant "More spouses are cheating (financially, anyway)" Your Money, Your Future. CNBC. https://www.cnbc.com/2014/02/07/more-spouses-are-cheating-financially-anyway.html
[497] Sarah Freeman "True confession: My Bipolar Disorder Wrecked My Finances", June 20, 2013. https://www.businessinsider.com/my-bipolar-disorder-wrecked-my-fiances-2013-6
[498] Marianne Bertrand, Emir Kamenica, Jessica Pan, "Gender Identity and Relative Income with households", March 2015, CEPR Discussion paper DP 10443. https://papers.ssrn.com/sol3/papers.cfm?abstract_id=2572421
[499] Michael Tobin, a savvy lawyer in Coral Gables, told me many years ago: "Remember that nobody ever got into any kind of trouble by saying *I can't remember*." As of then, I have faithfully followed his sage advice.
[500] Juju Chang, Victoria Thompson, and Kelly Harold, "Secrets of Gigolos: Why More Women say they are Willing to Pay for Sex" ABC News, February 26, 2012. https://abcnews.go.com/Business/secrets-gigolos-women-pay-for-sex.story?id_15644065
[501] There is a term in the Spanish language that says: "se quedo para vestir santos." It means that a woman remaining as a spinster until the end of her life or becoming a widow with an empty nest, would pitch in her local parish, instead of staying at home, to help with menial jobs like cleaning the floor or dusting the saints' garments.
[502] Susan Chira "Money is Power. And Women Need More of Both", News Analysis, The New York Times, March 10, 2018. https://www.nytimes.com/2018/03/10/sunday-review/women-money-politics-power.html
[503] David J. Ley, PhD, "Why Women love Romantic Threesomes?" Psychology Today, October 25, 2014. https://www.psychologytoday.com*/us/blog/women-who-stray/201410/why-women-love-romantic-threesomes
[504] "Alternativas. Dos hombres. ¿Una mujer…El trio menos pensado?" Entremujeres, Clarín, 23 Enero 2012. https://www.clarin.com/sexo/pareja-sexo-columnista-trio-mujer-hombre-cama-sexo_grupal-multiple-fantasias_0_SJbQl-5wXg.html
[505] Hollly Robinson, "A Blended Family United", Home, Parents magazine. https://www.parents.com/parenting/divorce/blended-families/navigating-the-challenges-of-blended-families
[506] Melissa Curley Bogner "From Stepchild to Stepmother: What I've Learned" Huffington Post, May 6, 2016. https://www.huffpost.com/entry/from-stepchild-to-stepmom_b_10248432
[507] Wednesday Martin "Why it's Easier to Love a Stepfather than a Stepmother?" Psychology Today, June 11, 2011. https://www.psychologytoday.com/us/blog/stepmonster/201106/why-its-easier-love-steepfather-stepmother
[508] "Stepfamilies: How to help your child adjust," Children's Health, The Mayo Clinic. https://www.mayoclinic.org/healthy-lifestyle/childrens-healthy/in-depth/stepfamilies/art-20047046
[509] Olivia Petter "Woman reveals what a real 'Knight in Shining Armor' looks like in vital Facebook post" Independent, November 2, 2017. https://www.independent.co.uk/life-style/love-sex/woman-knight-in-shining-armour-facebook-post
[510] Term in the French language that means "implicit terms."
[511] Lena Aburdene Dehally, "10 Tips for Choosing the Right Partner" The Huffington Post, June 30, 2015. https://www.huffpost.com/entry/choosing-right-partner_b_76888382
[512] This section was inspired by an old article that appeared in the newspaper *La Nación* from Buenos Aires. Unfortunately, we cannot remember its details but are willing to amend this deficiency if someone let us know them.

[513] Expression in the French language that means: "just in case."
[514] David Blumenthal, Shanoor Seervai, "Rising Obesity in the United states is a Public Health crisis" To the Point, April 24, 2018. https://www.coomonwealthfund.org/blog/2018/rising-obesity-unitede-states-public-health-crisis
[515] Rebecca M. Puhl, Chelsea A, Heuer "Obesity Stigma: Important considerations for Public Health" American Journal of Public Health, 2010 June: 100(6): 1019-1028. https://www.ncbi.nlm.nih.gov/pmc/articles/PMC2866597
[516] "Airline Passenger of Size Policies: Will you be forced to buy an extra seat?' Independent Traveler, April 16, 2019. https://www.smartertravel.com/airline-obesity-policies/
[517] https://www.amazon.fr/ne-na%C3%AEt-pas-grosse-ebook/dp/B071D6PNQ4
[518] Gaelle Dupont, "Il est urgent de lutter contre la grossophobie », Le Monde, 13 juin 2017. https://lemonde.fr/sante/article/2017/06/13/il-est-urgent-de-lutter-contre-la-grossophobie_5143496_1651302.html
[519] Term in the French language can be translated as "the phobia for fatness."
[520] Acronym for the "Institut National de la Santé et de la Recherche Medicale », the French equivalent of the « National Institute of Health" in the USA. https://www.inserm.fr/en/about-inserm
[521] Center for Disease Control and Prevention, "Overweight and Obesity." https://www.cdc.gov/obesity/data/prevalence-maps.htmleport
[522] Harvard T. H. Chan School of Public Health, "Obesity prevention source" https://www.hsph.harvard.edu/obesity-prevention-source/obesity-causes/diet-and-weight/
[523] Italian expression that can be translated as: "the occasion makes the thief."
[524] American Psychological Association (APA), "APA survey finds feeling valued at work linked to well-being and performance", March 8, 2012. https://www.apa.org/news/press/releases/2012/03/well-being
[525] American Psychological Association (APA). "Gender and Stress", web page. https://www.apa.org/news/press/releases/stress/2010/gender-stress
[526] "Eating your feelings? The link between job stress, junk food and sleep" Science News, June 22, 2017. https://www.sciencedaily.com/releases/2017/06/17062210387.htm
[527] Dan Lyons, "Congratulations! You're being fired." Opinion, The New York Times, April 9, 2016. https://www.nytimes.com/2016/04/10/opinion/sunday/congratulations-youve-been-fired.html?_r=0
[528] Name in the Italian language that refers to something or a process that was significantly reformed to conform to more modern standards or parameters.
[529] French expression that can be translated as: "the more it changes, the more it rests the same."
[530] Sigmund Freud, *New Introductory letters on Psychoanalysis*, George Allen and Unwin, London, January 1940,
[531] https://en.wikipedia.org/wiki/Ernst-Röhm/ .
[532] John Cleland, *Fanny Hill*, Gray Rabbit Publishing, London, 2018.
[533] The labia majora of the vagina are commonly referred as "the netherlips."
[534] Chrissie described this tool as a fast-paced messenger service that is commonly used in certain offices. "Messenger service on steroids," she said. https://slack.com/
[535] https://chrissie.blog/2020/05/13/are-you-okay/
[536] This term in the Latin language refers to the ancient act of contrition of Christians in front of the Holy Cross when they beat up their chests while they publicly assumed responsibility for their sins or faults.
[537] Ian Shapira, *Small businesses in high-rent cities face disaster. If they go under, urban life will change*, Local, The Washington Post, May 16, 2010. https://washingtonpost.com/local/small-businesses-in-high-rent-cities-face-disaster-if-they-go-under-urban-life-will-change/
[538] https://tinder.com/
[539] https://www.ashleymadison.com/
[540] Its motto is: "Life is short. Have an affair."
[541] https://www.usatoday.com/story/news/nation-now/2018/02/08/sex-intimacy-and-friendship-ashley-madison-survey-reveals-why-people-cheat/318668002/
[542] Popular expression that means: "to remain silent about something or somebody."
[543] https://www.psychologytoday.com/us/blog/love-and-gratitude/201310/oxytocin-the-love-and-trust-hormone-can-be-deceptive
[544] Jerald Bain, "The many faces of Testosterone" Clin. Interv. Aging 2007 Dec; 2(4): 567-576.

https://www.ncbi.nlm.nih.gov/pmc/articles/PMC2686330/

[545] This term was used by Ms. Maureen Dowd in an article that we are reading right now as we are editing this book. Every Sunday morning, we excitedly open the NY Times, filled with the fluttering heart of a teenager madly in love, so we can enjoy her acerbic, accurate and elegant political articles . *Merci beaucoup, ma chère Mau. Un gros bisou.*
https://www.nytimes.com/2020/01/18/opinion/sunday/starr-dershowitz-trump-epstein.html?action=click&module=Opinion&pgtype=Homepage

[546] Jake LaMotta was a great American middleweight boxer that became the central character in the fabulous Martin Scorsese's 1980 film "The Raging Bull"; Robert de Niro played the central character. My father Mario, my son Giani and I consider it one of the 10 very best films of all time. https://www.imdb.com/title/tt0081398/

[547] https://en.wikipedia.org/wiki/Nina_Simone

[548] Nina Simone speaks in "What happened Miss Simone?" A Netflix documentary watched on Valentine's day 2019.

[549] Term in the French language that refers to the pseudonyms taken by prostitutes to conceal their real identities.

[550] Ambassador Shabazz speaks in "What happened Miss Simone?" A Netflix documentary; watched on Valentine's Day 2019.
https://www.netflix.com/

[551] Sergio Guillen, Prólogo de "La Condena y otros relatos", Editorial Akal, Buenos Aires, 1987.

During the night of December 12 to December 13, 1912, Franz Kafka penned during one night of creative insomnia what many of his admirers have labelled as his "breakthrough" piece of writing, which clearly heralded what would be his unique literary style. It details the confrontation of Georg, his principal character, with his father.

This little book has special significance for us because we bought it with our children in a visit to Buenos Aires. When we entered the small Eudeba bookstore near the Congress, we were first attracted to a clearance table. Drawn by an irresistible *animal magnetism*, we first picked up this small, thin book amongst more alluring ones. When the old lady tending shop saw our gesture, she spontaneously exclaimed: "Oh, Kafka!" Yes, Franz all the time.

[552] Expression in Neapolitan slang that can be translated as: "Kulibaly, you are my life"

[553] It is hard to explain the intense passion of most Neapolitans, and by extension the inhabitants of the Campania Region, for their beloved football club. Everything is exaggerated, including love and its mirror feeling, hate.

[554] "Braccianti" referred to the laborers that worked for a meagre stipend; the term comes from "braccio", i.e. arm. "Mezzadri" referred to the laborers that worked for half the crop's profits; the term comes from "mezzo", i.e. half.

[555] Spanish saying that means: "a clean hog does not fatten up."

[556] Donna Britt, "A white mother went to Alabama to fight for civil rights. The Klan killed her for it." Retropolis, The Washington Post, December 15, 2017.

[557] Expression in the French language that means "done deal.'

[558] Expression in the French language that means "spiritual status."

[559] Term in the French language that can be translated as: "an irrefutable fact."

[560] Anupam B. Jena, Andrew R. Olenski, Daniel M. Blumenthal, "Sex differences in Physician Salary in US Public Medical schools", JAMA Internal Medicine, 2016; 176 (9); 1294-1304.
https://jamanetwork.com/journals/jamainternalmedicine/fullarticle/2532788

[561] Ibidem as above.

[562] Sloane Crosley, "Why women apologize and should stop", Op-Ed, The New York Times, June 23, 2015.
https://www.nytimes.com/2015/06/23/opinion/when-an-apology-is-anything-but.html

[563] Audrey Nelson "Who negotiates better, men or women?" Psychology Today, May 24, 2011.
https://www.psychologytoday.com/us/blog/he-speaks-she-speaks/201105/who-negotiates-better-men-or-women

[564] Bethanne Patrick, "Severe weather in the Sunshine State", Poets and Writers, July-August 2108, pages 38-43.
https://www.pw.org/content/severe_weather_in_the_sunshine_state

[565] Acronym for the "Royal Air Force."

[566] Official name of the German Army.

[567] "Edward R. Murrow reports the Dunkirk evacuation", You Tube,
https://www.youtube.com/watch?v=Ktvl2uJwv7A

[568] Acronym of the "British Broadcasting Corporation."

[569] "Great speeches of the 20th century/ We shall fight to the beaches." The Guardian, 20 April 2007.
https://www.theguardian.com/world/series/great-speeches-winston-churchill

[570] Edward Stourton, "Auntie's War: the BBC during the Second World War", Doubleday, November 2017.
https://www.penguin.co.uk/books/110/1109453/auntie-s-war/9781784160791.html

[571] Ian Jack, "Time for several whiskies", London Review of Books, Vol. 40, No. 16, pages 3-8. https://www.lrb.co.uk/v40/n16/ian-jack/time-for-several-whiskies
[572] Acronym for the "London Review of Books", perhaps the best literary magazine in the English language.
[573] Raymond Clayton, "Letter to the Editor', London Review of Books, Volume 40, Number 18, 27 September 2018, page 5. https://www.lrb.co.uk/v40/n18/letters
[574] Dr. Frank Luntz, "Words that work. It's not what you say. It's what people hear." Hyperion, 2007. https://www.amazon.com/Words-People-Luntz-Hyperion-Hardcover/dp/B00DWWISLG/ref=tmm_hrd_swatch_0?_encoding=UTF8&qid=&sr=
[575] According to the Merriam Webster dictionary, fantods refers to "a state of irritability and tension." The dictionary says that "the exact origin of fantod remains a mystery, but it may have arisen from English dialectical 'fantigue'—a word (once used by Charles Dickens) that refers to a state of great tension or excitement and may be a blend of "fantastic" and "fatigue." This word is our most humble recognition for one of our mentors, Charles Dickens. Ever since we started reading him as a child in the "Instituto Cultural Anglo-Uruguayo" (Anglo) where we studied English, he has been one of our favorite authors. https://www.merriam.webster.com
[576] This paragraph was inspired by the wonderful scenes of Christopher Nolan's 2017 masterpiece *Dunkirk*. https://www.youtube.com/watch?v=F-eMt3SrfFU
[577] Italian expression that literally means "under the desk." It refers to the widespread habitude of doing things outside of the established, and often legal and/or ethical, established channels, like offering bribes to functionaries.
[578] https://www.pewresearch.org/fact-tank/2017/03/20/despite-gains-women-remain-underrepresented-among-u-s-political-and-business-leaders/
[579] Erica Hersh, "Why Diversity matters: Women on Boards of Directors", *Harvard School of Public Health* web page. https://www.hsph.harvard.edu/ecpe/why-diversity-matters-women-on-boards-of-directors/
[580] Michael J. Silverstein and Kate Sayre, "The female economy", Harvard Business Review, September 2009. https://hbr.org/2009/09/the-female-economy
[581] Ibidem as above.
[582] "Fulfilling the promise: how more Women on Corporate Boards would make America and American companies more competitive", Statement by the Policy and Impact Committee of the Committee for Economic Development. https://www.ced.org/pdf/Fulfilling-the-Promise.pdf
[583] Adam J. Hampton, Amanda N. Fisher- Boyd, Susan Sprecher "You're like me and I like you; Mediators of the similarity- liking link assessed before and after a getting acquainted social interaction" Journal of Social and Personal Relationships, July 30, 2018. https://doi.org/10.1177%2F0265407518790411
[584] Gwendolyn Seidman, "Why do we like people who are similar to us?" Psychology Today. https://www.psychologytoday.com/us/blog/close-encounters/201812/why-do-we-people-who-are-similar-us
[585] Hampton et al. Ibidem as above.
[586] This is the ridiculous vainglorious term that the bosses of American corporations self- adopted in the 80s to boast about their privileged position in society and their supposedly infallible "supernatural powers" (sic)
[587] https://www.merriam-webster.com/dictionary/glass%20ceiling
[588] Michelle K. Ryan, S. alexander Haslam, « The Glass Cliff; evidence that Women are over-represented in Precarious Leadership Positions", British Journal of Management, Vol.16, No.2, pages 81-90, June 2005. https://papers.ssm.com/so13/paers.cfm?abstract-id+734677
[589] Susanne Bruckmuller, Nyla R, Branscombe, "How women end up on the 'Glass Cliff", Harvard Business Review, January-February 2011. https://hbr.org/2011/01/how-women-end-up-on-the-glass-cliff
[590] Ibidem as above.
[591] Term in the French language that refers to the histrionic gimmicks that actors used to please the popular classes massed in the more affordable gallery section of a theater in order to boost their enthusiasm and get their applause.
[592] Expression in Latin that can be translated as: "Fortune favors the audacious."
[593] Based on the famous quote from "The tragedy of Hamlet" by William Shakespeare.
[594] https://www.cnn.com/politics/live-news/kavanaugh-hearing-dle/index.html
[595] https://twitter.com/maggieNYT
[596] https://www.cdc.gov/nchs/data/vsrr/report004.pdf
[597] "America's fertility rate continues to decline", The Economist, October 31st, 2018. https://www.economist.com/democracy-in-america/2018/10/31/americas-fertility-rate-continues-its-deep-decline
[598] https://www.dol.gov/geeneral/topi/benefits-leave/fmla

[599] https://www.urban.org/urban-wire/what-changes-household-income-around-babys-arrival-tell-us-about-importance-paid-family-and-medical-leave
[600] Rasheed Malik, Katie Hamm, Leila Schochet, Cristina Novoa, Simon Workman and Steven Jessen-Howard, "America Child Care Deserts in 2018", Center for American Progress, December 6, 2018. https://www.americanprogress.org/issues/early-childhood/reports/2018/12/06/461643
[601] https://www.nhs.uk/using-the-nhs/about-the-nhs/the-nhs/www
[602] Denis Campbell, "Nye Bevan's dream: a history of the NHS", Society, The Guardian, January 18, 2016. https://www.theguardian.com/society/2016/jan/18/nye-bevan-history-of-nhs-national-health-service
[603] "What does the public think of the NHS?", The King's Fund, London, September 16, 2017. https://www.kingsfund.org.uk/publications/what-does-public-think-about--nhs
[604] https://www.gov.uk/govenment/organisations/department-of-health-and-social-care
[605] Laura Butler, "Male doctors earn 1,17 pounds for every pound earned by female doctors", Press release, March 29, 2019. https://www.surrey.ac.uk/news/male-doctors-earn-ps117-every-ps1-earned-female-doctors
[606] Denis Campbell, "Male NHS doctors earn 17% more than their female peers", The Guardian, March 28, 2019. https://www.theguardian.com/society/2019/mar/29/male-nhs-doctoors-earn-17-more-than-their-female-peers
[607] Expression in the French language that means: "it is only correct to say or do something"
[608] Christopher F. Karpowitz, Tali Mendelberg, Lee Shaker, "Gender Inequality in Deliberative Participation", American Political Science Review, Volume 106, Issue 3, August 2012, pp. 533-547, published online August 9, 2012. https://doi.org/10.1017/50003055412000329
[609] Lynn Smith-Lovin and Charles Brody, "Interruptions in group discussions; the effects of Gender and Z Group composition", American Sociological Review, Vol. 54, No.3 (June 1989) pp.424-435. https://www.jstor.org/stable/stable/2095614
[610] Ibidem as above.
[611] https://en.wikipedia.org/wiki/United_Statees_Military_Academyen.wikip
[612] Sean R. Martin, "Research: Men get credit for voicing Ideas, but not Problems. Women don't get credit for either" Harvard Business Review, November 2017. https://hbr.org/2017/11/research-men-get-credit-for-voicing-ideas-but-not-problems-women-dont-get-credit-for-either
[613] Eagly AH, Karau SJ, "Role congruity theory of prejudice toward female leaders", Psychology Review, 20012, July; 109 (3); 73-98. https://www.ncbi.nlm.nih.gov/pubmead/12088246
[614] https://www.pwc.com
[615] https://www.pwc.com/timetotalk
[616] Carol Stubbings, "What Women want in the Workplace", S+B blogs, Harvard Business Review, March 8, 2018. https://www.strategy-business.com/blog/What-Women-Want-in-the-Workplace
[617] This society, also known as the "Society of Saint Tammany" was the political machine of the Democratic Party that controlled the politics of New York City in the late nineteenth and early twentieth century, often controlled by the Irish immigrants. https://en.wikipedia.org/wiki/Tammany-Hall/
[618] "Women and Leadership", Pew Research Center, Social &Demographic Trends, January 18, 2015. https://www.pewsocialtrends.org/2015/01/14/women-and-leadership
[619] Carol Stubbings. Ibidem as above.
[620] Ibidem as above.
[621] Acronym for the "Vision Effects Society."
[622] https://www.siggraph.org
[623] https://youtu.be/O3cV5mzWZ5E
[624] Ellen Mccarthy "For female leaders, humor is a blessing. Unless it's a curse." Style, The Washington Post, January 16, 20120. https://washingtonpost.com/lifestyle/style/for-female-leaders-humor-is-a-blessing-unless-its-a-curse/2020/01/15
[625] Jonathan B. Evans, Jerel E. Slaughter, Aleksander P.J. Ellis and Jessi M. Rivin "Gender and the evaluation of humor at work" https://management.eller.arizona.edu.sites/default/files/leader_humor_jap_in_press.pdf
[626] www.wethepeoplesummit.org
[627] National Public Radio, "Presidential Politics; Does Likeability Matter", Podcast, October 7, 2012. https://www/npr.org/2012/10/07/162480455/presidential-politics-does-likeability-matter/
[628] Jennifer Rubin, "A study in contrasts: Klobuchar and O'Rourke", The Washington Post, April 2, 2019. https://www.washingtonpost.com/opinions/2019/04/02/

[629] Ibidem as above.
[630] Ibidem as above.
[631] Steve Peoples and Alexandra Jaffe, "O'Rourke's casual style to be tested by national campaign", The Washington Post, March 25, 2019. https://www.washingtonpost.com/politics/federal_government/
[632] Katie Galioto, "We'll make sure a space is cleared off for him: Shop owners clear off for him': Shop owners brace for Beto's next counter hop", Politico, March 20, 2019. https://www.politico.com/story/2019/03/20/
[633] Abigail Tucker, "How much is being attractive worth?" The Smithsonian Magazine, November 2012. https://www.smithsonianmag.com/science-nature/
[634] Claire Bond Potter, "Men invented 'Likability.' Guess Who benefits." The New York Times, May 4, 2019. https://www.nytimes.com/2019/05/04/opinion/sunday/likeable-elizabeth-warren-2010.html
[635] Kurt A. Gardinier, "The Beer President", The Huffington Post, October 30, 2012. https://www.huffpost.com/entry/the-beer-president_b_2043196
[636] Monica Hesse, "No, I don't want a beer with Elizabeth Warren. But can she come over for Settlers of Catan?", Perspective, The Washington Post, May 16, 2019. https://www.washingtonpost.com/lifestyle/style/no-I-don't
[637] Annie Linskey, "Warren bets detailed ideas will win over Trump-weary voters", Campaign 2020, The Washington Post, April 7, 2019. https://www.washingtonpost.com
[638] Ibidem as above
[639] Claire Bond Potter, "Men invented 'Likability.' Guess Who Benefits?", Opinion, The New York Times, May 4, 2019. https://www.nytimes.com/2019/05/04/opinion/sunday/likeable-elizabeth-warren-2020.html
[640] A popular rule in Sailing is that crew members older than 40 years old should work in the stern, behind the mast, and not in the bow of the ship, which has the most exacting physical challenges. After these three candidates quit the Democratic Party's primaries, only two politicians in their 70s (Joe Biden and Bernie Sanders) remained in the race.
[641] Harbans Kaijura, "Ganesh Chaturthi-Felicitations in abundance to all on the occasion birthday of Veghana-Harta on 13th September 2018" https://emulateme.worddpress.com/2018/09
[642] Adrian F. Ward "Men and Women Can't be 'Just Friends" Behavior and Society, Scientific American, October 23, 2012. https://www.scientificamerican.com/article/men-and-women-can-be-just-friends/
[643] April L. Bleske, David M. Buss, "Can men and women be just friends?" First published 20 May 2005. https://doi.org/10.111/j.1475-6811.2000.tb00008.x
[644] Term used by the character named Marcy in the 153rd episode of *Seinfeld* to abbreviate a long narration.
[645] Quoctrung Bui and Claire Cain Miller, "The Age that Women have Babies: How a Gap Divides America", The Upshot, The New York Times, August 4, 2108. https://www.nytimes.com/interactive/2018/08/04/upshot
[646] Marilyn Yalom, "The Social Sex: A History of Female Friendship", Harper Perennial, September 22, 2015. https://www.goodreads.com/books/show/24331389-the-social-sex
[647] https://en.wikipedia.org/wiki/Teresa_of_Avila/
[648] Benedetta Craveri, "La civiltà della conversazione", Adelphi Editore, Milano, 24 Maggio 2006. https://www.ibs.it/civilita-della-conversazione-benedetta-craveri/
[649] https://www.womenshistory.org/resources/geenral/woman-suffrage-movement
[650] Betty Boyd Caroli, "Eleanor Roosevelt; American Diplomat, Humanitarian and First Lady", Encyclopedia Britannica, February 27, 2019. https://www.britannica.com/biography/Eleanor-Roosevelt/
[651] Kristen Fuller, "The importance of Female Friendships Among Women", Psychology Today, August 16, 2018. https://www.psychologytoday.com/us/blog/happiness-is-state-mind/201808/the-importance-female-friendships-among-women/
[652] Rebecca Traister, "What Women find in Friends that they may not get from Love", Opinion, The New York Times, February 27, 2016. https://www.nytimes.com/2016/02/28/opinion/sunday/
[653] Michael Balint, "Thrills and Regressions", International University Press, January 30, 1959. https://www.goodreads.com/books/show/15000524-thrills-and-regressions
[654] A term of the German language that can be translated as: "the needed space by individuals to develop their potential."
[655] Term in Italian that refers to the sweeping incursions of the police and military in their enemy's territory, searching for opposition activists. The military dictatorships considered the civilian population of both countries largely as "their enemies."
[656] How does the pituitary gland work? InformedHealth.org. https://ncbi.nlm.nih.gov/books/NBK279389
[657] In the beginning of World War II, the *British Army* considered that their bastion of Singapore could not fall to the Japanese Army as high caliber artillery was arraigned against the sea entrance lanes and the *British Navy*

patrolled them round the clock. But the Japanese invaded Malaysia and swiftly approached the city from behind, where it was less powerfully defended.

[658] https://imdb.com/title/tt0050212/

[659] Pamela Hutchinson, "Last of the red-hot myths: what gossip over Rudolph Valentino's sex life says about the silent", The Guardian, Film, February 22, 2016. https://www.theguardian.com/film/2016/feb/22/

[660] Nadaj Savej, "It's not about nostalgia: re-examining gender roles in film posters", The Guardian, April 9, 2019. https://www.theguardian.com/film/2019/apr/09/

[661] Expression in Latin language that can be translated as : "and it moves, after all." It was supposedly defiantly said by Galileo Galilei at the end of his forced confession in the Inquisition's trial of 1633 for having dared to propose the "heresy" that the Earth was not at the center of our Universe and that it moved around the Sun.

[662] Quaint term of old English that means "a serious hang-over" ; it derives from the German "katz" (cat) and "jammer" (misery) It alludes to the distress felt by anyone listening to the wailing of a cat at night, something that we have certainly almost all of us experienced. https://www.merriam-webster.com

[663] https://britannica.com/science/psychoanalysis

[664] https://www.britannica.com/biography/Sigmund-Freud

[665] https://www.google.com/search?q==Brouillet/+Charcot%27s+class/+wikimedia

[666] Expression in the French language that can be translated as "the genital issue."

[667] Functional mental disorders that entail chronic stress and impaired conducts for the affected individuals. https://www.britannica.com/science/neurosis

[668] Frederick Crews, "The making of an illusion", Metropolitan, August 22, 2017. https://www.goodreads.com/book/sjow/31848259-freud

[669] "A jibe (US) or gybe (Britain) is a sailing maneuver whereby a sailing vessel reaching downwind turns its stern through the wind, such that the direction changes from one side of the boat to the other." https://en.wikipedia.org/wiki/jibe

[670] https://www.loc.gov/collections/sigmund-freud-papers/about-this-collection/

[671] F. Diane Barth L.C.S.W., "Whine, Whine, Whine: 4 steps for dealing with complainers", Psychology Today, posted on June 3, 2012. https://www.psychologytoday.com/us/blog/the-couch/201206/

[672] Ibidem as above.

[673] Miki Kashtan, "Why patriarchy is not about Men", Psychology Today, Posted August 4, 2017. https://www.psychologytodaay.com/us/blog/acquired-spontaneity/201708/

[674] Daniel López Rosetti, "Ellas, corazón y psicología de la mujer", Editorial Planeta, Buenos Aires, 2016.

[675] Gerda Lerner, "The Creation of Patriarchy", Oxford University Press, 22 October 1987. https://global.oup.com/academic/product/the-creation-of-patriarchy/

[676] Kathy E. Ferguson, "The Man Question", University of California Press, February 1993. https://www.ucpress.edu/book/97805200079915/the-man-question/

[677] https://en.oxforddictionaries.com/definition/patriarchy

[678] Cannel, Fenella, Green, Sarah (1996) "Patriarchy", in Kuper, Adam, Jessica (eds.) "The Social Science Encyclopedia", Taylor and Francis, December 28, 1995, p.592. https://www.barnesandnoble.com/p/the-social-science-encyclopedia-adam-kuper/

[679] Katherine Millet, "Sexual Politics", Garden City, New York, 1970. https://www.abebooks.com/book-search-title/sexual-politics/author/kate-millett/first-edition/

[680] Giddens, Anthony, Griffith, Simon, "Sociology", 5th edition, Polity. https://www.scribd.com/doc/212750572/Anthony-Giddens-sociology-5th-Edition/

[681] Bee Rowlat, "The original suffragette: the extraordinary Mary Wollstonecraft", The women's blog, The Guardian, October 5, 2015. https://www.theguardian.com/lifeandstyle/women-blog/2105/oct/2015/

[682] Ibidem as above

[683] Johann Jakob Bachofen, "Swiss jurist and anthropologist", Encyclopedia Britannica. https://www.britannica.com/biography.Johann-Jakob-Bachofen/

[684] Charlotte Higgins, "The age of patriarchy: how an unfashionable idea became a rallying cry for feminism today", The long read, The Guardian, June 22, 2018. https://www.theguardian.com/news/2018/jun/22/

[685] https://britannica.com/biography/Karl-Marx

[686] Friedrich Engels, "The Origin of the Family, Private Property and the State", Penguin Classics, Re-issue, ISBN-13:978-0141191119

[687] Expression in French language that can be translated as "follow the money."
[688] Virginia Woolf, "Three Guineas", Hogarth Press, London,1938. https://www.bl.uk/collection-items/three-guineas-by-virginia-woolf/
[689] Sylvia Walby, "Theorizing Patriarchy", ISBN -13:978-0631147695.
[690] https://britannica.com/biography/Frantz-Fanon/
[691] Frantz Fanon, "Peau Noire, Masques Blancs » Editions du Seuil, Paris, 1952.
[692] He was medically evacuated to the US Navy Hospital for specialized treatment by the Central Intelligence Agency (CIA) at the behest of the American administration. That gesture of great solidarity has been reciprocated over the years by the Algerian government (still controlled by the FLN) by becoming a bridge with the Arab world.
[693] https://hls.harvard.edu/faculty/directory/10540/MacKinnon/
[694] Catharine A. MacKinnon, "Towards a Feminist Theory of the State", 1991, ISBN 9780674896468.
[695] https://minnesota.universityprsscholarships.com/view/10.5749/minnesota/9780816680795.001.0001/upso-9780816680795-chapter-i
[696] Ibidem as above
[697] Amia Srinivasan, "Does anyone have the right to sex?" London Review of Books,22 March 2018. https://lrb.co.uk/v40/n06/amia-shrinivasan/does-anyone-have-the-right-to-sex
[698] www.pietaveneziaorg/istituto.cultura/il_tiepolo_restituito/
[699] Rodolfo Palluchini, "Giovanni Battista Tiepolo, Italian Artist", Encyclopedia Britannica. https://www.britannica.com/biography/Giovanni-Battista-Tiepolo
[700] Luigina Pizzolato, "Le putte di Vivaldi", Storia e Arte Veneta, 2 Marzo 2017. https://venetostoria.wordpress.com/2017/03/02/le-putte-di-vivaldi Our translation.
[701] https://en.wikipedia.org/wiki/Santa_Maria_della_Pieta_Venice
[702] Expression in the Italian language that can be translated as "commoner's girls."
[703] Expression in the Italian language that can be translated as "chorus girls."
[704] Term in Italian that can be translated as "musical school."
[705] Irene Marone, "Le Putte di Coro", Musica Barocca, 1° aprile 2008. https://www.baroque.it/arte-barocca/musica-barocca.le-putte-di-coro.html Our translation.
[706] Term in the Italian language used for patients with chronic respiratory ailments, including Tuberculosis, which was endemic at the time in the Italian peninsula.
[707] https://britannica.com/biography/Antonio-Vivaldi/
[708] Term in the Italian language that refers to "orphan girls."
[709] Irene Marone. Ibidem as above. Our translation.
[710] https://en.wikipedia.org/wiki/Antonio_Vivaldi
[711] Term in the French language that refers to the histrionic exclamations and acts of theatre players that pandered to the base instincts of the poorest spectators, seated in the upper parts, seeking an easy approval and applause.
[712] "Compact Oxford English Dictionary", page 366, Oxford University Press, Third Edition, 2005.
[713] Chris Beasley, "What is feminism?", Sage Books, New York. ISBN 9780761663356.
[714] https://en.wikipedia.org/wiki/Feminism/
[715] Henry, Astrid, "Not my mother's sister: generational conflict and third-wave feminism", Bloomington, Indiana University Press, 2004. ISBN 978-0-253—21713-4.
[716] Adela Cortina Orts, "Aporofobia, el rechazo al Pobre: un desafío para la sociedad democrática", Paidós Ibérica, Madrid, 2017. https://www.casadellibro.com/libro-aporophobia-el-rechazo-al-pobre3a-un-desafio-para-la-sociedad-democratica/
[717] https://www.fundeu.es
[718] Richard Partington, "Ballooning executive pay is at last coming under scrutiny", Business, The Guardian, April 24, 2019. https://www.theguardian.com/business/2019/apr/24/ballooning-executive-pay-is-at-last-coming-under-scrutiny/
[719] https://www.hbo.com/sex-and-the-city
[720] Angela McRobbie, "The Aftermath of Feminism: Gender, Culture and Social Change", Sage Publications, London, November 2008. https://uk.sagepub.com/en-gb/eur/the-aftermath-of-feminism/book211463
[721] Ibidem as above.
[722] Natalee D. Tucker, "Book Review: The Aftermath of Feminism: Gender, Culture and Social Change by Angela McRobbie", eScholarship, Open Access publications form the University of California, UC Santa Barbara, 2011. https://escholarship.org/uc/item/3m68352h

[723] The term refers to the unholy pact made by Faust with the Devil in Goethe's book.
[724] Silvia Walby, "Theorizing Patriarchy", Blackwell Pub, London, December 1, 1990. ISBN 978-0631147688.
[725] Sheryl Sandberg, "Lean in: Women, Work, and the Will to Lead", Deckle Edge, March 11, 2013. https://www.amazon.com/Lean-Women-Work-Will-Lead/dp/038549947
[726] Caitlin Gibson, "The end of the leaning in: How Sheryl Sandberg's message of empowerment fully unraveled", Style, The Washington Post, December 20, 2018. https://www.washingtonpost.com/lifestyle/style/the-end-of-lean-in-how-Sheryl-Sandberg's-message-of-empowerment-fully-unraveled
[727] https://metoomvmt.org/
[728] Ferdinand Magellan was a Portuguese explorer, working for the King and Queen of Spain, that commanded the first circumnavigation of the planet between 1519 and 1522. https://en.wikipedia.org/wiki/Ferdiannd-Magellan
[729] This term was coined in the now deceased Soviet Union to refer to any worker that toiled beyond expectations in order to contribute to the society's well-being. Alexey Stakhanov was a coal miner that appeared as a civic example in Soviet propaganda films and posters. https://en.oxforddictionaries.com/definition/stakhanovite
[730] Lewis A. Coser, "Greedy institutions; patterns of undivided commitment", Free Press, 1974.
[731] Claire Cain Miller, "The 24/7 Work Culture's Toll on Families and Gender Equality", The Upshot, The New York Times, May 28, 2015. https://www.nytimes.com/2015/05/31/upshot/the-24-7-work-culture-toll-on-families-and-gender-equality.html
[732] https://www.hbs.edu/gender/Pages/
[733] Claire Ann Miller, "Women Did everything Right. Then Work Got 'Greedy'", The Upshot, The New York Times, April 26, 2019. https://www.nytimes.com/2019/04/26/upshot/women-long-hours-greedy-prrofessions.html
[734] Kim A. Weeden, Youngjoo Cha and Mauricio Bucca, "Gender Gap in Pay, the Motherhood Wage Penalty, and the Fatherhood Wage Premium.". Project Muse, The Russelll Sage Foundation Journal of the Social Sciences, Volume 2, Number 4, August 2106, pp. 71-102. https://muse.jhu.edu/article/630321/pdf
[735] James Truslow Adams, "The epic of America", Little, Brown and Co., Boston, 1931.
[736] Raj Chetty, David Grusky, Maximilian Hell, Nathaniel Hendren, Robert Manduca, Jimmy Narang, "The Fading American Dream: Trends in Absolute Income Mobility since 1940", Science 356 (6336):398-406, 2017. https://science.sciencemag.org/content/356/6336/398
[737] Ibidem as above.
[738] https://news.gallup.com/po;;/1597/confidence-institutions.aspx
[739] Michael W. Kraus, "The Happiness Chronicles II: does Status Increase Happiness", Psychology Today, July 15, 2012. https://www.psychologytoday.com/us/blog/under-the-influence/201207/the-happiness-chronicles
[740] Claire Cain Miller, "The Relentlessness of Modern Parenting", The Upshot, The New York Times, December 25, 2018. https://www.nytimes.com/2018/12/25/upshot/the-relentlessness-of-modern-parenting.html
[741] This term derives from the novel *Il Gattopardo* from Giuseppe Tomasi di Lampedusa that narrates how a haughty Sicilian family had to change its ways to keep its privileged social standing after the fall of the Bourbon dynasty and the arrival of the Republic in Italy. Tancredi, the grandson of the Principe di Salina, the head of the clan, famously said: "bisogna cambiare tutto per non cambiare niente" (we must change everything so nothing changes)" This term, together with the related one of "transformismo" depicts the grand strategy of dominant classes to adapt to major social, political and economic changes by posing as "promoters of change" to maintain relevance.
Tomasi di Lampedusa "Il Gattopardo" Universale Economica Feltrinelli, Milano, 2013. https://www.lafeltrinelli.it/libri/giuseppe-tomasi-lampedusa/gattopardo/9788807810282
[742] https://www.eveensler.org/plays/the-vagina-monologues/
[743] Francesco Borgonovo, "L'era delle stregue. Cronache dalla guerra del sesso", Altoforte Edizioni, Roma, 10 Aprile 2019. https://www.amazon.it/delle-stregue-Cronache-dalla-guerra/dp/8832078074/
[744] Vijay Kumar Chattu, Mario O. Laplume, Soosanna Kumary, "Time for the Two-Spirits: shaping the inclusive policy environment for Hispanics and Transgenders through Global Health Diplomacy", Journal of Family Medicine and Primary Care, 2017 Oct-Dec; 6(4): 716-720 https://www.ncbi.nlm.nih.gov/pmc/articles.PMC5848
[745] National Center for Transgender Equality. Terminology. 2009. https://www.transequality.org
[746] Chattu, Laplume and Kumary. See above.
[747] Top Health Issues for LGBT Populations Information & Resource Kit. HHS Publications No.(SMA) 12-4684. Rockville, MD; Substance Abuse and Mental Health Services Administration; 2012. https://www.store.samhsa.gov/shin/content/SMA12-4684/pdf
[748] https://www.congress.gov/bill/115th-congress/house-bill/2282/text
[749] https://www.heritage.org

[750] www.womensliberationfront.org
[751] Tim Fitzsimmons. Ibidem as above.
[752] https://www.frc.org/
[753] https://www.splcenter.org/hatewatch/2017/10/23/christina-right-tips-fight-transgender-rights-separate-t-lgb
[754] Adam Liptak, Civil Rights Law Protects Gay and Transgender Workers, Supreme Court Rules, The New York Times, June 15, 2020. https://nytimes.com/2020/06/15/us/gay-transgender-workers-supreme-court.html/
[755] Marguerite Duras, « La Douleur », page 12, Gallimard, Paris, 1998. Our translation. www.gallimard.fr/catalogue/Gallimard/folio/la-douleur/
[756] https://www.britannica.com/biography/Marguerite-Duras
[757] Marguerite Duras, « L'amant », Les éditions de minuit, Paris, France, 1984.
[758] Florence de Chalonge, « La Douleur, le 'journal intemporel' de Marguerite Duras », literary review of Jean-Marie Paul, Anne-Rachel Hermelet « Ecritures autobiographiques », Presses Universitaires de Rennes. https://books.openedition.org/pur/38711?lang-es
[759] In the French language the verb "basculer" means to "pivot". This term refers to the proclivity of suffering women to go from one state of mind and/or spirit to the complete opposite one in a matter of seconds.
[760] Acronym for « Institucion Atlética Sud America" a football and social club in the Goes neighborhood of Montevideo, Uruguay.
[761] https://www.ancient.eu/hinduism/
[762] This avenue is one block away from the Medical School of the "Universidad de la Republica" in Montevideo, Uruguay. When the students occupied the school in the winter of 1973 to protest the military take-over of the government, we usually staged spontaneous protests in that place, after we stealthily left our bastion under siege.

[764] Expression in the French language that can be translated as : "the great ambition of women is to inspire love."
[765] Alberto López, "Alfonsina Storni, la relevancia artística de una mujer que renegó de serlo", Cultura, El País, 29 Mayo 2018. https://elpais.com/cultura/2018/05/29/actualidad/1527582166_036614.html/
[766] Alberto López, "Alfonsina Storni, la relevancia artística de una mujer que renegó de serlo", Cultura, El País, 29 de Mayo 2018. https://elpais.com/cultura/2018/05/29/actualidad/1527582166_036614.html/
[767] Ibidem as above.
[768] Sonia Jones, "Alfonsina Storni", Erser and Pond Publishers Limited, 2013. https://books.google.com/books/about/Alfonsina_Storni.html/
[769] Ibidem as above.
[770] Can be translated as "You want me White."
[771] Can be translated as "Little man."
[772] Alberto López, "Alfonsina Storni" See above.
[773] Term in the Spanish language that can be translated as "City Prize for Poetry."
[774] He was a Uruguayan physician and writer who had become her close friend and confidante. https://www.britannica.com/biography/Horacio-Quiroga/
[775] Can be translated as "I am going to sleep."
[776] "Julieta Lanteri, la primera mujer que pudo votar y fue olvidada por la historia", Sociedad, Orgullosa Feminista, Perfil, 10 de Mayo, 2019. https://www.perfil.com/noticias/sociedad/julieta-lanteri/
[777] This has changed dramatically in the last few years as there has been a revisionist aggiornamento of Argentine History. One of the stations of the new line H of the Buenos Aires subway, located below the Law School of the Universidad de Buenos Aires, will be named in her honor. https://www.buenosaires.gob.ar/noticias/la-nueva-estacion-de-la-linea-h-se-llamara-julieta-lanteri/
[778] Term in the Italian language that can be translated as "intersection" or "crossing". It usually refers to the railroad junctions but is also used metaphorically to label a critical intersection of thoughts, feelings, etc.
[779] There were two regular laborers in our grandfather Morizio's vineyard. Andrade was nicknamed "the stutterer" due to his evident physical defect. Leo was named "the German" but he was in fact Polish by birth; my brother and I had the chance to meet him when we were little boys. He was a husky man who nonetheless always received us with affection in his humble dwellings and offered us some of the legumes he was still growing in his garden. He had a cute cat nicknamed "the ophthalmologist" because he liked to play with his glasses laid on the table. ¡Que Dios los tenga a todos en su bendita Gloria!

[780] My mother had *Josefa* as a middle name, which is the translation of Giuseppa in Spanish, in honor of her grandmother. She did not it like it very much as its sounds a little quaint. We always enjoyed teasing her with it and one day she started telling us anecdotes about the original Giuseppa. Salve, carissima Nonna!

[781] Term in Italian that can be translated as "dear grandmother." Giuseppa was such a strong-willed woman that she explicitly forbade her husband to continue smoking. José Luis, their grandchild and our uncle, told us that one day at the winery he was chatting with Beppe at the end of a hard shift, when the latter dared to take a few puffs from a small pipe. When they heard that *La Nonna* was approaching, Beppe hid the pipe in his trousers' pocket without putting the fire off. As they were greeting her, a *fumata bianca* started to rise from his garments, exposing his transgression. As José Luis was rememorating this anecdote, we both laughed heartily. *Gracias Tío Querido.*

[782] Translation of Giuseppa in Spanish.

[783] Familiar term for those males named Giuseppe in the Piemontese dialect. They were all born and raised in Ricaldone, Provincia di Alessandria,

[784] This anecdote was personally narrated to us by Dr. Tsun-Nin Lee in one of his excellent conferences of the *Acupuncture Course* from the *Academy of Pain Research*, San Francisco, California, USA, 2009.

[785] Boxing term that means "to give up something or somebody after losing hope."

[786] Name of the inter-planetary ship of the original cult TV series "Star Trek." https://www/cbs/com/shows/star_trek/

[787] Middle ages term derived from the French Language that can be translated as "overlordship.". The dictionary defines it as: "the right of one country to rule over another country that has its own ruler but is not fully independent." Compact Oxford English Dictionary, Third Edition, Oxford University Press, 2005.

[788] "A Pyrrhic victory is a victory that inflicts such a devastating toll on the victor that it is tantamount to defeat…It is named after King Pyrrhus of Epirus, whose army suffered irreplaceable casualties in defeating the Romans at the battle of Heraclea in 280 B.C. and the battle of Asculum in 279 B.C." https://en.wikipedia.org/wiki/Pyrrhic_victory

[789] Rachel Cooke, "Sexism in advertising: 'They talk about diversity, but they don't want to change." The Observer, Advertising, The Guardian, April 14, 2019. https://www.theguardian.com/media/2019/apr/14/

[790] Name of the great novel written by George Orwell. https://www.barnesandnoble.com/w/1984-george-orwell/

[791] Samuel Beckett, *En Attendant Godot*, Les Editions de Minuit, Paris, 2002.

[792] Expression in the Spanish language that means: "See you later, Mommy."

[793] Friedrich Nietzsche, *Thus spoke Zarathustra*, First published 1883, Penguin Books, March 30, 1978.

[794] https://government.se/government-agencies/social-insurance-agency-forsakringskassan/

[795] Maddy Savage, "Burnout is rising in the land of work-life balance", BBC Worklife, July 29th, 2019. https://www.bbc.com/worklife/article/20190179-why-is-burnout-rising-in-the-land-of-work-life-balance

[796] Ibidem as above.

[797] Ibidem as above.

[798] Ibidem as above.

[799] Term in the French language that can be translated as "in a war path."

[800] Acronym for "too much information."

[801] These words in Latin were supposedly said by Julius Cesar when he was about to cross the Rubicon River with his expeditionary army in 49 BC. It marked the municipal boundary of the Roman Republic that, in order to avoid any military takeover, could not be crossed be any large military formation. It means: "the die has been cast."

[802] Heather Long and Andrew van Dam, *U.S. unemployment rate soars to 14.7 percent, the worst since the Depression era*, The Washington Post, May 8, 2020. https://washingtonpost.com/business/2020/05/08/april-20202-jobs-report/

[803] Ibidem as above.

[804] The Associated Press, *This Father's Day, Dads Have New Respect for Duties at Home*, The New York Times, June 18, 2020. https://nytimes.com/aponline/2020/06/18/us/ap-us-fathers-day-pandemic-lessons.html

[805] Céleste Albaret "Monsieur Proust (Souvenirs recueillies par Georges Belmont) » Robert Laffont, Paris, 1973.

[806] www.en.m.wikipedia.org/wiki/Celeste_Albaret/

[807] www.franceinter.fr/émissions/le-mag-de-l-été/

[808] www.larousse.fr/encyclopédie/personnage/Jean. Cocteau/13991

[809] This tape was played during the program *Le mag de l'été* in Radio France Inter on August 5,2019.

[810] This archaic term to describe some repulsive individuals was used by Democratic candidate Hillary Clinton to describe the "rough and tumble" supporters of the Republican candidate Donald Trump in one of her 2016 campaign rallies; as it generated an outcry in some political circles, she later expressed some remorse about using it.

[811] French expression that means : « To seduce is to distract."

[812] Catherine Balle, *Mort de Michel Piccoli, acteur de légende du cinéma français*, Le Parisien, Culture & Loisirs, Le 18 mai 2020.

[813] Hazel Rose Markus, Ph.D and Alana Conner, Ph.D., Clash. How to thrive in a Multicultural World, Plume, Penguin Group, 2013. https://penguinrandomhouse.com/books.308774/clash-by-hazel-rose-markus/

[814] A.H. Eagly, M.C. Johannesen-Schmidt, and M.L. van Engen, *Transformational, Transactional and Laissez Faire Leadership styles. A Meta-analysis comparing Women and Men*, Psychological Bulletin, 129 (2003); 569-91.

[815] This is a very ancient expression that was first recorded by Terence, a Roman playwright born in 195 or 185 B.C, who put these words in the mouth of Antipho, one of his characters. https://latinitium.com/blog/auribus-teneo-lupum

[816] Expression in the Latin language that means: "to hold a wolf by its ears."

[817] *Todo lo que pasa Edición Especial*, Radio Mitre AM 790, Buenos Aires, Argentina.

[818] https://www.merriam-webster.com/dictionary/sum-up

[819] The term "chauvinistic" drives from the name of *Nicolas Chauvin*, a retired soldier from the Napoleonic wars, that had been extremely satisfied with the small pension ha had gotten and extolled the virtues of ultra-nationalism. https://www.britannica.com/topic/chauvinism#ref171551
One of the commonest insults hurled at misogynistic individuals in the 1970s was "male chauvinistic pig." We took the French name for *pig (*cochon) to make a play with words and invent a new adjective for that abject condition.

[820] https://ir.blackrock.com/news-and-events/events-and-presentations/default.aspx

[821] https://www.imdb.com/title/tt0133093/

[822] Euphemism used in the French language to delicately refer to "an older lady."

[823] Ellie Williams, *Powerful Communication Skills for Women*, Chron. https://work.chron.com/powerful-communication-skills-women-8997.html

[824] This line is taken from the *New Colossus* by Emma Lazarus, dedicated to the *Statue of Liberty* in New York. https://en.wikipedia.org/wiki/The_New_Colossus

[825] These lines were delicately pronounced by a feminine voice-over in the RAI's live transmission of the Sunday Mass service in the Cathedral of Agrigento, Sicily, in *Cristianità* on April 28, 2019. It can be translated as:
"Whomever does not doubt, does not search
Whomever does not search, does not see
Whomever does not see, remains blind."

[826] "Get drunk…We have to get drunk without pause,
But with what? With wine, with poetry, with virtue,
Follow your taste…But get drunk." Our translation.

[827] Like the famous intrusion of the housemaid in Franz Kafka's bedroom when he was stuck at the end of "The Judgement", we had the unexpected interruption of a U.S. Navy officer when we were trying to finish the book. We had earlier responded to a cold call from a Navy recruiter to join the prestigious force as a physician and/or educator. We liked her unexpected "intrusion" so much that, in the final revision, we playfully added a sub-section titled *Diary USS Awareness* to sarcastically comment about the critical issues under discussion. **Castigat ridendo mores**. We follow the sage advice of Jean de Sauteuil, a 17th century French writer, who coined that term for the bust of the famous arlechino Domenico Biancolelli. That Latin expression means: to *criticize social customs with humor*.
Lieutenant Erika Olson was kindly responding to our phone call inquiring about the possibility of joining as a *Navy Reserve officer*; we eagerly discussed the practical possibility of setting up a study group about *Retention of Medical Personnel* in the force. Moreover, we discussed how we could contribute to any existing or future planned courses on *Gender and Minorities' Equality* at the prestigious *Naval Academy* in Annapolis, Maryland.
Our follow-up call was never responded so we assumed that they must have already solved all the critical issues related to the **Physician and Nurse Burn-out** and **Discrimination against Women and Minorities**, ensuring the force's well-being. Accepting that the U.S. Navy must already have a plethora of professionals *so well versed* in the intricacies of *gender* and *minorities psychology* and *politics,* we understand that our *humble contribution* would look sadly superfluous in the company of such a bounty. However, we are so grateful for having had the opportunity of studying and working in this great nation that we will never hesitate a second to respond every time *Uncle Sam* calls.

Thank you very much, dear Erika. Godspeed!

CPSIA information can be obtained
at www.ICGtesting.com
Printed in the USA
BVHW010220190921
616981BV00006B/88